"SAVING Those Who DOUBT"

CRISIS OF FAITH

EDWARD D. ANDREWS

CRISIS OF FAITH

Saving Those Who Doubt

Edward D. Andrews

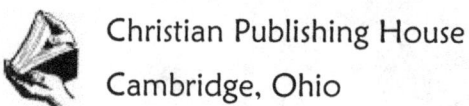 Christian Publishing House
Cambridge, Ohio

Copyright © 2015 Christian Publishing House

All rights reserved. Except for brief quotations in articles, other publications, book reviews, and blogs, no part of this book may be reproduced in any manner without prior written permission from the publishers. For information, write, support@christianpublishers.org

Unless otherwise stated, Scripture quotations are from *The Holy Bible, Updated American Standard Version (UASV)®*, copyright © 2016 by Christian Publishing House, Professional Conservative Christian Publishing of the Good News!

CRISIS OF FAITH Saving Those Who Doubt by Edward D. Andrews

ISBN-13: 978-0692580806

ISBN-10: 0692580808

Table of Contents

Preface 1
   Who Should Read CRISIS OF FAITH 1

INTRODUCTION What Is Doubt 3
   Divisions In the Church 5
   The Truth Will Set You Free 10
   Review Questions 10

CHAPTER 1 What Is Faith? 12
   Heroes of Faith (11:1–40) 14
   What Faith Is 15
   Faith and the Men of Old 22
   The Faith of the Patriarchs 26
   The Godly Devotion of the Patriarchs 32
   Faith Moves Us to Put God First 36
   Review Questions 39

CHAPTER 2 Do Not Let Doubts Destroy Your Faith 40
   Are Doubts Always Bad? 40
   Unfounded Doubts 41
   Examine Yourselves to See Whether You Are In the Faith 46
   Keep Testing Yourselves 48
   Keep Examining Yourselves 49
   Becoming Spiritually Strong 52
   Escape Spiritual Hunger 56
   No Unbelief Will Make Us Waver 60
   Review Questions 62

CHAPTER 3 Did the Miracles in the Bible Really Happen? 64
   Some Just Do Not Believe 65

    Violation of the Laws of Nature 66
    Fake Miracles Does Not Mean No Miracles 67
    Miracles Only In Times of Ignorance 67
    The Best Attested Miracle 68
    The Empty Tomb and the Report of the Guard 70
    Luke the Physician 71
    Eyewitnesses to the Resurrected Jesus 74
    Historical Confirmation of Jesus 75
    Miracles Are a Reality 76
    Review Question 77

CHAPTER 4 Is the Genesis Creation of the World a Myth and Legend? 78
    The Creation of the World 78
    Ancient Creation Stories 81
    Review Question 83

CHAPTER 5 Science and the Bible 84
    In The Beginning 85
    Earth's Orbit 86
    Oxygen and Photosynthesis 87
    From Self-Reproducing Cell to Man 88
    Did It All Happen by Chance? 89
    Review Question 89

CHAPTER 6 Why has God Permitted Wickedness and Suffering? . 90
    The Issues at Hand 93
    God Settles the Issues 94
    What Have Been the Results? 95
    Review Question 97

CHAPTER 7 Why is Life So Unfair? 98

    Unfairness the World Over 98

    God's View of Fairness 100

    From Where Does Unfairness Stem? 102

    Unfairness in the Last Days 104

    Unfairness Removed 105

    Do Not Love the World 105

    The End of the Age 106

    Signs of the End of the Age 110

    No One Knows That Day and Hour 116

    Fairness Restored 118

    Resurrection of Life and Judgment 124

    Passing Over from Death to Life 125

    Review Questions 127

CHAPTER 8 Does God Step in and Solve Our Every Problem Because We are Faithful? 128

    Praising God as the Grand Savior 128

    Wait for God 133

    Review Questions 134

CHAPTER 9 Bible Difficulties Explained 135

    Inerrancy: Can the Bible Be trusted? 139

    Inerrancy: Practical Principles to Overcoming Bible Difficulties .. 145

    Inerrancy: Are There Contradictions? 153

    Inerrancy: Are There Mistakes? 158

    Inerrancy: Are There Scientific Errors? 162

    Procedures for Handling Bible Difficulties 166

    Review Question 167

CHAPTER 10 Dealing With Bible Difficulties 168

    Honestly 168

    Humbly 168

    Determinedly 168

    Fearlessly 169

    Patiently 169

    Scripturally 169

    Prayerfully 169

    Review Question 170

CHAPTER 11 View of Bible Difficulties 171

    Turning the Tables 173

    Review Question 176

CHAPTER 12 Some Types of Bible Difficulties 177

    The Text from which our English Bible was Translated 177

    Inaccurate Translations 178

    False Interpretations of the Bible 179

    A Wrong Conception of the Bible 181

    The Language in Which the Bible was Written 184

    Our Defective Knowledge of the History, Geography and Usages of Bible Times 185

    The Ignorance of Conditions under Which Books Were Written and Commands Given 186

    The Bible has to do with the Infinite, and our Minds are Finite 187

    The Dullness of our Spiritual Perception 188

    Review Question 188

Bibliography 189

Preface

Inside of some Christians unbeknownst to their family, friends or congregation, they are screaming, "I doubt, I doubt, I have very grave doubts!" OURS is an age of doubt. Skepticism has become fashionable. We are urged to question everything: especially the existence of God and the truthfulness of his Word, the Bible. A half-brother of Jesus warned us against doubting: "the one who doubts is like a wave of the sea that is driven and tossed by the wind." (Jam. 1:6) When insidious doubts begin to creep into the mind and the heart, it is only a matter of time before a crisis faith gives way spiritual shipwreck. Since we have been warned "some will fall away from the faith," we should be ready "to save some."

In *CRISIS OF FAITH*, Edward D. Andrews guides in how we can restore them to the faith through an accurate knowledge that gives them the facts on which to rebuild their faith. We can restore their confidence in a world beset by doubts. We can help them once again to make the Word of God their own. *CRISIS IN FAITH* will make them sure that the Bible truly is from God. Those who have doubts need to have their questions answered, and this book will fill the need for honest-hearted persons who sincerely want to know.

Who Should Read CRISIS OF FAITH

(1) Anyone who has had doubts about any aspect of the Bible as to its trustworthiness or accuracy should read CRISIS OF FAITH.[1] If one believes, there are historical inaccuracies, scientific inaccuracies, geographic and geologic inaccuracies, and the like. In addition, if ones believe that there are contradictions, myths and legends within the Bible, they should read CRISIS OF FAITH.

(2) Anyone who has a friend or family member, even a coworker, who is struggling with doubts, as Jude, Jesus half-brother tells us

---

[1] Doubt (to feel unconvinced or uncertain) is normal even in the most mature and knowledgeable Christian. Why? We can know many things with certainty but cannot know all things with certainty, so we may be uncertain on a particular doctrine. However, after enough research, we can believe beyond a reasonable doubt, to use a legal term, that we have the truth of the matter. Therefore, if we are struggling with a particular doctrine, it need not weigh us down emotionally. However, if we have excessive doubts, this is needs to be addressed before we suffer spiritual shipwreck.

that we are to "have mercy on those who doubt; save others by snatching them out of the fire."

(3) Anyone who beliefs their faith is so strong that they would never doubt God's Word. The apostle Paul warned the Corinthians, "let him who thinks he stands take heed that he does not fall." (1 Cor. 10:12, NASB) "Followers of Christ who are overly confident and **think** they are **standing firm** should **be careful** not to **fall**." (Pratt Jr 2000, p. 166)

INTRODUCTION What Is Doubt

Below is a section taken from *The Baker Encyclopedia of Psychology and Counseling*, Second Edition, which will help our readers better understand what doubt is ad when it has become a problem to the point of being concerned.

Doubt. A state of mind characterized by an absence of either assent or dissent to a certain proposition. It is a suspension of commitment to belief or disbelief, either because the evidence pro and con is evenly balanced (positive doubt) or because evidence is lacking for either side (negative doubt, exemplified by the apostle Thomas). Doubt is thus an integral part of each person's belief system, since it is impossible for anyone to believe or disbelieve with complete certainty all propositions of which he or she is aware. Yet in spite of the natural occurrence of doubt in human cognition, many people view doubt as a negative mindset to be avoided if at all possible.

Doubt is a topic of interest to scholars from three academic disciplines. Philosophers study doubt because of its epistemological implications in relation to knowledge, truth, and awareness of existence. Theologians are concerned with doubt because it often occurs as a prelude to belief or as a precursor of disbelief. Psychologists investigate doubt because of the emotions that often accompany it (anxiety, depression, or fear) and because in certain pathologies doubt can become obsessional and debilitating.

Doubt, Unbelief, and Ambivalence. One can differentiate between doubt and unbelief. Unbelief is a positive conviction of falsity regarding an issue and hence is a form of belief. Doubt does not imply a belief in a contrary position; it is simply being unconvinced. If, however, doubt becomes pervasive and dominates the thinking of a person regarding all issues, it is more appropriately called skepticism or definitive doubt. The skeptic despairs of ever knowing truth with certainty.

One can also distinguish doubt from ambivalence. Ambivalence is a state of mind characterized by the concurrent presence of two or more differing feelings toward the same object. Indecisiveness and vacillation, although related to doubt, refer more to a lack of commitment to a proposition or to a frequent change of opinion. Ambivalence in massive quantities is classically seen as a primary indicator of schizophrenia, whereas massive doubt is more often a part of obsessional disorders.

One can differentiate between normal doubt and abnormal doubt chiefly by the degree to which the doubt impairs daily living. Doubt is normal when it does not dominate a person's thinking, when it is overshadowed by stable beliefs, and when the goal of the doubt is resolution into belief or disbelief. Doubt is also normal when employed, as René Descartes advocated, for the purpose of seeking truth. Normal doubt is a type of mental clarification and can help a person better organize his or her beliefs. Developmental theorists have noted several phases of life when doubts are characteristically found: in adolescence, when the teenager moves from childhood credulity toward a personalized belief system, and in the middle years, when issues of competence and direction predominate (Grant, 1974). Abnormal doubt, unlike normal doubt, focuses on issues having little consequence or issues without grave implications of error.

Religious Doubt. Religious doubt has been a concern of believers from biblical days to the present. In the garden of Eden the serpent used doubt as a tool to move Eve from a position of belief to one of disobedience. Abraham, Job, and David all had times of doubt that were painful yet growth-producing. The best-known example of doubt in the Bible is Thomas, who was absent when Jesus made a post resurrection appearance to the ten apostles. Jesus showed the ten his hands and his side (John 20), evidence that dispelled their doubt as to his identity. When told of Jesus' appearance, Thomas replied that he would not believe until he too had seen the evidence. Eight days later Jesus reappeared, showed Thomas his wounds, and made a gracious plea for faith.

By way of contrast, Jesus consistently condemned unbelief wherever he found it. Jesus presumably tolerated doubt because it was a transitory, nonpermanent state of mind, whereas he condemned unbelief because it was a fixed decision often accompanied by hardness of heart. Guinness (1976) cautions, however, that Scripture sometimes uses the word *unbelief* to refer to doubt (Mark 9:24). Hence exegetical care is needed when interpreting the Bible's teachings regarding doubt.

Doubt is a problem in theological systems committed to inscripturated truth. For example, evangelical Christians are generally not tolerant of doubt if it is prolonged, unyielding, and centered on cardinal truths. Doubt is not so much a problem in liberal theologies since truth in those systems is more relative and less certain. Thus the conservative Christian community sees doubt as risky and dangerous, whereas the liberal Christian community sees doubt as a sign of healthy intellectual inquiry. Some psychologists of religion even see doubt, particularly as envisioned within a questing religious orientation (see Batson, Schoenrade, & Ventis, 1993), as an indication of religious maturity.

Normal doubt tends to appear when a person's belief system "does not protect the individual in hislife experiences and from its more painful states" (Halfaer, 1972, p. 216). Doubt is resolved into belief or disbelief in any of four ways: through conversion, through liberalization, through renewal, or through emotional growth. Individuals can construct rigid defenses designed to ensure belief and prevent doubt at all costs such as sometimes occurs in cults that discourage any reexamination of beliefs. (Benner and Hill 1985, 1999, P. 368)

In short, doubt as it relates to God or his Word is when we feel unconvinced or uncertain about some biblical teaching or some trustworthy aspect of God's Word. Someone might say, "I feel, I think, or I believe that the Bible is unlikely to be completely without error." Some may have a feeling or state of uncertainty, especially as to whether a certain biblical position on a particular teaching is true, or as to whether the Word of God as a whole is accurate or trustworthy. Some may feel that it is unlikely that the Bible is one hundred present true, or beneficial for the world we live in today.

Divisions In the Church

There are 41,000 different denominations, each of which teaches different views on the various Bible doctrines, such as salvation, sanctification, eternal security, the charismatic gifts, women in the ministry, the length of the Genesis creation days, the human constitution

(Christian anthropology), and the like. Each Bible doctrine has at least two different views, with some having four or more. Therefore, not all of the various views of a particular doctrine can be true. For example, under the human constitution or Christian anthropology, there are three views: Two parts (Dichotomism), Three parts (Trichotomism), and One part (Monism).

The traditional position of many theologians in some denominations is the **Dichotomist view**, which believes that the human being is formed of two components: material (body/flesh) and spiritual (soul/spirit). The **Trichotomist** believes that human beings are made up of three distinct components: body or flesh, soul, and spirit. A significant minority of theologians in some denominations holds this view. The **Monist** believes that the body and soul are **not** considered separate components of a person, but rather as two facets of a united whole. Modern theologians more and more are taking this position, as well as modern neuroscience. Now, the point being, not all three views can be correct. Thus, not all doubts are necessarily a bad thing. Let us suppose that one of these is the absolute truth and we hold one of the other two positions. After much research, our conclusion based on previous knowledge is revised, so that we now take the position that is absolutely true, meaning that the doubts about our former position were warranted.

A recently new belief among liberal and some moderate Bible scholars is relativism. Relativism is the belief that concepts such as right and wrong, goodness and badness, or truth and falsehood are not absolute but change from culture to culture and situation to situation, even person to person. Thus, as silly as it might sound, a relativist would argue that all three of the above positions on the human constitution would be true for different people that hold those positions. Episcopal bishop John Shelby Spong (liberal theologian) commented: "We must ... move from thinking we have the truth and others must come to our point of view to the realization that ultimate truth is beyond the grasp of all of us."[2] As conservative Christians, we hold that there is absolute truth. Jesus said, "You will know the truth, and the truth will set you free." (John 8:32, ESV) The apostle Paul wrote, "This is good, and it is acceptable in the sight of God our Savior, who desires all men to be saved and to come

---

[2] But Mr. Myers...! | Uncommon Descent, http://tiny.cc/xar64x (accessed October 26, 2015).

to an accurate knowledge[3] of truth." (1 Tim. 2:3-4) Jesus also said, "True worshipers will worship the Father in spirit and truth, for the Father is seeking such people to worship him. God is spirit, and those who worship him must worship in spirit and truth." (John 4:23-24, ESV) Therefore, true Christians believe that absolute truth exists. As it relates to God's Word, we must carry out an exegetical investigation, to discover it.

There are a large number of books on biblical interpretation, with different rules and principles for interpreting the Scriptures, which is one reason as to why there are so many different views on a given Bible doctrine. Other reasons for different views of the same doctrine would be church tradition, lack of knowledge or interpretative skills, theological bias, and human imperfection, among other things. However, just as was true of liberal scholarship and their relativistic belief that there is no such thing as absolute truth when we know otherwise, so it is the liberal and moderate Bible scholars who use a method of interpretation that contributes to subjective interpretation, i.e., the historical-critical method. Conservative scholarship uses the objective form of interpretation, namely, the Historical-grammatical interpretation. Thus, we can see how Christians might struggle with what is the correct way to interpret Scripture. In addition, they are overwhelmed with what is the correct view of each of our Bible doctrines.

In his forward to R. C. Sproul's *Knowing Scripture*, J. I. Packer observes that Protestant theologians are in conflict about biblical interpretation. To illustrate the diversity of biblical interpretations, William Yarchin pictures a shelf full of religious books saying different things, but all claiming to be faithful interpretations of the Bible. Bernard Ramm observed that such diverse interpretations underlie the "doctrinal variations in Christendom." A mid-19th century book on biblical interpretation observed that even those who believe the Bible to be "the word of God" hold "the most discordant views" about fundamental doctrines."[4]

Below are just a few examples of the "discordant views," i.e., conflicting views of different Bible doctrines.

---

[3] *Epignosis* is a strengthened or intensified form of *gnosis* (*epi*, meaning "additional"), meaning, "true," "real," "full," "complete" or "accurate," depending upon the context. Paul and Peter alone use *epignosis*.

[4] Biblical hermeneutics - Wikipedia, the free encyclopedia, https://en.m.wikipedia.org/wiki/Biblical_hermeneutics (accessed October 26, 2015).

Four Views of Hell	Four Views of Salvation	Two Views of Inspiration	Three Views of Atonement
Four Views of creation	Four Views of Eternal Security	Four Views of Inspiration	Four Views of Works in Final Judgment
Four Views of Inerrancy	Four Views of Sanctification	Two Views of Fasting	Four Views of the Book of Revelation
Two Views of Christology	Three Views of Image of God	Three Views of Grace	Three Views of Human Constitution
Four Views of Providence	Two Views of Lord's Supper	Four Views of Free Will	Two Views of Charismatic Gifts
Two Views of Baptism	Three Views of Jesus' Return	Two Views of Sabbath	Four Views of Predestination
Three Views of Purgatory	Four Views of the Church	Four Views of End Times	Four Views of Christian Spirituality
Four Views of Antichrist	Three Views of Neutrality	Three Views of Heaven	Two Views of Foreknowledge

Some begin to doubt, wondering how are they ever going to know what is true. Moreover, many have misrepresented just how difficult and complex the Bible is, suggesting that it is easy to understand. The Danish philosopher Søren Kierkegaard offered a similarly provocative diagnosis: "The matter is quite simple. **The bible is very easy to understand**. But we Christians are a bunch of scheming swindlers. We pretend to be unable to understand it because we know very well that the minute we understand, we are obliged to act accordingly." If a churchgoer is sitting in the pews hearing how easy the Bible is to understand and at the same time struggling to understand it, this alone could be so overwhelming, it could contribute to a bout of depression. One might ask, "If the Bible is easy to understand and I cannot understand it, what does that say about me?" Relax; take a deep breath, the Bible is not even close to being easy to understand. Those who make such claims are likely the ones that are furthest from having a correct understanding of it. Even the inspired apostle Peter stated that he found the apostle Paul's letters 'difficult to understand.' (2 Pet. 3:16) If the Bible is so easy to understand, how on earth can Dr. Craig S. Keener (PhD, Duke University), pen a four-volume commentary on the book of Acts alone, which has 4640 pages?

Keeping the truth from people will inevitably lead to a spiritual shipwreck. Religious leaders can no longer hide the truth from their flock. There are several thousand Bible difficulties from Genesis to Revelation. Bible critics call these mistakes, errors, and contradictions. These would have never been discussed in our church 20-years ago because elders and pastors did not see the need for dealing with such hot topics, nor were they qualified to do so. Occasionally, in the 1980s, a flock member might happen upon a book in a store that attacked the Bible and the Christian faith, walking its reader through many of these so-called mistakes, errors, and contradictions. The Christian end up being heartbroken, keeping these doubts bottled up inside, falling away from the faith eventually. Some had even gone to the pastor or elder, showing them the book, who then blew it off by saying, "Why are you feeding your mind on such a book? This is simply a bunch of lies spread by false teachers." Of course, the pastor or elder was unable to explain how any of the Bible difficulties were lies. So few Christians were lost to this danger that it was felt that there was no need to talk about Bible difficulties, how many tens of thousands of different denominations there are, the different views on all of the Bible doctrines, and the like.

However, the internet has exploded into the lives of every Christian; even the elderly are texting their friends. There is access to social media sites such as Facebook, Twitter, YouTube Pinterest, LinkedIn, Google + and dozens of others. There are now over 2 billion social media users worldwide and more than half (52 percent) of those use two or more social media sites. Thus, the proverbial cat is out of the bag, or the beans have been spilled, meaning that the secret has been revealed unintentionally.

The flood of books, movies, and media by the Bible critics is so pervasive that we now have universities that are apologetic universities. **Christian apologetics** [Greek: *apologia*, "verbal defense, speech in defense"] is a field of **Christian theology** that endeavors to offer a reasonable and sensible basis for the **Christian faith**, defending the faith against objections. It is reasoning from the Scriptures, explaining and proving, as one instructs in sound doctrine, many times having to overturn false reasoning before he can plant the seeds of truth. It can also be earnestly contending for the faith and saving one from losing their faith, as they have begun to doubt. Moreover, it can involve rebuking those who contradict the truth. It is being prepared to make a defense to anyone who asks the Christian evangelist for a reason for the hope that is in him or her. – Jude 1.3, 21-23; 1 Pet 3.15; Acts 17:2-3; Titus 1:9.

The Truth Will Set You Free

The truth is,

- The Bible is a very complex and deep book, which is difficult to understand, but we have great study tools today, and anyone wanting to understand it, need only to buy out the time.
- There are over 41,000 different denominations and all are not the truth and the way. In fact, many are false. However, it is true that one or more may be the truth and the way. Alternatively, it may be that it is true that there are many true Christians in some denominations, which Jesus will unite before the end comes.
- It is true that every Bible doctrine has more than one view, but not all are true. However, it is also true that the meaning of each of those doctrines is found in God's Word and only needs to be discovered.
- It is true that salvation is open to everyone. However, it is also true that few will find it because most are too lazy to buy out the time to study.
- It is true that God wants everyone to be saved. However, it is also true that he is interested only in saving those with a receptive heart.

Review Questions

- Who should read Crisis of Faith?
- What is doubt and what are its different levels?
- Just how serious are the divisions within the church?
- Why can we say the Bible is not easy to understand?

- What is Christian apologetics?
- How has the truth set us free?

CHAPTER 1 What Is Faith?

Hebrews 12:1 Updated American Standard Version (UASV)

12 Therefore, since we have so great a cloud of witnesses surrounding us, let us also lay aside every weight and the sin which so easily entangles us, and let us run with endurance the race that is set before us,

We might think of a runner in an Olympic race, say the 100 metres, or 100-meter dash. The current men's world record is 9.58 seconds, set by Jamaica's Usain Bolt in 2009 while the women's world record of 10.49 seconds set by American Florence Griffith-Joyner in 1988 remains unbroken. The reigning 100 m Olympic champion is often named "the fastest man in the world." Then, there are the 10,000 metres, which is the longest standard track event. The international distance is equal to approximately 6.2137 miles. Kenenisa Bekele is the current 10,000 m world record holder, 26:17.53. We think of the strain and stress on every fiber of their body whether it be for the quick 100-meter dash or the long 10,000 m marathon.

What about the figurative Christian runner that Paul spoke of in the above text, how does this correlate? They are running in the race of life. We might compare the Olympic 100-meter runner to a Christian making it through each and every day, while the 10,000 meter marathon runner to a Christian running his entire life. John Macarthur writes, "The deceased people of [Hebrews] chapter 11 give witness to the value and blessing of living by faith. Motivation for running "the race" is not in the possibility of receiving praise from 'observing' heavenly saints. Rather, the runner is inspired by the godly examples those saints set during their lives.

The great crowd is not comprised of spectators but rather is made up of ones whose past life of faith encourages others to live that way (cf. 11:2, 4, 5, 33, 39). **let us.** The reference is to those Hebrews who had made a profession of Christ, but had not gone all the way to full faith. They had not yet begun the race, which starts with salvation. The writer has invited them to accept salvation in Christ and join the race. **every weight.** Different from the "sin" mentioned next, this refers to the main encumbrance weighing down the Hebrews, which was the Levitical system with its stifling legalism. The athlete would strip away every piece of unnecessary clothing before competing in the race. The outward things emphasized by the Levitical system not only impede; they also "ensnare." **sin.** In this context, this focuses first on the particular sin of unbelief, refusing to turn away from the Levitical sacrifices to the perfect sacrifice, Jesus Christ (cf. John 16:8–11), as well as other sins cherished by the unbeliever. **endurance.** Endurance is the steady determination to keep going, regardless of the temptation to slow down or give up (cf. 1 Cor. 9:24, 25). **race.** The athletic metaphor presents the faith-filled life as a demanding, grueling effort. The English word agony is derived from the Greek word used here."[5]

Reflecting on the Bible background of Hebrews 12:1, Clinton E. Arnold has, "**IT DOES NOT TAKE LONG EXPERIENCE** in the Christian faith to learn that maintaining a resolute commitment to Christ is not easy and demands endurance. We can find help, however, from several directions. The "cloud of witnesses" reminds us that God's people of the past have walked similar paths as the ones we are walking presently and have done so keeping faith. The exhortation of Scripture to put off those things that hinder us reminds us that the weights we embrace in life—whether unwholesome activities or attitudes of questionable value—can impede our progress in the faith. Finally, we must look to Jesus as the ultimate example of endurance. His attitude of scorning shame gives us a powerful reference point from which to evaluate the difficulties of life, especially those that come because we are committed to God's path." He goes on to write, "So too the author of Hebrews challenges his readers to 'strip' off everything that hinders them in the race of endurance. An ancient writer could use the term *onkos*, translated in 12:1 as [something] 'that hinders,' to refer to a mass, weight, or bodily fat. In the context of running, it could refer to burdensome clothing or excess bodily weight.

---

[5] MacArthur, John (2005-05-09). *The MacArthur Bible Commentary* (Kindle Locations 62741-62752). Thomas Nelson. Kindle Edition.

Therefore, believers are to run the Christian race with endurance, laying aside those things that bind or weigh us down."[6]

The apostle Paul may have had the figurative runners of a race in a stadium in mind when he penned the book of Hebrews for the Jewish Christians in Jerusalem (c. 61 C.E.).[7] The Jewish people were heading into their great tribulation in 66-70 C.E., when the Roman was to come and destroy Jerusalem, so they need firm faith. (Heb. 10:32-39) It would only be by faith that they would heed the prophetic warning of Jesus and flee Jerusalem in 66 C.E., a few short years before to would be destroyed (70 C.E.), wherein over one million Christians were executed by being impaled on a stake and over one hundred thousand were taken back to Rome to be sold as slaves. Faith would also sustain them when they were "who are persecuted for righteousness' sake." – Matthew 5:10; Luke 21:20-24.

In Hebrews chapter 11 Paul reviewed great persons of faith who lived centuries, even millenniums before the Christian era. He then urged in Hebrews 12:1, "Therefore, since we have so great a cloud of witnesses surrounding us, let us also lay aside every weight [that would hinder us spiritually] and the sin [lack of faith], which so easily entangles us, and let us run with endurance the race [for life eternal] that is set before us." Paul's review of faith highlighted several facets of it and will help us as well today. The question that might seem obvious to some is, "what is faith?" What are the specific aspects that can be beneficial to us? First, Bible scholar David S. Dockery will give us an overview of Hebrews chapter 11.

Heroes of Faith (11:1–40)

As an incentive to endurance before God, the writer presented a gallery of Old Testament heroes of faith. Faith gives reality to things that cannot be seen. By this faith the Old Testament believers received a positive witness from God. In the generations before the flood, Abel, Enoch, and Noah all responded by faith to demonstrate obedience to God. Their faith pleased Him. Abraham demonstrated his faith by forsaking

---

[6] (Arnold, Zondervan Illustrated Bible Backgrounds Commentary Volume 4: Hebrews to Revelation 2002, p. 75)

[7] B.C.E. means "before the Common Era," which is more accurate than B.C. ("before Christ"). C.E. denotes "Common Era," often called A.D., for *anno Domini*, meaning "in the year of our Lord."

the comforts of Ur and Haran to follow God to the promised land. By faith Abraham and Sarah bore Isaac as a child of their old age. Moses showed his faith by leaving the wealth of the Egyptian palace to suffer hardship with the Hebrew people. The writer presented Gideon, Samson, David, Samuel, and many other heroes as examples whose faith Christians should follow. The promises the Old Testament believers had expected were coming true in the events New Testament Christians were experiencing.[8]

What Faith Is

Hebrews 11:1-3 Updated American Standard Version (UASV)

11 Now faith is the assurance[9] of things hoped for, the conviction[10] of things not seen. **2** For by means of it, the men of old[11] had witness borne to them. **3** By faith we understand that the worlds[12] were prepared by the word of God, so that what is seen was not made out of things which are visible.

The apostle Paul defined faith as "the assurance[13] of things hoped for." The one who has faith has an absolute guarantee that everything God says will come to pass, will be fulfilled. Faith is also, "the conviction[14] of things not seen." The convincing evidence of the unseen is so powerful that faith is viewed as bring the same to that evidence.[15]

---

[8] (D. S. Dockery, HOLMAN CONCISE BIBLE COMMENTARY Simple, straightforward commentary on every book of the Bible 1998, p. 625)

[9] Lit *a sub-standing*; Gr *hypostasis*

[10] Or *convincing evidence*

[11] Or *of ancient times*; Lit *older men*; Gr *presbyteroi*.

[12] Or *universe*; Lit *ages*

[13] Lit *a sub-standing*; Gr *hypostasis*

[14] Or *convincing evidence*

[15] "This verse is written in a style of Hebrew poetry (used often in the Psalms), in which two parallel and nearly identical phrases are used to state the same thing. Cf. 1 Peter 1:7—God tests our faith in the crucible. **Substance**. This is from the same Greek word translated "express image" in 1:3 and 'confidence' in 3:14. The faith described here involves the most solid possible conviction, the God-given present assurance of a future reality. **evidence of things not seen**. True faith is not based on empirical evidence but on divine assurance, and is a gift of God (Eph. 2:8)." – MacArthur, John (2005-05-09). *The MacArthur Bible Commentary* (Kindle Locations 62577-62581). Thomas Nelson. Kindle Edition.

By means of faith, "the men of old[16] had witness borne to them" that they had a righteous standing before God. In addition, "by faith we understand that the worlds[17] [earth, the sun, the moon, and the stars] were prepared by the word of God," "so that what is seen was not made out of things which are visible." (Gen. 1:1; John 4:24; Rom. 1:20) Below, we will let several different leading Bible scholars address Hebrews 11:1-3, as it is the foundation of this book. We will begin with the author that is easiest to understand and work our way to the more difficult, so by the time we get to the more difficult we have the basic knowledge, to grasp the deeper things.

Faith

On Hebrews 11:1-3, William Barclay writes, "TO the writer to the Hebrews, faith is a hope that is absolutely certain that what it believes is true and that what it expects will come. It is not the hope which looks forward with wistful longing; it is the hope which looks forward with utter conviction. In the early days of persecution, a humble Christian was brought before the judges. He told them that nothing they could do could shake him because he believed that, if he was true to God, God would be true to him. 'Do you really think', asked the judge, 'that the likes of you will go to God and his glory?' 'I do not think,' said the man, 'I know.' At one time, John Bunyan was tortured by uncertainty. 'Everyone doth think his own Religion rightest,' he said, 'both Jews and Moors and Pagans; and how if all our Faith and Christ and Scriptures should be but a "Think so" too?' But, when the light broke, he ran out crying: 'Now I know! I know!' The Christian faith is a hope that has turned to certainty. This Christian hope is such that it dictates every aspect of the way Christians conduct themselves. They live in it and they die in it; and it is the possession of it which makes them act as they do."[18]

On Hebrews 11:1-3, Thomas D. Lea writes, "**11:1.** Eyesight produces a conviction about objects in the physical world. Faith produces the same convictions for the invisible order. Faith shows itself by producing assurance that what we hope for will happen. Faith also provides an insight into realities which otherwise remain unseen. A person with faith lets these unseen realities from God provide a living, effective power for daily life. **11:2–3.** These verses present two illustrations of the use of faith.

---

[16] Or *of ancient times*; Lit *older men*; Gr *presbyteroi*.

[17] Or *universe*; Lit *ages*

[18] Barclay, William (2010-11-05). *The Letter to the Hebrews (New Daily Study Bible)* (pp. 152-153). Westminster John Knox Press. Kindle Edition.

First, faith enabled the heroes of the Old Testament to receive a good standing with God. God gave his approval to the faith of these saints. Second, believing that God created the world involves a leap of faith. Faith points to an unseen power who made the world we see. The **universe** involves more than the physical world. It includes the ages that God had planned, beginning with the act of creation and extending to the consummation of all things in Christ. By faith we know that all we see around us and all that takes place on earth came from one we cannot see. By observing creation we may learn of God's power. We learn the manner of God's creation only by responding in faith to the statements of Scripture." (T. D. Lea, Holman New Testament Commentary: Hebrews, James 1999, p. 201)

On Hebrews 11:1-3, Simon J. Kistemaker writes, "The heroes of faith have one thing in common: they put their undivided confidence in God. In spite of all their trials and difficult circumstances, they triumphed because of their trust in God. For the author, faith is adhering to the promises of God, depending on the Word of God, and remaining faithful to the Son of God. When we see chapter 11 in the context of Hebrews, the author's design to contrast faith with the sin of unbelief (3:12,19; 4:2; 10:38–39) becomes clear. Over against the sin of falling away from the living God, the writer squarely places the virtue of faith.[19] Those people who shrink from putting their trust in God are destroyed, but those who believe are saved (10:39)."[20]

Assurance

Kistemaker goes on, "The author of Hebrews expresses that same assurance in much more concise wording: "Faith is being sure of what we hope for." The expression *being sure* of is given as 'substance' in other translations. The difference between these translations arises from understanding the original Greek word *hypostasis* subjectively or objectively. If I am sure of something, I have certainty in my heart. This is a subjective knowledge because it is within me. Assurance, then, is a subjective quality. By contrast, the word *substance* is objective because it refers to something that is not part of me. Rather, substance is something

---

[19] F. W. Grosheide, *De Brief aan de Hebreeën en de Brief van Jakobus* (Kampen: Kok. 1955), p. 255.

[20] (S. J. Kistemaker, Baker New Testament Commentary: Hebrews 1984, P. 310)

on which I can rely. As one translation has it, 'Faith is the title-deed of things hoped for.'[21] That, in fact, is objective."

He goes on, "To come to a clear-cut choice in the matter is not easy, for the one translation does not rule out the other. The translation *confidence* or *assurance* has gained prominence, perhaps because 3:14 also has the same word: "We have come to share in Christ if we hold firmly till the end the confidence we had at first." In the case of 11:1, even though the objective sense has validity, the subjective meaning is commended."

Kistemaker concludes, The author [Paul] teaches the virtue of hope wherever he is able to introduce the topic (3:6; 6:11, 18; 7:19; 10:23). Hope is not an inactive hidden quality. Hope is active and progressive. It relates to all the things God has promised to believers: "all things of present grace and future glory."[22] (S. J. Kistemaker, Baker New Testament Commentary: Hebrews 1984, P. 311)

Certainty

Faith

is

being sure of	certain of
what we hope for	what we do not see

Kistemaker writes, "In short, assurance is balanced by certainty. These two nouns are in this text synonymous. Certainty, then, means 'inner conviction.'[23] The believer is convinced that the things he is unable to see are real. Not every conviction, however, is equal to faith. Conviction is the equivalent of faith when certainty prevails, even though the evidence is lacking. The things we do not see are those that pertain to the future that in time will become the present. Even things of the present, and

---

[21] James Hope Moulton and George Milligan, *The Vocabulary of the Greek Testament Illustrated from the Papyri and Other Non-Literary Sources* (London: Hodder and Stoughton, 1930), pp.659–60.

[22] John Owen, *An Exposition of Hebrews*, 7 vols. in 4 (Evansville, Ind.: Sovereign Grace, 1960), vol. 7, p. 7.

[23] Bauer, p. 249.

certainly those of the past, that are beyond our reach belong to the category of 'what we do not see.' Comments B. F. Westcott, 'Hope includes that which is internal as well as that which is external.'[24] Hope centers in the mind and spirit of man; sight relates to one of his senses (Rom. 8:24–25). Faith, therefore, radiates from man's inner being where hope resides to riches that are beyond his purview. Faith demonstrates itself in confident assurance and convincing certainty."[25]

Some Christians who claim to have faith are confusing it with a somewhat, easygoing, good-natured sentimentality, a more or less 'faith in faith.' These ones feel that they believe in God, so they emotionally know that God exists. However, to be honest, this lukewarm faith will have little effect on their life when tragedy strikes. Therefore, faith based on emotions is impractical, although it will seem quite real until difficult times befall them.

However, the genuine, true faith that the Bible encourages is very different. It is "the assurance[26] of things hoped for, the conviction[27] of things not seen." – Hebrews 11:1.

The Greek word behind our English translation "assurance" (*hypostasis*) carries the idea of something that lies beneath or guarantees what is expected. Therefore, this Biblical faith is not some meager, emotional, ambiguous feeling or an unsupported hope; real assurance is involved. The Greek word behind our English translation "conviction" (*elenchos*) carries the thought of presenting convincing evidence (literally, the proof) particularly evidence that establishes something other than what many might believe not to so. Accordingly, even though we live in a world filled with people who say there is no God; our faith in him comes not from emotionalism, but rather convincing evidence.

Where are we on this? Can we say that we have assurance, maintained by convincing evidence that God exists?

---

[24] B. F. Westcott, *Commentary on the Epistle to the Hebrews* (Grand Rapids: Eerdmans, 1950), p. 350.

[25] (S. J. Kistemaker, Baker New Testament Commentary: Hebrews 1984, P. 311)

[26] Lit *a sub-standing*; Gr *hypostasis*

[27] Or *convincing evidence*

Faith Is the Evidence of Things Not Seen

The definition of faith continues: "faith is ... the evidence of things not seen." The author uses a reference to one of the senses of the human body through which we gain knowledge, the sense of sight. There is a popular expression today, "Seeing is believing." Similarly, people from Missouri like to say, "Show me." This attitude is not opposed to biblical faith, for the New Testament calls us to put our trust in the gospel not on the basis of some irrational leap into the darkness but on the basis of the testimony of eyewitnesses who report in Scripture about what they saw.

Think, for example, of the apostolic testimony of Peter: "For we did not follow cleverly devised myths when we made known to you the power and coming of our Lord Jesus Christ, but we were eyewitnesses of his majesty" (2 Peter 1:16). Likewise, when Luke begins his Gospel, he addresses it to Theophilus, saying, "it seemed good to me ..., having followed all things closely for some time past, to write an orderly account for you" (v. 3). He is talking about things he has substantiated on the basis of eyewitness testimony. In the same way, when Paul defends his confidence in the resurrection in 1 Corinthians 15, he appeals to the eyewitnesses of the risen Christ: Cephas, the Twelve, the five hundred, James, and all the apostles (vv. 5–7). Then he writes, "Last of all, as to one untimely born, he appeared also to me" (v. 8). Paul is saying, "I believe in the resurrection because many eyewitnesses saw the resurrected Christ, and I saw Him myself."

So there is a link in the New Testament between faith and seeing, and yet the author of Hebrews describes faith as the conviction of things *not* seen. Maybe this is why some people argue that there is a biblical ground for regarding blind faith as virtuous. After all, if one cannot see, one is said to be blind, so if faith is evidence for that which cannot be seen, that must mean that the faith of which the author is speaking is blind faith.

I cannot think of anything that is farther from the meaning of Hebrews 11:1–2 than blind faith. Those promoting blind faith say: "We believe what we believe for no reason whatsoever. It's totally gratuitous." The idea is that there's some kind of virtue in closing our eyes, taking a deep breath, and wishing with all of our might that something is true—then saying, "It's true." That is credulity, not faith.

The Bible never claims that we should jump into the darkness. In fact, the biblical injunction is for people to come out of the darkness and into the light (cf. John 3:19). Faith is not blind in the sense of being arbitrary, whimsical, or a mere expression of human desire. If that were the case, why would the author of Hebrews say that faith is "the evidence of things not seen"?

When faith is linked to hope, it is put into the time frame of the future, and the one thing that I cannot see at all is tomorrow. None of us has yet experienced tomorrow. As I said earlier, I have hope that the Pittsburgh Steelers will win their football games. But I cannot know in advance whether that will happen or not.

However, Hebrews says that faith is the *evidence* of things not seen. Evidence is tangible. Evidence is something we can know through our five senses. Evidence is what police officers inspect and try to collect at a crime scene—fingerprints, traces of gunpowder residue, articles of clothing that are left behind, and so on. All these things are visible and point beyond themselves to some important truth. That's why people analyze evidence.

The idea is this: I don't know what tomorrow is going to bring, but I know that God knows what tomorrow is going to bring. So if God promises that tomorrow will bring something, and if I trust God for tomorrow, I have faith in something I have not yet seen. That faith serves as evidence because its object is God. I know Him; He has a track record—He is infallible and never lies. God knows everything and is perfect in whatever He communicates. So if God tells me that something is going to happen tomorrow, I believe it even though I haven't seen it yet.

That's not credulity or irrationality. On the contrary, it is irrational *not* to believe something that God says regarding some future event.

What does God say regarding the future? He not only reveals to us events of tomorrow that we haven't yet seen, He also reveals to us much about the supernatural realm that our eyes cannot penetrate. We cannot see angels at this time. We cannot see heaven. But God reveals to us the reality of these things, and by faith we see that they have substance because God is credible. (Sproul 2010, pp. 5-8)

Faith and the Men of Old

Hebrews 11:4 Updated American Standard Version (UASV)

⁴ By faith Abel offered to God a better sacrifice than Cain, through which he obtained the testimony that he was righteous, God testifying about his gifts, and through faith,[28] though he is dead, he still speaks.

There are two aspects of Cain's offering, which found him unapproved before God: **(1)** his attitude and **(2)** the type of offering.

It seems that Abel, the second born of Adam and Eve, was capable of discerning the need for blood to be involved in the atoning sacrifice, while Cain was not, or simply did not care. Therefore, it was the heart attitude of Cain that resulted in his sacrifice being rejected. Consequently, "but on Cain and his offering he did not look with favor. So Cain was very angry, and his face was downcast." (Gen 4:5, NIV) It may well be that Cain had little regard for the atoning sacrifice, giving it little thought, going through the motions of the act only. However, as later biblical history would show, God is not one to be satisfied with formal worship. Cain had developed a bad heart attitude, and God well knew that his motives were not sincere. The way Cain reacted to the evaluation of his sacrifice only evidenced what God already knew. Instead of seeking to improve the situation, 'Cain grew very angry.'

One of the many aspects of faith is our understanding and appreciating that there is a need for a sacrifice for sins. Just after Adam and Eve were expelled from the Garden of Eden, Abel demonstrated faith in a blood sacrifice. Clearly, Abel must have discerned that he had inherited sin (missing the mark of perfection) from his parents. (Gen. 2:16-17; 3:6-7; See Rom. 5:12) Obviously, Abel must have seen the fulfillment of God's decree on Adam, cursing the ground, saying that in pain he would eat of it as growing food would be very difficult. God concluded, "By the sweat of your face you shall eat bread, till you return to the ground, for out of it you were taken; for you are dust, and to dust you shall return." (Gen 3:17-19) He must have also been aware of the fulfillment of God's decree on Eve, "I will surely multiply your pain in childbearing; in pain you shall bring forth children. Your desire shall be for your husband, and he shall rule over you." (Gen. 3:16, ESV) Therefore, Abel had "the assurance of" God's word coming true. (Heb. 11:1) This would include the prophetic word concerning Satan the Devil,

---

[28] Lit *it*

who had projected his voice through the serpent in Eden, contributing to the rebellion of Adam and Eve. God said to the serpent, i.e., Satan, "I will put enmity between you and the woman, and between your offspring and her offspring; he shall bruise your head, and you shall bruise his heel." – Genesis 3:15, ESV.

Abel demonstrated his faith in the promised seed spoken of By God by his discerning the need to offer up an animal sacrifice, which could substitute for Abel's blood, though not completely. However, Cain and his bloodless vegetables evidenced a lack of faith or a failure to understand. Moreover, his attitude showed that he really did not care to understand. (Genesis 4:1-8) As Abel struggled for his life, he could know that he had a righteous standing before God,[29] as Paul said "God testifying about his gifts." How did God testify about Abel's gifts? The Father accepted Abel's sacrifices that he offered in faith. Clearly, "though he is dead, he still speaks." Can we say that we evidence faith in Jesus Christ's greater ransom sacrifice? – 1 John 2:1-2.

Hebrews 11:5-6 Updated American Standard Version (UASV)

⁵ By faith Enoch was transferred[30] so as not to see death, and he was not to be found because God had transferred him; for before he was transferred he obtained the witness that he was pleasing to God. ⁶ And without faith it is impossible to please him, for whoever would draw near to God must believe that he is and that is the rewarder of those seeking him.

These rebel angels had the power at one time to materialize in human form, just like those who had remained faithful to God, when they delivered messages for Him to Abraham, Moses and others. (Gen. 18:1, 2, 8, 20-22; 19:1-11; Jos 5:13-15) The "proper dwelling" that Jude spoke of is Heaven, which these angels abandoned, to take on human form, and have relations that were contrary to nature with the "the daughters of man." (Dan. 7:9-10) The Bible intimates that these rebel angels were stripped of their power to take on human form, as you never hear of it taking place again after the Flood, only spirit possession

---

[29] **1 John 3:23** English Standard Version (ESV)

²³ And this is his commandment, that we believe in the name of his Son Jesus Christ and love one another, just as he has commanded us.

[30] **to convey from one place to another, *put in another place, transfer* –** BDAG, p. 642.

thereafter. These disobedient angels are now "spirits in prison," who have been thrown into "eternal chains under gloomy darkness [Tartarus],"[31] which is more of a condition of limited powers, **not** so much a place, like a maximum-security prison.--1 Peter 3:19; 2 Peter 2:4; Jude 6

The offspring of these unnatural relations between materialized angels and women were the Nephilim, giant humans of about 9.5 feet tall, who were half angel and half human, demigods. The world had become so corrupt and violent that this is why God brought the Flood. It is in this environment that Enoch courageously preached the message of condemnation, which he was commissioned to deliver to that evil world. We know that "all the days of Enoch were three hundred and sixty-five years. And **Enoch walked with God**, and he was no more, for God took him." – Genesis 5:23-24.

Enoch lived in a very violent world, where he was the only faithful follower of God at that time. Enoch only lived 365 years in an era where everyone else lived over 900 years. The "sons of God" mentioned in Genesis 6 were disobedient angels. The same expression "sons of God" is found in Job 1:6 and Job 38:7, and is applied to angels. The apostle Peter supports this interpretation as well, for he writes, "he [Jesus] went and proclaimed to the spirits in prison, because they formerly did not obey, when God's patience waited in the days of Noah while the ark was being prepared." (1 Pet 3:19-20) Moreover, Jude adds weight to this position as well, when he writes, "the angels who did not stay within their own position of authority, but left their proper dwelling, he has kept in eternal chains under gloomy darkness until the judgment of the great day." – Jude 1:6.

It would seem that Satan began his rebellion in Eden by himself, having no other angels take his side at that time. The issues that he raised had never been raised before human creation. Therefore, he had no real arguments to get other angels to join him in the Garden of Eden. However, they were certainly waiting and watching, seeing how things developed. Some 1,500 years later, in Noah's day, Satan could make the claim that he had misled all of humankind up unto that point, possibly thousands, with the exception of only three men Abel, Enoch and Noah. His argument to the angelic body could have been something like this, 'I alone misled thousands by myself, just imagine if I had help, with an army

---

[31] Tartarus is found only in 2 Peter 2:4. Tartarus is not to be confused with Hades or Gehenna. It is more of a condition than a place.

of angels, I could have completely thwarted God's plan, and humans would be worshiping us!'

Satan could have gone on to bolster his argument, by saying that he was winning against God, as fifteen centuries has passed since the rebellion in Eden, and where is this so-called promised "seed"? (Gen 3:15) He could have sold the plan that if the angels would use their powers to materialize in human form, having relations with the women of earth, they would produce an offspring of being who were half human and half angel, who could rule the earth, defeating God's plan of saving humankind. These demigods, Satan could argue, could take over and rule the earth, but be under Satan and the angels, who would receive the worship that rightly was going to go to God. While this is certainly, an inference of how the argument, behind the scenes, with Satan and the angels, could have gone, the Scriptures tell us, this is, in fact, how it went historically, leaving out the conversation behind the scenes.

The world had become so corrupt and violent that this was why God brought the flood. It is in this environment that Enoch courageously preached the message of condemnation, which he was commissioned to deliver to that evil world.

Hebrews 11:7 Updated American Standard Version (UASV)

⁷ By faith Noah, being warned by God about things not yet seen, **in reverence** prepared an ark for the salvation of his household, by which he condemned the world, and became an heir of the righteousness which is according to faith.

By faith, Noah "prepared an ark for the salvation of his household." (Heb. 11:7; Gen. 6:13-22) Noah was also "a proclaimer of righteousness" who also possessed great courage in preaching under the same conditions Enoch had; warning all that a great flood was coming. (2 Peter 2:5) Try to picture that evil world. You had the giant Nephilim causing everyone to live in fear, powerful angels materializing to take women, all living in debauchery, yet Noah and his family were walking with God, living a righteous life, doing all that God had commanded. Now, imagine having to go out and preach condemnation to these ones, saying that 'a worldwide flood is coming because God has judged you, repent now and be saved!' Imagine the ridicule, the threats that Noah and his family must have faced. How much faith it must have taken to work on the ark, day after day, month after month, all the while being threatened, taunted and mocked. Nevertheless, Noah did not allow fear of man, demigod, or even rebel angels to keep him from his commission as a preacher of righteousness. Unlike Adam and Eve, his love for God was greater than his love for man.

Genesis 6:13-22 Updated American Standard Version (UASV)

¹³ Then God said to Noah, "The end of all flesh has come before me; for the earth is filled with violence because of them; and behold, I am about to destroy them with the earth … ²² Thus **Noah did; according to all that God had commanded him**, so he did.

2 Peter 2:5 Updated American Standard Version (UASV)

⁵ and did not spare the ancient world, but preserved Noah, a **proclaimer of righteousness**, and seven others when he brought a flood on the world of the ungodly;

Yes, God thwarted Satan and his army of rebel angels, in the days of Noah. At the Flood, the giant Nephilim were destroyed, and the angels who had materialized in human form had to give up that body by dematerializing and going back to heaven. The angels, who were once "sons of God," did not return to the positions they previously held, they were in heaven with their new master, Satan, becoming his demon army. Yes, God did not spare the angels who sinned but held them captive in Tartarus, a prison-like condition, with chains of darkness he handed them over to be kept for judgment. (2 Pet. 2:4) However, the war was far from over, for the next 4,000 years, the battles for the minds of humankind continued.

The Faith of the Patriarchs

Hebrews 11:8-12 Updated American Standard Version (UASV)

⁸ By faith Abraham, when he was called, obeyed in going out[32] into a place he was destined to receive as an inheritance; and he went out, not knowing where he was going. ⁹ By faith he lived as an alien in the land of promise, as in a foreign land, dwelling in tents with Isaac and Jacob, fellow heirs of the same promise; ¹⁰ for he was looking for the city that has foundations, whose architect and builder is God. ¹¹ By faith Sarah herself received power to conceive,[33] even when she was past the age, since she considered him faithful who had promised. ¹² Therefore there was born even of one man who was as good as dead in these things, as

---

[32] Lit *to go out*

[33] Lit *power into throwing down of seed*

many descendants as the stars of heaven in number and as innumerable as the sand by the seashore.

Genuine faith includes our having complete confidence in God's promises. It was by faith that Abraham (Abram at the time) obeyed God and left the city of "Ur of the Chaldeans," a city that offered much to its citizens, meaning Abraham sacrificed materially, comforts like running water, and the safety of living in a big city. He believed God when he was told him, "Go from your country and your kindred and your father's house to the land that I will show you. And I will make of you a great nation, and I will bless you and make your name great, so that you will be a blessing. I will bless those who bless you, and him who dishonors you I will curse, and in you all the families of the earth shall be blessed." God also promised, "To your offspring I give this land, from the river of Egypt to the great river, the river Euphrates," (Gen. 12:1-9; 15:18-21, ESV) Both "Isaac and Jacob, [were] fellow heirs of the same promise." "By faith he lived as an alien in the land of promise, as in a foreign land." He looked "for the city that has foundations, whose architect and builder is God." While Abraham would not have known the specifics of this heavenly Kingdom and its King that Christians have had unlocked for them by the apostle Paul, he believed.

EXCURSION Faith of Abraham

ABRAHAM: When famine hit Canaan, Abraham went down to Egypt. In this, we find two incidents that are taken negatively toward Abraham. Before delving into them, let us preface this with almost all commentators read negative things into Abraham's life. To mention just a few,

(1) Ur was a place of idol worship in which Abram and his family participated (Josh. 24:2, 14).

(2) Abraham fled to Egypt because of the Famine in Canaan, as he lacked or lost faith in the promise that God would bless him.

(3) Abraham lied about his wife Sarai, saying she was his sister when they went to Egypt because he was only concerned about how he would be treated.

We will address each one of these, but let us take number **(2)** first, because Holman Commentary deals with it correctly initially, and then fails in every other place. Stephen Bramer and Kenneth O. Gangel in the *Holman Old Testament Commentary* Genesis wrote,

Commentators have offered numerous reasons why Abram took this trip: he was lonely in Canaan, he was depressed by Canaanite idolatry, his wife was barren. But the text only allows one—survival. The people of Canaan realized that Egypt was the bread basket of the world at that time [see "Deeper Discoveries"]. Griffith Thomas criticizes Abram for this decision and adds, "It would certainly seem that Abraham was now thinking solely of the land and its famine, and forgetting God and His promises" (Thomas, 119). Kidner adds, "His craven and tortuous calculations are doubly revealing, both of the natural character of this spiritual giant and of the sudden transition that can be made from the plane of faith to that of fear" (Kidner, 116). **But the text never faults Abraham for making the trip, only for lying about Sarai.**[34]

Notice the logic in the author's reasoning, "the text never faults Abram for the trip." We will build on this logic, for our setting the record straight about Abraham. Now, notice, in the very next sentence he drops the ball, calling Abraham a liar in the negative sense. He also states that the text faults Abraham about lying about Sarai. This is not true, but rather his reading it into the text. More on that in a moment, as we now, will go to number **(1)** Ur was a place of idol worship in which Abram and his family participated. – Joshua 24:2-14.

Response: Living in the midst of idolatry it is likely that Terah and his family engaged in it idol worship, which is what the text says, "Thus says the Lord, the God of Israel, 'Long ago, your fathers lived beyond the Euphrates, Terah, the father of Abraham and of Nahor; and they served other gods." However, the text says Terah and his family, which would have made up many people, including their slaves. We could be considering dozens of people, if not more. Thus, Abraham is mentioned because he is one of the most prominent persons within Scripture and he is the Son of Terah and the father of the Israelites. The reference "they" of "they served other gods," need not include Abraham.

Moreover, God specifically chose Abraham for his great faith. In fact, the rest of the Scriptures are founded on this man of faith. Faith is not based on simple belief, but rather on knowledge, understanding and wisdom. Abraham was the only one from the postflood era, who was evidencing faith in God. In addition, it is truly likely that his knowledge,

---

[34] Anders, Max; Gangel, Kenneth; Bramer, Stephen J. (2003-04-01). *Holman Old Testament Commentary - Genesis*: 1 (pp. 121-122). B&H Publishing. Kindle Edition.

understanding and wisdom came from a preflood person, i.e., Shem, the son of Noah, the only son to remain faithful. Shem lived 150 years into Abraham's life, meaning that Abraham's first 75 years before leaving Mesopotamia could very well have been personally associated with Shem. (Gen 9:26) Shem lived 500 years after fathering Arpachshad, dying at the age of 600 years. (Gen 11:10-11) He actually dies about 13 years after the death of Sarah. Returning to Joshua, the verse reads, "your fathers lived beyond the Euphrates, Terah, the father of Abraham and of Nahor; and **they served other gods**." Again, the "they" does not have to refer to Abraham just because he is mentioned in the verse. Yes, he is mentioned in the verse, but Terah was the father, the patriarch, and he had a very big family, so it is not as if Joshua could list them all. Abraham was referred to because of his being the most prominent one in Scripture. I say that since it does not out and out point the finger at Abraham and, when we consider that God explicitly chose Abraham because of his great faith, it is not likely Joshua was including Abraham. Would this be the case if Abraham had been an idol worshiper? No, it is because Abraham displayed great faith in God that he picked him to be the line to the Messiah. He earned the reputation "the righteousness of the faith which he had while uncircumcised, so that he might be the father of all who believe without being circumcised, that righteousness might be credited to them." – Romans 4:11.

What about accusation number **(3)** Abraham lied about his wife Sarai, saying she was his sister when they went into Egypt because he was only concerned about how he would be treated. Now, notice that the Homan commentators again find fault with Abraham. The Holman Commentary has,

> The Bedouin scheme he concocted was to speak a half-truth about his sister-wife. This was a subtle way to salve his own conscience. She was indeed his sister (actually a half-sister; cp. 20:12), so he conveyed to the Egyptians only what he wanted them to know. His motive was undoubtedly based on patriarchal society laws (cp. Laban, 24:29-61). In enemy territory a husband could be killed for his wife. But if Abram were known as her brother, someone wanting her would have to make marriage arrangement with him, which would possibly give him time to react in his own interest" (Ross, 49). 12:14-16. Abram had not counted on Sarai being approached by the one man in Egypt who needed no special permission to take a woman. Abram's selfish concern of verse 13 ["so that I will be treated well"] may have stuck in his throat, for Moses writes of

Pharaoh, he treated Abram well. Wealth in the ancient Middle East was not measured in gold but in animals, slaves, and land. 12:17-20. Abram's sin brought God's judgment on Pharaoh's house. But in a true demonstration of biblical grace, God overcame Abram's sin, forgave his lie, and sent him back to the land. Egyptian ethics insisted on absolute truthfulness, so Abram's behavior offended his hosts. Abram probably learned two important spiritual lessons from this side trip to Egypt—truth and trust. The lesson of trust he exemplified throughout the rest of his life. The issue of truth, unfortunately, gave him difficulty on at least one other occasion.[35]

Response: The standard of God is that there is no lying, which Exodus 20:16 makes all too clear, "You shall not bear false witness against your neighbor." However, When Abram was forced to go down to Egypt, because of a famine, he "said to Sarai his wife, 'I know that you are a woman beautiful in appearance, and when the Egyptians see you, they will say, 'This is his wife.' Then they will kill me, but they will let you live. Say you are my sister, that it may go well with me because of you, and that my life may be spared for your sake.'" (12:12-13) In Genesis chapter 20, we find Abraham repeating this behavior, even though it did not bode well for him the first time. Did Abraham lie these two times, and if so, why does the entire account of Abraham present him as righteously walking with God, the epitome of faith?

First, it should be mentioned that Sarah was the half-sister and wife of Abraham. Therefore, in essence, he did not lie about their relationship; he only withheld information that would have been used by the enemy, resulting in Abraham being possibly killed. It is true malicious lying is prohibited in the Bible, which is to say something that is not true in a conscious effort to deceive or hurt somebody that is deserving of the truth. However, the Bible has examples or cases where a person has withheld information from the enemy, who would have used that information to hurt or cause harm to a person or another. The Bible seems to suggest that we are not under obligation to divulge information to the enemy, which would result in our harm or the harm of another. The American legal system allows something like this as well. It is called The Fifth Amendment (Amendment V), which guarantees you do not have to testify against yourself.

---

[35] Anders, Max; Gangel, Kenneth; Bramer, Stephen J. (2003-04-01). *Holman Old Testament Commentary - Genesis*: 1 (p. 122). B&H Publishing. Kindle Edition.

Jesus Christ counseled, "Do not give dogs what is holy, and do not throw your pearls before pigs, lest they trample them underfoot and turn to attack you." (Matt 7:6) Even Jesus himself, who is incapable of malicious lying, on occasion, withheld information from those who were not worthy of it, and would have only used it to hurt him. (Matt 15:1-6; 21:23-27; John 7:3-10) We see this same principle under way with Abraham, Isaac, Rehab, and Elisha, as all pointed in the wrong direction or withheld all the facts from the enemies or nonworshipers.[36]

- A crazed gunman breaks into our house, and asks you, "Is anyone else here?" Are we obligated to tell him that your two little girls are upstairs hiding under the bed?
- What if we see a woman run into an alley to escape someone who is trying to kill her, and he asks us, "Where is she?" What do we do? Do we send him on a wild goose chase to protect the woman's life? Or do we lead them to him to the victim? – William Lane Craig
- During World War II, we are bringing a food box into a concentration camp. The guard asked us if there is any contraband inside. Would we be obligated to tell him that we have a small Bible smuggled into one of the packages?
- Are we to endanger a human life, or do we withhold information that the enemy does not deserve, nor have the right to, even giving them misinformation?

The advice offered here is twofold: **(1)** Do not read anything into the text that is not clearly stated, especially if it shines a negative light on someone like the father of all having faith, i.e., Abraham. All Scripture is inspired, meaning that the inspired writers of the New Testament can often settle gray areas in the Old Testament. **(2)** If the verse does not say it explicitly but, seems to suggest a negative on the first glance; then, look at the whole book for context, as well as the entire Bible. If it is a man or woman that God had special dealings with, give them the benefit of the doubt. If it is a person like wicked Nimrod; then, we can suggest such things. Use the entire Bible, as it is one book, by one author, with 40 plus writers, who wrote under inspiration, being led along by Holy Spirit. Again, many commentators tend to project negative unnecessary perceptions of Bible characters when the Bible itself has them in a positive light. Readers should ignore this. – **End of Excursion**

---

[36] Genesis 12:10-19; chap 20; 26:1-10; Jos 2:1-6; James 2:25; 2 Kings 6:11-23

The wives of the patriarchs, Sarah, Rebekah, and Rachel also had faith in God's promises. Many times, we tend to overlook the faithful women of Scripture. Scripture encourages us to 'consider the outcome of faithful one's way of life, and imitate their faith.' It also says, 'be imitators of those who through faith and patience inherit the promises. Dear Christian sisters; imagine what it would be like to have been neighbors, even friends with Rachel, Rebekah, Ruth, Hannah, Abigail, Esther, Mary, and the like. How might have they affected your life? For example, by faith Sarah, who had been barren for 90 years, "received power to conceive, even when she was past the age, since she considered him [God] faithful who had promised." Soon enough, Sarah gave birth to Isaac. Therefore, Abraham, who was one hundred at the time, "who was as good as dead in these things [reproduction]," had "as many descendants as the stars of heaven in number and as innumerable as the sand by the seashore." – Genesis 17:15-17; 18:11; 21:1-7.

EXCURSION Understanding Abraham and Sarah's Laughter (Genesis 17:17-18; 18:9-15)

Both Abraham and Sarah laughed when the angel announced that, they were to have a son when Abraham was 100 years old, and Sarah was 90. (Gen 18:16–21:7) We can note from the account that Abraham was **not** rebuked for his laughing, but Sarah was, which she even tried to deny. Therefore, there is no reason to see Abraham's laughter as nothing more than that of joy, for he was finally going to have a son with his beloved Sarah. However, Sarah's laughter was something more, as she saw this amazing prospect as humorous. In other words, the idea of having a child at the age of 90, when she had been barren all these years, struck her as funny. Maybe she was picturing her 90-year-old body being nine months pregnant and what she would have looked like. However, no one can rightfully look at the account, and come away with either Abraham or Sarah laughing because of contempt, disrespect or deliberate sarcasm as both are recorded as demonstrating faith in the promise God made. (Rom 4:18-22; Heb. 11:1, 8-12) – **End of Excursion**

The Godly Devotion of the Patriarchs

Hebrews 11:13-16 Updated American Standard Version (UASV)

[13] These all died in faith, not having received the things promised, but having seen them and greeted them from afar, and having acknowledged

that they were strangers and temporary residents in the land.[37] **14** For those who say such things make it clear that they are seeking a home territory of their own. **15** And indeed if they had been thinking of that territory from which they went out, they would have had opportunity to return. **16** But as it is, they desire a better territory, that is, a heavenly one.[38] Therefore God is not ashamed to be called their God, for he has prepared for them a city.

Faith will help us to remain devoted to God even when we do not even see the fulfillment of his promises. The patriarchs were promised that the new land (Canaan) would be theirs, and they would have descendants that outnumbered the stars or the sands of the seashore, yet they died without seeing that promise fulfilled. However, they saw [the promises] "from afar, and having acknowledged that they were strangers and temporary residents in the land." Yes, they faithfully lived very long lives in tough times, as they faced life and death, for centuries would pass before future generations would take possession of the Promised Land.

EXCURSION "in the land" vs "on the earth" and "a heavenly one"

It can be a bit misleading if the text is translated literally in verse 13, "on the earth," as opposed to interpretively, "in the land." This is especially so when verse 16 says the patriarchs were looking for a better 'land' or 'territory,' namely a heavenly one.' These texts could cause the reader to believe that the patriarchs were looking for some spiritual, heavenly kingdom.

Abraham and his family left Ur of the Chaldeans, and he no longer wanted that city. If the patriarchs had been "thinking of that territory from which they went out [Ur of the Chaldeans], they would have had opportunity to return." Abraham and his son Isaac, as well as his grandson Jacob and his great grandson Joseph 'desired a better territory,' that is, "a heavenly one," i.e. they looked for a heavenly like territory prepared by God. Bible commentators Dods and Lane, take it in reference to the land of Canaan, i.e., the Promised Land, which was described as

---

[37] Lit on the earth; the Greek (*ges*) literally means "earth, land, region, humanity," and it is the context that determines our word choice. The Greek here means the surface of the earth as the habitation of humanity. (BDAG) Dods and Lane, take it in reference to the land of Canaan. (Dods, "Hebrews," 357; Lane, *Hebrews 9–13*, 357) See vs 16 note

[38] The patriarchs were not looking for any spiritual, heavenly resurrection

being like the Garden of Eden.[39] It should be added that Jerusalem was the "city of our God" (Psa. 46:4; 48:1, 8; 87:3; Heb. 12:22) and the city of Jehovah (Psa. 48:8; 101:8; Isa. 60:14, ASV), its name means "two-fold peace." The things promised to these patriarchs were possession of the land, the founding of a nation, and blessing that would come through Abraham's offspring. These are the things the patriarchs looked for, which would have been encompassed in the land of Canaan, known as the Promised Land.

In 30 C.E., Jesus told Nicodemus, "No one has ascended into heaven except he who descended from heaven, the Son of Man." (John 3:13) In essence, Jesus said that Abraham, Isaac and Jacob, nor Joseph, not even David were in heaven. Some three years later, Pentecost 33 C.E., the apostle Peter said similarly, "For David did not ascend into the heavens." If David did not ascend into the heavens, the same would be true of Abraham, Isaac, Jacob and Joseph. The opportunity for life in heaven was not available to imperfect humans when they died, until the death, resurrection, and ascension of Jesus Christ. (Jn. 14:2-3; Heb. 9:24; 10:19-20) This is why we are told in 2 Kings 2:10, "then David slept with his fathers [he died] and was buried in the city of David." In other words, David had the hope of a future resurrection, once the ransom was paid. (Gen 3:15) The hope of a heavenly resurrection is not discussed in the Old Testament, or any time prior to Christ, as he is the first to bring it up. (Matt. 19:21, 23-28; Lu 12:32; John 14:2-3) The resurrection hope was not fully understood until after Pentecost 33 C.E. (Acts 1:6-8; 2:1-4, 29-36; Rom. 8:16-17) Even Job expected that at his death, he would be asleep in death in the grave, until a future resurrection. (Job 14:13-15) What these patriarchs looked for was a heavenly like city prepared by God. The patriarchs were **not** looking for some spiritual, heavenly kingdom. **End of Excursion**

Just because the prophetic promises were not fulfilled within their lifetime, this did not embitter Abraham, Isaac, Jacob, and Joseph. This did not cause them to turn away from the only true God. No, they did not take the easy way out by running back to Ur of the Chaldeans, where life was easier, having many relatives that were likely involved in worldly activities.[40] No, those patriarchs "desire a better territory, that is, a heavenly one," namely, looking for a heavenly like territory prepared by

---

[39] See Num. 13:23; Deut. 8:7-9; 11:9, 11-15; 26:15; Isa. 51:3; 58:11; Jer. 31:12; Eze. 36:35

[40] Compare John 17:16; 2 Timothy 4:10; James 1:27; 1 John 2:15-17.

God, in the land of Canaan, known as the Promised Land, containing the city of God, Jerusalem. 'Therefore, God is not ashamed to be called their God, for he has prepared for them a city.' They remained faithful until death having a hope of a future resurrection, where the Messiah, Jesus Christ, whom they were never able to see will bring them back. (John 5:28-29; Acts 24:15)[41] What about us, have we been walking with God for some time? We must maintain our confidence in the return of Christ, even if it does not happen in our lifetime. (3 John 1:4; 2 Pet. 3:11-13) The reward is well worth anything we might suffer for the faith, and the promises are true.

Hebrews 11:17-19 Updated American Standard Version (UASV)

¹⁷ By faith Abraham, when he was tested, offered up[42] Isaac, and he who had received the promises was offering up[43] his only begotten son, ¹⁸ of whom it was said, "In Isaac your seed[44] shall be called," ¹⁹ having reasoned that God was able even to raise him from the dead, from which, figuratively speaking,[45] he did receive him back.

One of the most important aspects of genuine faith is unquestioning obedience to God. Since Abraham obeyed God without question, he offered up Isaac, his only begotten son, i.e., the only one he had by Sarah. How could Abraham have listened to a command to offer Isaac? Because he "reasoned that God was able even to raise him from the dead, from which" the promised offspring would come. Abraham held the knife high above his head ready to plunge it into Isaac, ending his life, when an angel's voice brought him to a halt. Therefore, Abraham received Isaac

---

[41] **Resurrection Hope - Where?**

http://www.christianpublishers.org/resurrection-hope-where

[42] An interpretive translation could read, "as good as offered up Isaac." The Greek verb here (*prosenenochen*) translated "offered up" is in the perfect tense, where the writer describes "a completed verbal action that occurred in the past but which produced a state of being or a result that exists in the present (in relation to the writer). The emphasis of the perfect is not the past action so much as it is as such but the present 'state of affairs' resulting from the past action." (GMSDT) Dods and Moffatt take the perfect tense to refer only to a past act with no emphasis being suggested by the author. (Dods, "Hebrews," 358; Moffatt, Hebrews, 176.)

[43] The Greek verb here (*prosepheren*) translated "was offering up" is in the imperfect tense, "where the writer portrays an action in process or a state of being that is occurring in the past with no assessment of the action's completion." (GMSDT) Therefore, this rendering is in harmony with what actually happened.

[44] Or *descendants*; *offspring*

[45] Lit *in a parable*; Gr *enparabolei*

back from the dead in a figurative way. We too should be ready to obey God even if life is in jeopardy, as there will be a future resurrection. (1 John 5:3) It should be mention that, Abraham and Isaac portrayed how the Father would offer up his only-begotten Son, Jesus Christ, as a ransom sacrifice so that those having faith in him might receive eternal life. – Genesis 22:1-19; John 3:16.

Hebrews 11:20-22 Updated American Standard Version (UASV)

²² By faith also Isaac blessed Jacob and Esau concerning things to come. ²¹ By faith Jacob, as he was dying, blessed each of the sons of Joseph, and worshiped, leaning on the top of his staff. ²² By faith Joseph, when he was dying, made mention of the exodus of the sons of Israel, and he gave a command⁴⁶ concerning his bones.

If we truly have genuine faith; then, we would be very eager to help our family to place their hope in the promises of God. Even though the promises of God was not fulfilled in the lifetime of these patriarchs, their faith was so great, their priority was sharing that hope with each generation, making sure their children cherished their relationship with the Father. Therefore, "Isaac blessed Jacob and Esau concerning things to come." 'In addition, "Jacob, as he was dying, blessed each of the sons of Joseph [Ephraim and Manasseh], and worshiped, leaning on the top of his staff." Joseph had such great faith in the promises of God, especially that his people would inherit the Land of Canaan, he commanded them that they take his bones with them when they departed long after his death. (Genesis 27:27-29, 38-40; 48:8-22; 50:24-26) Are we operating by faith?

Faith Moves Us to Put God First

Hebrews 11:23-26 Updated American Standard Version (UASV)

²³ By faith Moses, when he was born, was hidden for three months by his parents, because they saw he was a beautiful child; and they did not fear the edict of the king. ²⁴ By faith Moses, when he had grown up, refused to be called the son of the daughter of Pharaoh, ²⁵ choosing to be ill-treated with the people of God rather than to have the temporary enjoyment of sin, ²⁶ considering the reproach of Christ greater riches than the treasures of Egypt; for he was looking to the reward.

If we truly have genuine faith; then, we will place God ahead of everything this world has to offer us. The Israelites were made slaves in

---

⁴⁶ Or *gave instructions; gave orders*

Egypt after the death of Joseph, in dire need of being delivered, when the parents of Moses took action. "They did not fear the edict of the king," which was to kill every Hebrew male at birth. Rather, when Moses was born, they hid him for three months. "But when she could hide him no longer, she got a papyrus basket for him, and she coated it with tar and with pitch. She put the child in it and placed it among the reeds by the bank of the Nile. And his sister [Miriam] stood at a distance to know what would be done to him. Now the daughter of Pharaoh came down to bathe at the river while her young women walked beside the river. She saw the basket among the reeds and she sent her slave girl, and she took it." (Ex. 2:1-10) The daughter of Pharaoh had a Hebrew woman nurse baby Moses, which actually was his mother, Jochebed. Therefore, Moses was initially nursed and spiritually trained by his father Amram and his mother, Jochebed. Then, growing up under the roof of the Pharaoh's daughter, Moses was instructed in all the wisdom of the Egyptians, and he was mighty in his words and deeds. – Acts 7:20-22.

However, an Egyptian education and the wealth of the Egyptian Empire did not result in Moses abandoning his faith in the only true God. Rather, "when he had grown up, refused to be called the son of the daughter of Pharaoh," a path underscored when he defended a Hebrew brother. (Exodus 2:11-12) Moses chose "to be ill-treated with the people of God [Fellow Israelites] rather than to have the temporary enjoyment of sin." If we are a true servant of God, who has maintained a prayer life, regular meeting attendance, personal Bible study, preparing for Christian meetings, and sharing God's Word, we are following Moses' example, taking a firm stand for pure worship. The battle for true worship is raging even more so today than any other time and, we need to take a stand.

Moses left the house of Pharaoh to join God's chosen people, "considering the reproach of Christ greater riches than the treasures of Egypt; for he was looking to the reward." In other words, Moses valued the reproach of being the ancient type of Christ (Messiah), i.e., anointed one, as greater riches than the treasures of Egypt. John Macarthur writes, "Moses suffered reproach for the sake of Christ in the sense that he identified with Messiah's people in their suffering (v. 25). In addition, Moses identified himself with the Messiah because of his own role as leader and prophet (cf. 12:2; Deut. 18:15; Pss. 69:9; 89:51). Moses knew of the sufferings and glory of the Messiah (cf. John 5:46; Acts 26:22, 23; 1 Pet. 1:10–12). Anyone who suffers because of genuine faith in God and for the redemptive gospel suffers for the sake of Christ (cf. 13:12, 13; 1 Pet.

4:14)."[47] Being a member of Pharaoh's house, Moses could have enjoyed a life of luxury, wealth, power, and prestige. However, by faith, he was "looking to the reward."

Hebrews 11:27-29 Updated American Standard Version (UASV)

[27] By faith he left Egypt, not fearing the wrath of the king; for he endured, as seeing him who is invisible. [28] By faith he kept the Passover, and the sprinkling of the blood, that the destroyer of the firstborn should not touch them. [29] By faith they passed through the Red Sea as on dry land, but when the Egyptians attempted it, they were swallowed up.[48]

Faith can also make us fearless in the face of difficulty, even death, because we have complete trust in God as a deliverer. When Pharaoh heard of it that Moses had killed an Egyptian, he sought to kill Moses. However, Moses fled from Pharaoh and stayed in the land of Midian. (Ex. 2:11-15) In the above, the book of Hebrews is alluding to forty years later, when the Israelites had to exodus Egypt, saying, "By faith he [Moses] left Egypt, not fearing the wrath of the king [who threatened Moses with death for being a representative of God to the Israelites]; for he [Moses] endured, as seeing him who is invisible." (Ex. 10:28-29) Even though Moses had never seen God, His interactions with Moses were so real; it was as though Moses was "seeing him who is invisible." (Ex. 33:20) If we fully commit ourselves to God, fully trusting in him, he will act on our behalf. Can we say that our relationship with God is that strong, or do we waver in difficult times? – Psalm 37:5; Proverbs 16:3.

Just before their exodus from Egypt, "By faith he kept the Passover, and the sprinkling of the blood, that the destroyer of the firstborn should not touch them [i.e., the Israelites]." There is little doubt; it had to of taken faith to keep the Passover, being certain that the firstborn of Israel would come away unscathed while those of the Egyptians would die. Moses faith was rewarded. (Exodus 12:1-39) God proved to be a great deliverer, as the Israelites "passed through the Red Sea as on dry land, but when the Egyptians attempted it, they were swallowed up." The book of Exodus tells us "Israel saw the great hand[49] that Jehovah used against Egypt, and the people feared Jehovah, and they believed in Jehovah and

---

[47] MacArthur, John (2005-05-09). *The MacArthur Bible Commentary* (Kindle Locations 62689-62692). Thomas Nelson. Kindle Edition.

[48] Or *they were drowned*

[49] Or *power*

in Moses his servant." (Exodus 14:21-31) The faith of the patriarchs and Moses are a great model for Christians today.

Review Questions

- How is the Christian race for life like the Olympic runner?
- What do the Bible scholars say about Hebrews 12:1
- What does Hebrews 11:1 mean by "assurance of faith"?
- What do the Bible scholars say about Hebrews 11:1-3?
- What does Kistemaker say about "assurance" and "certainty"?
- What are some Christians confusing with faith?
- What do the Greek words behind "assurance" and "conviction" mean?
- What was the difference between Cain and Abel's sacrifices and what was Abel capable of discerning?
- What is faith?
- What does Enoch's example teach us about faith?
- How can we view the two incidents where Abraham use Sarah being his sister, hoping it would save his life?
- How can we understanding Abraham and Sarah's laughter?
- What did the patriarchs show us about having complete confidence in God's promises?
- What action did Abraham take that evidenced his unquestioning obedience to God, showing us that obedience is a vital facet of faith?
- How did the life of Moses show us that faith means putting God and his people ahead of everything in the world?

CHAPTER 2 Do Not Let Doubts Destroy Your Faith

Life is going well for us, we are in perfect health; and then, suddenly we fall ill. Unexpectedly, we have no strength or vitality. Then, as suddenly, we have intense headaches and our entire body is afflicted with pain. What is going on, we might be asking? The dangerous bacterium, virus, or other microorganisms that can cause disease have infiltrated our body's defenses and are attacking our vital organs. If we ignore these symptoms, hoping everything will get better; these invading pathogens could destroy our good health permanently, even causing death.

Certainly, if we had not been in good health to begin with, we would have been even more helpless and defenseless. Suppose we ate poorly, suffering from malnutrition. In other words, we are lacking healthy foods in our diet, or just not taking in enough calories each day, which can lead to poor health all by itself. Suffering from malnutrition can lower or resistance to infectious pathogens, it could be fatal, even if we seek medical help.

When we pause to consider, who would choose to live in a famine like condition? If we knew what was happening to our body, slowly, over time, we would take appropriate actions to avoid exposing ourselves to a dangerous bacterium, virus, or any other microorganisms. Of course, this was all leading to the importance of being and remaining "healthy in faith." (Titus 2:2) Are we like the young person, who believes nothing bad physically can happen to them, so they eat poorly, and similarly we think our faith is so strong, we would never stumble spiritually, or we would never doubt? Are we, for example, alert to all of the misleading information by Bible critics today? If we take these in without being healthy spiritually, prepared, they can invade our minds and hearts, ruining our relationship with God. Sadly, many Christians are unaware of this danger; others, ignore warning signs while some even seek this kind of information out. Some actually believe they are not susceptible to doubts, not realizing they have been starving themselves spiritually because they have simply been snacking on the Word of God.

Are Doubts Always Bad?

Most of us can conclude that not all doubts are bad. If we were considering something where we did not have all of the facts, we would want to hold off on accepting it, until we are sure. We hear the mantra in the different Christian denominations today, "Don't be afraid – just believe." (Mark 5:36) Some feel that faith is merely believing and doubting nothing at all. This is very naïve, dangerous, and deceptive. Yes, it is true that certain Bible verses can be used to suggest that all we need to do is, 'just believe,' like "Love ... believes all things," at 1 Corinthians 13:7. Even the demons believe, and yet they shudder. (Jam. 2:19) A genuine Christian, who has the love of Christ in their heart, should believe those who have proved trustworthy over the years. However, God's Word also warns against 'believing every word.' (Pro. 14:15, LEB) Jesus said, "Beware of false prophets, who come to you in sheep's clothing but inwardly are ravenous wolves." (Matt 7:15, ESV) Does this not suggest there will be some who appear as innocent as sheep, but really are false prophets to the point of being ravenous wolves?

The apostle John warns Christians against believing things blindly. He wrote, "Beloved ones, do not believe every spirit, but test the spirits to see whether they are from God, for many false prophets have gone out into the world." (1 John 4:1) John Stott notes, "Neither Christian believing nor Christian loving is to be indiscriminate. In particular, Christian faith is not to be mistaken for credulity [i.e., gullibility]. True faith examines its object before reposing confidence in it." (Stott 2009, p. 156) Daniel L. Akin writes, "His [John's] warning is clear: behind every statement is a spirit, a pneuma, but not every spirit is the Spirit of God." (Akin 2001, p. 170) This spirit, i.e., statement or teaching, may seem as though it has come from God; then, in fact, it has come from a deceiver, and to be generous, someone who is simply mistaken or misinformed. We need to have some doubt, or let us say a level of cautiousness, which will serve as a protection, as the apostle John wrote, "Many deceivers have gone out into the world." – 2 John 7, ESV.

Unfounded Doubts

Certainly, we are on the safe side of things, if we honestly, humbly examine the facts of any situation, to arrive at the truth. However, this is **not the same as,** allowing unfounded, destructive doubts to grow in our mind and heart, doubts that can ruin our firmly established beliefs and relationships. Nevertheless, the objective way of believing certain Bible doctrines as being the truth is as follows. The biblical view of the doctrine _____ is _____, and it is the truth, unless, enough evidence comes along to say otherwise. If we grow in knowledge and understanding, our conclusions based on previous knowledge may need to be revised. For increased knowledge can require adjustments in one's thinking. We must remember the Apostle Paul studied under the renowned Pharisee Gamaliel, who was the grandson of Hillel, the Elder (110 B.C.E.[50] – 10 C.E.), the founder of one of the two schools within Judaism. Paul describes himself as "circumcised on the eighth day, of the people of Israel, of the tribe of Benjamin, a Hebrew of Hebrews; as to the law, a Pharisee; as to zeal, a persecutor of the church; as to righteousness under the law, blameless." (Phil 3:5-6) He also states, "But whatever gain I had, I counted as loss for the sake of Christ. Indeed, I count everything as loss because of the surpassing worth of knowing Christ Jesus my Lord. For his sake I have suffered the loss of all things and count them as rubbish, in order that I may gain Christ" (Phil. 3:7-8) Thus, we know that the Israelites were God's chosen people and the only way to God for some 1,500 years. However, Jesus brought a new way, Christianity. Saul/Paul was slow to accept this because he could not see Jesus Christ as the long-awaited Messiah. Nevertheless, after Jesus visited Paul on the road to Damascus and Ananias, a Christian disciple of Damascus, visited Paul, he saw the Old Testament Scriptures pointing to the Messiah accurately, he was able to humble himself and accept a different belief, i.e., Christianity was the truth and the way.

To believe without enough support, to believe in the face of contrary evidence is irrational. Therefore, we must humbly examine the facts behind what we believe, to establish the truth continually. Just as the apostle Paul exhorted the Christians at Corinth to "examine yourselves, to see whether you are in the faith. Test yourselves" (2 Cor. 13:5), we could say the very same thing about our beliefs. We could say, 'examine our beliefs, to see whether they are the truth, test our beliefs.' Now, this is not to suggest that our beliefs are to be ever changing, but that they should be able to stand up to scrutiny when they are challenged by something we have heard or read. However, this refinement of our beliefs should not be confused with allowing unfounded, damaging doubts to grow in our hearts and minds, doubts that can destroy our confidently established beliefs and our relationship with our heavenly Father. **Unfounded doubt** is defined as something that is not supported by any evidence or a minuscule amount of evidence, to cause uncertainty of belief or opinion that often interferes with our decision-making skills.

Let us go back to the first unfounded doubt in human history, Adam and Eve. Satan the Devil by way of the serpent caused Eve to question her

---

[50] B.C.E. years ran down toward zero, although the Romans had no zero, and C.E. years ran up from zero. (100, 10, 3, 2, 1 ◄B.C.E. | C.E.► 1, 2, 3, 10, and 100)

beliefs,[51] i.e., by planting *unfounded doubt* in her mind. Satan said to Eve through the serpent, "Did God actually say, 'You[52] shall not eat of any tree in the garden'?" (Gen. 3:1) Without saying it, the insinuation here was that God was withholding something from Adam and Eve, and this was unbelievable that he would do such a thing. Satan placed uncertainty in the mind of Eve with this innocent-appearing question, which influenced her decision-making.[53] This is similar to a **poison pen letter**, which contains unpleasant, abusive or malicious statements or accusations about the recipient or a third party. It is usually sent anonymously. Poison pen letters are usually composed and sent to upset the recipient. They differ from blackmail, which is intended to obtain something, in that they are purely malicious. Saran is the father of the lie. (John 8:44) He will deceive with outright lies, half-truths, hint or an indirect remark or gesture

---

[51] As we can see from most English translations at Genesis 3:16, the plain sense of the text is, Adam was with her, which creates a real Bible difficulty. The reason for the difficulty is this, they are taking it as though Adam and Eve are standing before the tree of knowledge of good and evil, and the serpent, Satan, starts to speak to Eve. They carry on a conversation, with Adam simply passively listening. Satan deceives Eve, but Adam is not deceived, yet he does not argue with the serpent, snatch the fruit from Eve, but rather just stands there letting Eve eat the fruit, knowing she will die. Really? I just cannot see how that can rationally be the case. I would argue that Eve was alone before Adam joined her.

Was Adam standing beside Eve when she had the conversation with the serpent, was deceived and chose to rebel against God? The Bible shows no indication that this is the case. The translations above make it appear as though that is the case, "she took of its fruit and ate, and she also **gave** some to **her husband who was with her**, and he ate."

The Hebrew verb translated "gave" is in the imperfect waw consecutive, as a result, it points to a temporal or logical sequence (usually called an "imperfect sequential"). Hence, a Bible translator or committee can translate the several occurrences of the waw, which tie together the chain of events in verse 6, with "and" as well as other transitional words, such as "subsequently," "then," "after that," afterward," and "so."

Genesis 3:6 Updated American Standard Version (UASV)

6 So when the woman saw that the tree was good for food, **and** that it was a delight to the eyes, **and** that the tree was to be desirable to make one wise, **and** she took of its fruit **and** ate, *then* she also gave some to her husband when with her, **and** he ate.

[52] In Hebrew *you* is plural in verses 1–5

[53] Eve was the newest person to the Garden of Eden, which is why Satan chose her instead of Adam. Moreover, serpents could not talk, which is why Eve likely felt that what the serpent was saying might not be true. Imagine, she was walking by the **tree of knowledge** and a serpent that cannot speak is hanging from a limb, eating the fruit, and it turns its head and begins to speak to Eve. The fact Eve is not surprised makes some commentators believe the Serpent must have been able to speak. No, rather Eve is not surprised because it seems the fruit of the tree can give you special knowledge, for the snake is likely eating of the fruit from this **tree of knowledge**. Satan is actually using the serpent as a modern day ventriloquist uses a dummy when he projects his voice. Satan was and is a very powerful demon.

that usually carries a suggestion. Now, we can recognize that the doubt placed in the mind of Eve is unfounded when we go back to what God really said. "God commanded the man, saying, "From **every tree of the garden** you may freely eat, **¹⁷** but from the tree of the knowledge of good and evil you shall not eat,⁵⁴ for in the day that you eat from it you shall surely die."⁵⁵ (Gen 2:16-17) What Satan did was take Eve's mind off the fact she had tens of thousands of fruit trees to eat from, meaning she lacked nothing, and place her focus on a supposed negative, God prohibiting one tree. Satan was asking an inferential question, "Did God actually say, 'You shall not eat of any tree in the garden'?" First, he is overstating what he knows to be true, not "any tree," just one tree. Second, Satan is inferring, 'I can't believe that God would say ... how dare he say such a thing.'

How did Eve respond? She said to the serpent, "From the fruit of the trees of the garden we may eat, but from the tree that is in the midst of the garden, God said, 'You shall not eat from it, **nor shall you touch it**, lest you die.'" (Gen. 3:2) Notice that Eve has been told so thoroughly about the tree that she even goes beyond what Adam told her, not just that you 'do not eat from it,' no, 'you do not even touch it!' Then, Satan out and out lied and slandered God as a liar, saying that 'they would not die.' To make matters much worse, he infers that God is withholding good from them, and by rebelling they would be better off, being like God, 'knowing good and bad.'⁵⁶ This knowing good and bad was the ability to choose for themselves what was good and what was bad, i.e., independence from God, rejecting his sovereignty.

---

⁵⁴ Lit *eat from it*

⁵⁵ Lit., *dying you* [singular] *shall die.* Heb., *moth tamuth*; the first reference to death in the Scriptures

⁵⁶ This latter point is not knowledge of; it is the self-sovereignty of choosing good and bad for oneself and act of rebellion for created creatures. What was symbolized by the tree is well expressed in a footnote on Genesis 2:17, in The Jerusalem Bible (1966):

> This knowledge is a privilege which God reserves to himself and which man, by sinning, is to lay hands on, 3:5, 22. Hence it does not mean omniscience, which fallen man does not possess; nor is it moral discrimination, for unfallen man already had it and God could not refuse it to a rational being. It is the power of deciding for himself what is good and what is evil and of acting accordingly, a claim to complete moral independence by which man refuses to recognize his status as a created being. The first sin was an attack on God's sovereignty, a sin of pride.

The Issues at Hand

(1) Satan called God a liar and said he was not to be trusted, as to the life or death issue.

(2) Satan's challenge, therefore, took into question the right and legitimacy of God's rightful place as the Universal Sovereign.

(3) Satan also suggested that people would remain obedient to God only as long as their submitting to God was to their benefit.

(4) Satan all but said that humankind was able to walk on his own, there being no need for dependence on God.

(5) Satan argued that man could be like God, choosing for himself what is right and wrong.

(6) Satan claimed that God's way of ruling was not in the best interests of humans, and they could do better without God.

We can turn to the disciple James to understand how Eve, a perfect human could choose to sin. How she could be so easily influenced. James warns, "The one who doubts is like a wave of the sea that is driven and tossed by the wind." One who doubts is "a double-minded[57] man, unstable in all his ways."[58] (Jam. 1:6-8) How did this doubt come about in the perfect woman's mind? Satan offered her unfounded doubt, by suggesting, inferring, supposing certain things, which were not supported by any evidence, and it caused uncertainty of belief or opinion that interfered with our decision-making skills. James goes on to write, "each one is tempted when he is carried away and enticed by his own desire.[59] Then the desire when it has conceived gives birth to sin, and sin when it is fully grown brings forth death." (Jam. 1:14-15) Just as it happened to Eve,

---

[57] Or "*indecisive*," i.e., wavering in mind

[58] "**With no doubting**. This refers to having one's thinking divided within himself, not merely because of mental indecision but an inner moral conflict or distrust in God (see note on v. 8). **Wave of the sea.** The person who doubts God's ability or willingness to provide this wisdom is like the billowing, restless sea, moving back and forth with its endless tides, never able to settle (cf. Josh. 24:15; 1 Kin. 18:21; Rev. 3:16). 1:8 double-minded man. A literal translation of the Greek expression that denotes having one's mind or soul divided between God and the world (see note on 4:4). This man is a hypocrite who occasionally believes in God but fails to trust Him when trials come, and thus receives nothing. The use of this expression in 4:8 makes it clear that it refers to an unbeliever. **unstable.**" – MacArthur, John (2005-05-09). *The MacArthur Bible Commentary* (Kindle Locations 63042-63049). Thomas Nelson. Kindle Edition.

[59] Or "own *lust*"

a perfect human, with her uncertainty of belief, we can become vulnerable to all sorts of false teachings and empty, deceitful philosophy that is according to human traditions and the elemental spirits of the world, and not according to Christ."

Examine Yourselves to See Whether You Are In the Faith

2 Corinthians 13:5 Updated American Standard Version (UASV)

⁵ Keep testing yourselves to see if you are in the faith. Keep examining yourselves! Or do you not realize this about yourselves, that Jesus Christ is in you, unless indeed you fail to meet the test?

When was the last time that we truly took a good look at ourselves? How did we feel about what we saw? When we ponder over our personality, what are we actually projecting to others? Most of us are very complex people when it comes to our thoughts, feeling and beliefs, so it might be difficult to lock down what kind of personality that we have. As a man, are we faithful like Abraham one moment and then blown back and forth like doubting Thomas the next? As a female, are we submissive like Sarah when we are in public and then like domineering Jezebel in private? As a Christian, are we devoted and energetic for the truth on Christian meeting days and then loving the world like Demas[60] the other days out of the week? As a Christian, have we entirely taken off the old person with its practices and clothed ourselves with the new person? – Colossians 3:9-10; Ephesians 4:20-24.

Some women are known to spend much time every morning, 'putting on their face,' as it is commonly expressed. So much so, it has been commonly joked about, and men know not to interfere until the project is over. However, truth be told, men are very much concerned with how they look when going out into public. Thus, all of us are conscious of whether our hair is out of place, if we have a pimple or a cold sore, or if there is something about us that is unkempt, ruffled, scruffy, or messy. We want to look our best. What we may have not considered is, our personality, is always showing as well. The deeper question though is "are we putting on our personality to cover over before we go out in public while our real personality is on display in

---

[60] A "fellow worker" with Paul at Rome (Col. 4:14; Philem. 24), who eventually, "in love with this present world," forsook the apostle and left for Thessalonica (2 Tim. 4:10). No other particulars are given concerning him. (ISBE, Volume 1, Page 918)

private?" Is what the public sees, who we really are? Does our real personality bring honor to God?

A man walking the roads of the countryside in a small European country comes to a fork in the road. He is uncertain as to which way he should go. Therefore, he asks several who are passing by for directions, but some told him to take the left fork, and others said to make the right. After receiving contradictory information, he simply did not know what to do, how was he to go on, without knowing for certain which path led to the destination. He was unable to move on until he knew what the right path was. Having doubts about our faith, our walk with God, his Word can influence us similarly. It can actually cause severe emotional turmoil as we go about our Christian life.

There was a similar situation in the first-century Corinthian congregation. Some known as "super-apostles" were actually taking the apostle Paul to task, as to Paul's walk with God, saying, "His letters are weighty and strong, but his bodily presence is weak, and his speech of no account." (2 Cor. 10:7-12; 11:5-6, ESV) Certainly, we can see how a Christian in that congregation could wonder if they were truly walking with God when the apostle Paul himself was being called into question.

Paul founded the Corinthian congregation in about 50 C.E.[61] on his second missionary journey. "When Silas and Timothy arrived from Macedonia, Paul was occupied with the word, testifying to the Jews that the Christ was Jesus. And the Lord said to Paul one night in a vision, 'Do not be afraid, but go on speaking and do not be silent, for I am with you, and no one will attack you to harm you, for I have many in this city who are my people.' And he stayed a year and six months, teaching the word of God among them." (Acts 18:5-11, ESV) The apostle Paul was deeply interested in the spiritual well-being of the brothers and sisters in Corinth. Moreover, the Corinthian Christians were interested in their spiritual welfare as well, so they wrote Paul for his counsel on certain matters. (1 Cor. 7:1-40) Therefore, Paul, under inspiration offered them inspired counsel in what would be his second letter to them.

"Keep testing yourselves to see if you are in the faith. Keep examining yourselves! Or do you not realize this about yourselves, that Jesus Christ is in you, unless indeed you fail to meet the test?" (2 Cor. 13:5) If these brothers in the days of having Paul found their

---

[61] B.C.E. means "before the Common Era," which is more accurate than B.C. ("before Christ"). C.E. denotes "Common Era," often called A.D., for *anno Domini*, meaning "in the year of our Lord."

congregation, who spent sixteen months under the guidance of the greatest, inspired Christian, needed to self-examine themselves, how much more should we need to do so, as we are 2,000-years removed. If these brothers followed this advice to examine themselves, it would have offered them direction on how to walk with God and let them know if they were on the right path.

Remember, Jesus warned, "Not everyone who says to me, 'Lord, Lord,' will enter the kingdom of heaven, but **the one who does** the will of my Father who is in heaven." (Matt 7:21, ESV) In other words, not every Christian was going to enter into the kingdom, even though they felt that they were walking with God. Jesus spoke of their mindset in the next verse, "On that day many will say to me, 'Lord, Lord, did we not prophesy in your name, and cast out demons in your name, and do many mighty works in your name?'" (Matt. 7:22, ESV) Yes, these ones, who felt that they were walking with God, on that day they were supposing that they were truly Christian, were in for a rude awakening. What is Jesus going to say to these ones, "And then will I declare to them, 'I never knew you; depart from me, you workers of lawlessness.'" (Matt. 7:23) What were and are these ones lacking?

Jesus said they were **not doing the will of the Father**, even though they believed they were. Notice that in 98 C.E., the apostle John, the last surviving apostle, in one of his letters offered that same warning too. He wrote, "The world is passing away, and its lusts; but the one who does the will of God remains forever." (1 John 2:17) Thus, we can see the wisdom of the apostle Paul's counsel to 'Keep testing ourselves to see if you are in the faith. Keep examining ourselves!' Thus, the next question is, what do we need to do to follow this advice? How does one test whether or not they are in the faith? In addition, what does it mean to 'keep examining ourselves after we have tested ourselves?

Keep Testing Yourselves

In a **test**, there is an examination of a person or an object to find something out, e.g. whether it is functioning properly or not. In this **test**, there must be a standard by which the person or object is measured. For example, the "normal" human body temperature is 98.6°F (37°C). Therefore, if we were testing our temperature, it would be measured against the normal body temperature. Anything above or below that would be considered high or low. Another example is the normal resting heart rate for adults, which ranges from 60 to 100 beats a minute.

However, our test in this publication is to see if we are truly Christian. However, what we are looking for when we 'test ourselves, to see if we are in the faith,' **is not** the faith, that is the basic Bible doctrines. In our test, we are the subject. What we are testing is, if we are truly walking with God. If we are to test our walk as a Christian, we need to have a perfect standard. Our perfect standard by which to measure ourselves is,

Psalm 19:7-8 Updated American Standard Version (UASV)

⁷ The law of Jehovah is perfect,
 restoring the soul;
the testimony of Jehovah is sure,
 making wise the simple.
⁸ The precepts of Jehovah are right,
 rejoicing the heart;

Yes, the Word of God, the Bible is the standard by which we can measure our walk with God. On this, the author of Hebrews wrote, "For the word of God is living and active and sharper than any two-edged sword, and piercing as far as the division of soul and spirit, of both joints and marrow, and able to judge the thoughts and intentions of the heart." (Heb. 4:12) Thus, we must test our walk with God by examining our life course as outlined by Scripture, to find his favor, to be in an approved standing, to be declared righteous before him. Herein, each of the twenty chapters will have a text that they will be built around, a text that defines **what we should be** in the eyes of God. For example, several times Jesus says 'if we are doing _____, we are truly his disciples.' Well, the objective would be to discover what all is involved in doing _____.

Keep Examining Yourselves

While the phrase to keep *examining yourselves* is self-explanatory, but to spell it out, it involves a self-examination. We may have been a Christian for a number of years, but how many times have we had a spiritual checkup. Every six months we are to go in for a dental cleaning, and unless there is a problem, we should get a health screening once a year. The problem with our spirituality is it is far more susceptible to injury than we are physically. The author of Hebrews warns us, "We must **pay much closer attention** to what we have heard, lest we **drift away** from it." (2:1) One chapter later, we are told, "**Take care**, brothers, lest there be in any of you *an evil, unbelieving heart*, leading you to **fall away** from the living God. But exhort one another every day, as long as it is called "today," that none of you may be **hardened by the**

deceitfulness of sin." (3:12-13) This same author warns us about falling away (6:6), becoming sluggish (6:12), and growing weary or fainthearted (12:25).

Why would this be the case? If we are saved, why is it necessary that we keep examining ourselves? Why would we still be susceptible to bad behaviors to the point of drifting away, to the point of having an unbelieving heart, falling away, becoming sluggish, growing weary or fainthearted?

There are four reasons. **(1)** First and foremost, we have inherited sin, which means that we are missing the mark of perfection. **(2)** In addition, our environment can condition us into the bad thinking and behavior. **(3)** We have our human weaknesses, which include inborn tendencies that we naturally lean toward evil, leading us to bad behaviors. **(4)** Moreover, there is the world of Satan and his demons that caters to these human weaknesses, which also leads us down the path of bad thinking and behaviors. After our self-examination, what is needed if we are to overcome any bad thinking or behaviors and how are we to avoid developing them in the future? We will offer more on this in each chapter as well as two appendices at the end, but we offer this for now. It is paramount that we fully understand what all is involved in our human imperfection and never believe that we are so strong spiritually that we would never fall away, slow down, or becoming sluggish in our walk with God.

Obviously, this should be of the greatest concern to each one of us. We may be a person of good character, and believe that in any situation, we will make the right decisions. However, the moment that **innocent appearing situation** arises, we are plagued with the inner desire toward wrong. We need to address more than what our friends, or our workmates or our spouse may see. We need to look into our inner self, in the hopes of determining, who we really are, and what do we need to do to have a good heart (i.e., inner person).

As we know, we could not function with half a heart. However, we can operate, albeit dysfunctional, with a heart that is divided. Yes, we have things outside of us that can contribute to bad thinking, which if left unchecked will lead to bad behavior, but we also have some things within. The apostle Paul bewailed about himself, "For I do not do the good I want, but the evil I do not want is what I keep on doing. Now if I do what I do not want, it is no longer I who do it, but sin that dwells within me." (Romans 7:19-20) This is because all of us are mentally bent toward the doing of wrong, instead of the doing of good. (Gen 6:5;

8:21; Rom 5:12; Eph. 4:20-24; Col 3:5-11) Jeremiah the prophet informs us of the condition of our heart (our inner person), "The heart is deceitful above all things and desperately sick; who can understand it?" These factors contribute to our being more vulnerable to the worldly desires and the weak human flesh than we may have thought. One needs to understand just how serious human imperfection is before they can fully implement the right **Christian Living Skills**.

Returning to the book of Hebrews, we are told, "solid food belongs to the mature, to those who through practice have their discernment trained to distinguish between good and evil." (5:14) We will have evidence that we are one of the mature ones by training ourselves to make a distinction between good and evil. We likely believe that we are already spiritually mature, which may very well be the case. Nevertheless, we are told by Paul to carry out this self-examination and to keep on examining ourselves, to remain that way, and even to improve upon what we currently have by way of maturity. Just as a man or woman in a marathon must continually train their muscles to surpass others in the sport, our discernment (perception) needs to be trained through regularly and rightly applying the Word of God. Throughout this publication, we will apply the inspired words of James, Jesus' half-brother.

James 1:22-25 Updated American Standard Version (UASV)

22 But be doers of the word, and not hearers only, deceiving yourselves. 23 For if anyone is a hearer of the word and not a doer, he is like a man who looks intently at his natural face[62] in a mirror.

24 for he looks at himself and goes away, and immediately forgets what sort of man he was. 25 But he that looks into the perfect law, the law of liberty, and abides by it, being no hearer who forgets but a doer of a work, he will be blessed in his doing.

When we are inundated in the Word of God, it serves as the voice of God, telling us the way in which to walk. On Hebrews 5:14, Thomas D. Lea writes, "The readers did not know and understand these truths because they had not applied themselves to them. The solution to this dilemma [becoming and remaining a mature Christian] lay in developing their spiritual senses through practice. The training they needed involved a steady application of spiritual discipline. Spiritual maturity would not develop primarily from a sudden burst of insight. It would come from dogged usage of spiritual resources. God has given believers faculties to

---

[62] Lit *the face of his birth*

make spiritual judgments and to develop understanding. God gives Christians training in understanding (Heb. 12:11) so that it can produce **a harvest of righteousness and peace for those who have been trained by it** (Heb. 12:11). Christians are able to distinguish between good and evil. The terms **good** and **evil** may have both a moral sense and a theological sense. Christians are those who can spot moral evil and avoid it. They can see moral good and attach themselves to it. Christians also can distinguish between true and false doctrine. They will turn aside from the false and faithfully follow the true. Living the Christian life demands the spiritual skills of stamina seen physically in a long-distance runner. Unswerving, relentless applications of Christian truth and practice will equip us for a lifetime of usefulness, which will continue into eternity."[63]

Becoming Spiritually Strong

1 Peter 5:8-10 Updated American Standard Version (UASV)

⁸ Be sober-minded; be watchful. Your adversary the devil prowls around like a roaring lion, seeking someone to devour. ⁹ Resist him and be **firm in the faith**, knowing that the same sufferings are being experienced by your brothers in the world. ¹⁰ After you have suffered for a little while, the God of all grace, who called you to his eternal glory in Christ, will himself will restore, support, strengthen and establish you.

Peter helps us to see how we can protect ourselves from damaging doubts. He gives the simple way out of the downward spiral of doubts, which lead to spiritual shipwreck. We simply prepare our mind for the stannic propaganda that is out there. Yes, some Christian leaders might suggest that Christians never listen to or read what the Bible critics say or write. Well, how can we save those who doubt, if we are unaware of what the critic is saying or writing? Is the truth so frail that it cannot stand up to the lie? Peter says that we are to resist Satan, which will make us firm in the faith. We can resist Satan's minions, i.e., Bible critics, by knowing the lie and overshadowing it with the truth.

If we are to continue to grow spiritually, minimizing the number of stumbles along the way, we need to feed our mind and heart spiritual food. Returning to the analogy of our physical body, even when are sleeping at night, it requires a continuous supply of energy to maintain the organs and bodily functions. This holds true of our spiritual health as well.

---

[63] (T. D. Lea, Holman New Testament Commentary: Hebrews, James 1999, p. 97)

We are supposed to be continuously taking in spiritual food, not just when we are at Christian meetings. Sadly, many Christians

- they do not have any personal Bible study,
- they do not have a family Bible study,
- they do not prepare for the Christian meetings,
- they do not participate at the Christian meetings,
- they barely pay attention at the Christian meetings, and
- they do not have any avenue for regularly sharing the Christian faith.

Can we even imagine if we ate food to nourish our bodies this way? Why do they fail to take care of their spiritual health? One reason is, they do not truly believe in the things they profess to believe. Look, if we absolutely knew that on January 07, 2037, Armageddon was coming, Jesus was returning, and we was going to be receiving eternal life, we would not waste a moment, we would prepare like it was the spiritual Olympics, and we certainly would spend more time trying to save as many lives as we can. Without taking in constant spiritual food throughout every day, our faith will eventually grow weakened, and we will likely die out before we finish our life course, or before the return of Christ. Jesus said, "'Man shall not live by bread alone, but by every word that comes from the mouth of God.'" (Matt. 4:4, ESV) Let us return to the analogy of our physical health once more.

"If you don't take in enough calories every day, you may not be as fast and as strong as you could be, and may even break down rather than build up your muscles. If you are a healthy weight (in other words you don't need to gain or lose weight), here are some general guidelines to help you eat enough:"

- Do not skip meals. It is too hard to make up the lost food later.
- Add a healthy snack between breakfast and lunch, lunch and dinner, and right before bed.

- Make higher calorie healthy foods part of your daily routine (nuts and nut butters, bananas, granola and other cereals, whole grain breads and muffins, dried fruit, juices, and smoothies).[64]

Let us repeat everything tis health expert said but turn it into spiritual health.

If you do not take in enough biblical food every day, you may not be as fast at making life decisions based on God's Word and as spiritually strong as you could be, and may even stumble spiritually rather than grow into spiritual maturity. If you are an average Christian (in other words doing the fundamentals in Christian service), here are some general guidelines to help you take in enough spiritual food:

- Do not skip taking in Bible knowledge daily. It is too hard to make up the spiritual food later when you need the strength to survive a tribulation.

- Add a daily personal Bible study between weekly Christian meetings, prepare for each Christian meeting so you can fully participate, share your faith with others, and right before bed pray to God that you may faithfully take in his Word as vigorously the tomorrow.

- Make deeper Bible study tools part of your daily, personal Bible study (commentary volumes, Bible dictionaries, word study books, Bible encyclopedias, Bible background), and read books that are designed to help you earnestly fight for the faith.

Whether we are relatively new to the faith, or we have been a Christian for decades, we all can remember when we first became a Christian. The apostle Paul, speaking of bringing new ones into the faith said, "Faith comes from hearing, and hearing through the word of Christ." (Rom 10:17, ESV) What Paul meant was that the new person builds his faith and confidence in God by feeding his mind on the Word of God. I hope that we had a healthy doubt and did not just blindly accept everything we heard. I also hope that we were like the people from the first century, living in the city of Beroea. They "received the word with all eagerness, examining the Scriptures daily to see if these things were so." (Ac 17:11, ESV) I hope that we were 'transformed by the renewal of our mind, that by testing we may have discerned what is the will of God,

---

[64] What happens if I don't eat enough? - Nutrition - Sharecare, https://www.sharecare.com/health/nutrition-diet/what-happens-dont-eat-enough (accessed November 11, 2015).

what is good and acceptable and perfect.' (Rom. 12:2, ESV) This renewal of our mind takes place over time as we feed on the Word of God. On 1 Thessalonians 5:21-22, Knute Larson writes,

> Paul advised the Thessalonians to **Test everything**. The word *everything* is universal; it leaves nothing free from examination by spiritual standards and understanding. Paul did not explain how to carry out this testing. But certainly the fire of the Spirit (his convicting, guidance, and illumination), the instructions from the apostles and missionaries, and the written revelation of God are the lenses through which we must scrutinize everything. The clear purpose of this testing was to **hold on to the good**, and to **avoid every kind of evil**. The good has its origin in God; evil is a distortion of that good. Evil is twisting and destructive. We must not flirt with evil. (Larson 2000, p. 76)

From this moment forward, whether we are new to the faith or have been walking with God for years, let us reinforce our faith as we come to know ever more precisely what the Word of God means and how we might better defend it and our faith. The Word of God will never fail us; it is we alone, who will let us down. Joshua was a general in the Israelite fighting forces and a man of great faith. Joshua replaced Moses as the leader of the Israelite nation and he led them well, saying to them just before his death,

Joshua 23:14 Updated American Standard Version (UASV)

[14] "Now behold, today I am going the way of all the earth, and you know in all your hearts and in all your souls that not one word of all the good words which Jehovah your God spoke concerning you has failed; all have come to pass for you; not one word of them has failed.

Isaiah wrote,

Isaiah 55:10-11 Updated American Standard Version (UASV)

[10] "For as the rain and the snow come down from heaven
and do not return there but water the earth,
making it bring forth and sprout,
giving seed to the sower and bread to the eater;
[11] so shall my word be that goes out from my mouth;
it shall not return to me empty,

but it shall accomplish that which I purpose,
   and shall succeed in the thing for which I sent it.⁶⁵

Regardless of what his creation, spirit or human, may have done or will do, his will and purposes will be accomplished; God's word will not return to him empty.

Escape Spiritual Hunger

The objective of every Christian should be to grow his faith and to maintain that growth, avoiding any uncertainty of belief that can weaken our assurance of things hoped for, the conviction of things not seen. If we are to accomplish this, we must with all eagerness, examining the Scriptures daily. The apostle Paul warns those who may even have strong faith, "the Spirit explicitly says that in later times some will fall away from the faith, paying attention to deceitful spirits and doctrines [or teachings] of demons." (1 Tim. 4:1) Larson writes, "Paul predicted that some will abandon the faith. Apostasy has been around as long as human history. Paul dealt with it in his own day (1 Tim. 1:19; 2 Tim. 2:17–18), and the casualty list is high in our time." (Larson 2000, p. 203) These deceitful spirits and doctrines form doubts in the minds of some, which cause them to draw away from God, as opposed to drawing close to God. (Jam. 4:8) How are we to protect against this? Paul says we should be continuously "nourished on the words of the faith and of the good teaching that you have followed closely." – 1 Timothy 4:6.

Sadly, what we have today is anything but Christians being "nourished on the words of the faith and of the good teaching," as many are too busy making a name for themselves in this world that has Satan for its ruler. There has never been a time when so much Bible study literature has been available, much of it freely or at least very affordable. At Proverbs 19:24 and 26:15, "we find a tongue-in-cheek portrait of the lazy man. He refuses to be hurried, and though he buries his hand in a dish of food, he is too lazy to bring it back up to his mouth! If this description were literally true, the person would soon starve."⁶⁶ How can

---

⁶⁵ "Moisture from heaven invariably accomplishes its intended purpose in helping meet human physical needs. The word of God will likewise produce its intended results in fulfilling God's spiritual purposes, especially the establishment of the Davidic kingdom on earth (vv. 1–5)." – MacArthur, John (2005-05-09). *The MacArthur Bible Commentary* (Kindle Locations 29443-29445). Thomas Nelson. Kindle Edition.

⁶⁶ Anders, Max (2005-07-01). Holman Old Testament Commentary - Proverbs (p. 290). B&H Publishing. Kindle Edition.

we be surrounded by so much spiritual food and yet be starving spiritually?

If we believe that we can survive off of the basic Bible knowledge that we acquired in the beginning and the simple snacks we receive at each Christian meeting, we are sadly mistaken because our spiritual health with deteriorate. If we neglect to have our regular personal Bible study daily, prepare for and participate in our Christian meetings, as well as share our faith, we will grow spiritually weak. Paul wrote, "For in view of the time you ought to be teachers, you have need again for someone to teach you from the beginning the elementary things of the words of God, and you have come to need milk and not solid food." (Heb. 5:12) He had warned the Hebrew Christians about neglect earlier in the letter, "For this reason we must pay much closer attention to the things that have been heard so that we do not drift away from it." Paul was well aware of how easy it is to drift away from the faith, if "we neglect so great a salvation." – Hebrews 2:1, 3

Many Christians sitting in the pews of the church may not look like they are suffering from spiritual malnutrition. It may be that the person themselves may not feel that they are starving spiritually. It is not until we are challenged physically that we realize we are suffering from physical malnutrition. The same is true with us spiritually. All may seem well until a great tribulation falls upon us and then it is too late, for we crash and burn spiritually because we do not have the strength to overcome the unfounded doubts. Imagine the family that has had some difficulties in life but, for the most part, no real serious tragedies. Then, one day, the father and the mother come home to find that some criminal broke in the home, where he raped, tortured and killed their three daughters (16, 13, and 9). This is a great tribulation like no other, and if they had never fully grasped why an all-loving God, who is also all-powerful, would allow pain, suffering and death to continue, they are going to end up blaming him for this evil act.

"On December 14, 2012, 20-year-old Adam Lanza fatally shot twenty children and six adult staff members in a mass murder at Sandy Hook Elementary School, in the village of Sandy Hook in Newtown, Connecticut. Before driving to the school, Lanza shot and killed his mother Nancy at their Newtown home. As first responders arrived, he committed suicide by shooting himself in the head."[67] Life is full of these

---

[67] Newtown Public Schools - Wikipedia, the free encyclopedia, https://en.wikipedia.org/wiki/Newtown_Public_Schools (accessed November 11, 2015).

type of accounts the world over. We have social depravities everywhere we look. In the United States, there are hundreds of thousands living in homeless shelters, under bridges, eating at soup kitchens, and many have young children with them as well. On the other hand, the United States throws away more food than any other country. Sadly, the hungry in the United States, while truly unfair, is not very serious, when we consider the inhumane conditions of other countries. In some countries, like Mexico, you have a millionaire living in a mansion, with a poor person living in a shack next door, and a person living in a car, living next door to him. Almost two billion people live in such hopeless poverty and inhuman conditions that those in the Western part of the world could never relate.

Should we understand that the Scriptures teach that because we are wisely walking with God that he will miraculously step in to protect each servant personally from difficult times, diseases, mental disorders, injury or death? No. These sorts of miracles are the extreme exception to the rule. Of the 4,000 plus years of Bible history, from Adam to Jesus, with tens of millions of people living and dying, we have but a few dozen miracles that we know of in Scripture. Even in Bible times, miracles were not typical, far from it. Hundreds of years may pass with no historical record of a miracle happening at all.

If we are wisely walking with God, we can be confident that bodily disease, mental disorders, injury or early death is far less likely than if we were not. Moreover, we can draw on the resurrection hope. Does God miraculously move events to save us out of difficult times or miraculously heal us? Yes, he certainly can, but it is an extreme exception to the rule. He miraculously heals those who are going to play a significant role in his settling of the issues that were raised in the Garden of Eden.

What God's Word teaches us is this, that if we walk by using discernment and exercising sound judgment from Scripture unless unexpected events befall us, we can be sure that we will not stumble into the difficulties that the world of humankind alienated from God faces every day. Conversely, the wicked do not have this protection as they reject the Word of God as foolish. In other words, Christians live by the moral values of Scripture, which gives them an advantage over those who do not. Therefore, God answers our prayers by our faithfully acting on behalf of those prayers, by applying Scripture in a balanced manner. If we have not taken in a deep understanding of God's Word, how can we have the Spirit-inspired wisdom, the very knowledge of God to guide and direct us in our ways? Just because we are not being rescued when we feel that we should, this does not mean that we have lost faith, or that God is displeased. Even though we have no doubt that God is coming to our aid, be it by his Word, by a miracle because we are one play an intricate role in his will and purposes, or by a resurrection, we still experience grief.

If we ever find ourselves in tough times, we need to follow the pattern set by the Psalmist. We need to remember that God is well aware of our circumstances, and he will not forsake us. We must realize that the issues that were raised by Satan in the Garden of Eden, the sovereignty of God, the rightfulness of his rulership, and the issues raised by Satan to God in the book of Job, the loyalty of God's creatures, are greater than we are.

If we are to remain rational in our thinking, we need to grasp the fact that God does not always step in when we believe he should, nor is he obligated to do so. God has larger issues that need resolving, which have permanent effects for the whole of humankind. There are far more times that when God does not step in, meaning that our relief may come in the hope of the resurrection. However, for his servants that apply his Word in a balanced manner, fully, God is acting in their best interest by way of his inspired, inerrant Word. If we are not regularly feeding our mind and heart on the Word of God, we will become susceptible to unfounded doubts, leaving us unable to "contend earnestly for the faith." (Jude 1:3, NASB) Each of us is personally responsible for our own personal spiritual feeding program.

We cannot repeat the need for regular, daily, personal Bible study, which of focused on the right subject areas; it will defeat doubts before they can even arise. Returning to the analogy of our physical health, would we ever ignore a minor infection from a cut or scrape? A minor infection can become an acute infectious disease that causes severe muscular spasms and contractions, especially around the neck and jaw, i.e., tetanus. This is why we receive a tetanus vaccine as a child. Now, carry this over to our spiritual health, would we ever want to ignore nagging doubts, as it too could lead to disastrous consequences. (2 Cor. 11:3) How can a person be sure that the Bible, the basis for knowing the future, truly is from God? Is the Genesis account of creation fact or fiction? Was there an earth-wide flood? Can you expect secular history always to agree with the Bible? Are the miracles of the Bible true? Does the Bible contradict itself? Is the Bible practical for our day? Can you believe everything the Bible says? Questions by the thousands exist about the Bible and God, and if we ignore one that is nagging us, soon it will become two; then, ten, which Satan would love to fester until it becomes a spiritual infection. This author can offer the reader this comfort, of the tens of thousands of questions that could cause doubt almost everyone has an answer, and for the handful that have not, follow R. A. Torrey's advice. "Do not be discouraged because you do not solve every problem in a day. If some difficulty persistently defies your very best efforts at a solution, lay it aside for a while. Later it will likely be resolved, and you will wonder how you were ever perplexed by it."

No Unbelief Will Make Us Waver

When we consider Abraham and Sarah, we might feel like he had good reasons for doubting. God had said he was to be the father of many nations, and things were certainly not going as planned. However, Abraham "**did not weaken in faith** when he considered his own body, which was as good as dead (since he was about a hundred years old), or when he considered the barrenness of Sarah's womb. **No unbelief made him waver** concerning the promise of God, but he **grew strong in his faith** as he gave glory to God, **fully convinced** that God was able to do what he had promised." (Rom. 4:18-21, ESV) Abraham had a long history of trusting God that went back decades before he was ever called out of Ur of the Chaldeans at the age of seventy-five. He dismissed any doubts that may have weakened his relationship with God. Moreover, he Grew his faith.

We can do the same if we "Follow the pattern of the sound words ... in the faith and love that are in Christ Jesus." (2 Tim. 1:13) We must never take doubts lightly and realize that none of us is beyond having them. We must understand that Satan is very real as are his demons, and they are very powerful spirit creatures. They enemies have the world under their control so that it caters to the fallen flesh, which includes the weakness of doubts. We must understand and appreciate that spiritual warfare is very real. If we fail to take in the Word of God in by personal Bible study daily, regularly prepare for and attend Christian meetings, and shared and defended our faith, we are susceptible to having unbelief to cause us to waver. We must realize that the depth of our studies will dictate the state of our spiritual strength. If all we do is take in spiritual milk, which is for babes and not solid food that belongs to the spiritually mature, we will be blown back and forth, wavering in our faith. (Heb. 5:13-6:2; Jam. 1:5-8) Sadly, churches have small Bible study groups that are studying booklets, written on a 6th-7th-grade level, leaving their members spiritual babes.

"Deep study is no guarantee that mature faith will result, but shallow study guarantees that immaturity continues." – Dr. Lee M. Field

SPIRITUAL MILK (Shallow Study):

- Discovering the Joy of Jesus: A Guide to Philippians (2013, 160 pages)
- Who Is Jesus? A Guide to Jesus (2012, 144 pages)
- Connecting With God: A Guide To Prayer (2012, 144 pages)
- Growing in the Christian Life: A Guide to James (2013, 144 pages)

SOLID FOOD (Deep Study)

- Fool's Gold?: Discerning Truth in an Age of Error (2005, 224 pages)
- Knowing God (1993, 286 pages)
- Searching for the Original Bible (2007, 293 pages)
- Misquoting Truth: A Guide to the Fallacies of Bart Ehrman's "Misquoting Jesus" (2007, 176 pages)
- Fabricating Jesus: How Modern Scholars Distort the Gospels (2008, 290 pages)
- Basic Bible Interpretation (1991, 324 pages)

It is just not that the depth of the book is of paramount importance; it is that we must avoid "anyone [who] teaches a different doctrine and does not agree with the sound words of our Lord Jesus Christ and the teaching that accords with godliness." (1 Tim. 6:3, ESV) Do not believe that deeper books have to mean necessarily difficult to understand because many of those books are now written in easy to understand language. In addition, a babe, i.e., young child has the vocabulary that is indicative of their age. The same is true of the spiritual babe. Thus, these ones will simply have to grow their vocabulary, so that some of these deeper books can be easily understood. For example, before reading *Searching for the Original Bible* or *Misquoting Truth* or *Fabricating Jesus* above, the reader may want to read *Introduction to New Testament Textual Criticism* (1993, 174 pages) or the Text of the New Testament, From Manuscript to Modern Edition (2008, 144 pages) because our book recommendations are on that subject matter. Which do we think to be better: (1) having faith that the Bible is the Word of God and is trustworthy, or (2) knowing that the Bible is the Word of God and is trustworthy?

Our three book recommendations *Searching for the Original Bible* (2007), *Misquoting Truth* (2007), and *Fabricating Jesus* (2008) are the direct result of New York Times Bestselling author Dr. Bart D. Ehrman and his book *Misquoting Jesus: The Story Behind Who Changed the Bible and Why* (2007, 242 pages). *Misquoting Jesus* is an incredibly easy to understand book on the Greek text of the New Testament that lies behind our English translation. Ehrman in a very misleading way casts extreme doubt on the trustworthiness of the Greek text, which would mean that we could not trust the English translation of that text, regardless of the translation we choose. Over ten very good books deal with *Misquoting Jesus*. *Misquoting Jesus* is just one of over twenty Ehrman books, and it is a New York Times Bestseller, meaning that it is getting into the hands of hundreds of thousands of Christians, creating doubt in the trustworthiness of God's Word. In addition, *Misquoting Jesus* is getting in the hands of hundreds of thousands of Bible critics, who are bent on tearing down the faith of as many Christians as possible.

If the reader of this book were to read *Searching for the Original Bible* (2007), *Misquoting Truth* (2007), and *Fabricating Jesus* (2008), followed by *Misquoting Jesus* (2007), what would be the benefit? First, by reading the recommended books before reading the lies of Ehrman, the reader would be able to identify the misleading information in *Misquoting Jesus*. Why is that important? Second, they would grow their faith. Third, they would be able to defend their faith in God and his Word. Fourth, they would be able to assist God in saving some who have begun to doubt. We do not want doubts to destroy our faith. Moreover, we do not want doubts to destroy our spiritual brothers and sisters' faith. Thus, it is imperative that we grow our faith with books such as those listed above.

Review Questions

- How can our human immune system be compared to our spiritual health? What questions should we ask ourselves?
- Are doubts always bad? Explain.
- What are unfounded doubts?
- How did Satan place unfounded doubt in the mind of Eve?

- What issues did Satan raise with his inferential, suggestive, supposing comments and questions?
- How can we test whether we are truly Christian?
- What warning did Jesus and the apostle John give to those who believed they were doing the right things?
- What is involved in examining what we ourselves are?
- Why must we keep testing ourselves?
- Why must we keep examining ourselves?
- Why do we need to understand just how bad human imperfection is before we can fully implement the right Christian Living Skills?
- What is it that will make us spiritually strong and will help us to maintain that strength?
- How can we escape spiritual hunger?
- How can we make sure that no unbelief ever makes us waver?

CHAPTER 3 Did the Miracles in the Bible Really Happen?

"That evening they brought to him [Jesus Christ] many who were oppressed by demons, and he cast out the spirits with a word and healed all who were sick." (Matt. 8:16, ESV) "And he awoke and rebuked the wind and said to the sea, 'Peace! Be still!' And the wind ceased, and there was a great calm." (Mark 4:39, ESV) When we read these statements, can we say that we truly believe they are actual historical events, or do we agree with the liberal Bible scholars, who say they are allegorical stories, mere myths?

Many express serious doubts about any miracles in the Word of God. We live in the era of the computer, a network that links computer networks all over the world by satellite and telephone (i.e., the internet), and the $27 million electron microscope. Its ability to make images to a resolution of half the width of a hydrogen atom, space exploration and of genetic engineering, which has actually contributed to doubts about miracles, rather than support them. Many view Jesus' miracles as nothing more than fraud.

Luke 7:11-16 J.B. Phillips New Testament (PHILLIPS)

Jesus brings a dead youth back to life

11-13 Not long afterwards, Jesus went into a town called Nain, accompanied by his disciples and a large crowd. As they approached the city gate, it happened that some people were carrying out a dead man, the only son of his widowed mother. The usual crowd of fellow-townsmen was with her. When the Lord saw her, his heart went out to her and he said, "Don't cry."

14 Then he walked up and put his hand on the bier while the bearers stood still. Then he said, "Young man, wake up!"

15-16 And the dead man sat up and began to talk, and Jesus handed him to his mother. Everybody present was awe-struck and they praised God, saying, "A great prophet has arisen among us and God has turned his face towards his people."

This is one of the most moving accounts in the Gospels, if not the Bible. However, many would argue that it is not true. Many people do not believe that miracles[68] are possible because they seem unreasonable. Others have a more philosophical perspective, following what is known as naturalism, which is belief in a religious truth from the study of science and nature. Naturalism is a belief that all religious truth is derived from nature and natural causes, and not from revelation. Additionally, naturalism rejects all spiritual and supernatural explanations of the world and contends science is the sole basis of what can be known. Thomas W. Clark, from the Center for Naturalism makes just that point in an online website:

> For a philosophical and scientific naturalist such as myself, the traditional Christian god is ruled out simply because the existence of the supernatural in general is ruled out. If you stick with science as your guide to what's ultimately real, and critique your assumptions in open philosophical inquiry, there are no good reasons to believe that reality is split between two categorically different realms, the natural and the supernatural. Instead, science reveals that the world is of a piece, what we call the natural world. Disbelief in God, therefore, is a corollary of the rationally defensible claim that nature is all there is, the basis for the world-view known as naturalism.[69]

If naturalists are correct, we must scrap the Bible as the inspired, fully inerrant Word of God, and accept it as the Word of man alone. Why? According to Scripture, the Bible exists because of the supernatural and miraculous. The Apostle Paul wrote, "All Scripture is inspired by God." (2 Tim. 3:16) The Apostle Peter wrote, "Men spoke from God as they were carried along by the Holy Spirit." (2 Pet. 1:21) Moreover, the Bible is filled with miracles from Genesis to Revelation. Therefore, to believe in the Bible as the written Word of God requires believing in miracles. In truth, the Christian faith hangs on the greatest miracle of them all, Jesus Christ's resurrection.

Some Just Do Not Believe

The deeper we get into the scientific age, a two-fold effect has occurred: (1) many are abandoning Christianity because they feel it is irrational to believe in miracles; and (2) naturalists do not accept miracles,

---

[68] A miracles is an event that appears to be contrary to the laws of nature, and surpasses all know human or natural powers, and is regarded as supernatural, an act of God.

[69] http://www.naturalism.org/Toogoodtobetrue.htm

but the intricacy of creation has moved them to speak of design, which means creation had a designer. There are three reasons Scottish philosopher David Hume raised in his objection to miracles. First, "A miracle is a violation of the laws of nature." Second, people are prone to accept the unusual and incredible, which excites agreeable passions of surprise and wonder. Those with strong religious beliefs are often prepared to give evidence they know is false, "with the best intentions in the world, for the sake of promoting so holy a cause." Third, miracle stories tend to have their origins in "ignorant and barbarous nations."[70] Let us investigate these three arguments, which are still used today.

Violation of the Laws of Nature

Certainly, this statement would move a reasonable person because it seems logical on the surface. A miracle is an event that appears to be contrary to the laws of nature, surpasses all known human or natural powers, and is regarded as supernatural, or an act of God.

Educated people today, in the era of such epoch scientific achievements, suggest we fully grasp the laws of nature. What may appear to be outside the laws of human nature may not be after all, and are certainly not outside the Creator's laws. While we have always known the three dimensions of length, breadth, and height, a fourth dimension has been discussed. "In mathematics, four-dimensional space ('4D') is an abstract concept derived by generalizing the rules of three-dimensional space. It has been studied by mathematicians and philosophers for over two centuries, both for its own interest and for the insights it offered into mathematics and related fields."[71]

While in Hume's day in the eighteenth century it might have been easy to accept miracles are outside the laws of nature, it is not so easily accepted by science today. If something seems to occur outside the laws of nature, we should not automatically assume it could not happen. When the naturalist scientist has made such strides, to the point of seeing design everywhere, but hesitating to see a designer, the concept of a Creator is ever closer to a scientific reality, as our knowledge of the natural world grows. God is outside the natural universe, and therefore, his powers far exceed anything we could imagine, as well as his being the engineer of the natural world.

---

[70]Hume, *An Enquiry concerning Human Understanding* X, i, 86

[71]http://en.wikipedia.org/wiki/Four-dimensional_space

Isaiah 40:13 Updated American Standard Version (UASV)

¹³ Who has directed the Spirit of Jehovah,
or as his counselor has informed Him?

Isaiah 40:15 Updated American Standard Version (UASV)

¹⁵ Behold, the nations are like a drop from a bucket,
and are counted like dust of the scales;
behold, he lifts up the islands like fine dust.

Fake Miracles Does Not Mean No Miracles

My goodness, the televangelist with their fake healing miracles has caused more damage to the integrity of the Christian faith than one can possibly know. These frauds of Christianity should not be the poster child, which is then used by Bible critics as evidence that all Christianity is false. It is irrational to suggest fraudulent miracles equal no such thing as genuine miracles. Think of the hucksters in the nineteenth century who sold elixirs (**cure-all**) that would supposedly heal anything. Should we suggest there are no medicines, which can cure or relieve ailments, because scammers sold fake cure-all medicines? Hardly!

Miracles Only In Times of Ignorance

Certainly, no writer wishes to be arrogantly dogmatic about a belief because an understanding of Scripture could be overturned or adjusted before his eyes as he grows in knowledge and understanding. The evidence says miracles of tongues and healings, as well as resurrections, were given to some in the infant Christian congregation. Why? The objective was to establish it as the new way to God, to give witness to God's mighty acts that include the ransom sacrifice of Christ, his resurrection and ascension, and to communicate rapidly to those who spoke other languages.

Did miracles happen after the first century? Yes. What about today? If we remain rational, we must realize God has not always intervened when we believed he should, nor is he obligated to do so. As was stated earlier, he has greater issues that need resolving, which have eternal effects for humankind. There are far more times when God does not step in, which means our relief may come in the hope of a resurrection. However, for servants who apply his Word in a fully balanced manner, God is acting in their best interest by way of his inspired, fully inerrant

Word. Nevertheless, God does step in and it would be disheartening to seek the tens of thousands of fraudulent cases, to find genuine miracles.

Is it possible to appease the critics who refuse to accept miracles are even possible? No. Not just because they are stubborn, but how do you explain what might actually be within the laws of nature, but are beyond our understanding? It is like a man time traveling from one thousand years ago to the twenty-first century, seeing all of our technology, and then going back. How could he get them to believe what he had seen with his own eyes and touched with his own hands?

The Best Attested Miracle

Whether you wish to accept the reality of it or not, the resurrection of Jesus Christ has all of the evidence of being the greatest miracle of all time. Below is an **overview** of the account. For greater detail, read the cited texts in full in the ESV, NASB, HCSB, or the LEB.

The betrayer had given them a sign. He had said, "The one I kiss will be the man. Get hold of him and you can take him away without any trouble." So he walked straight up to Jesus, cried, "Master!" and kissed him affectionately. And so they got hold of Jesus and held him. So they marched Jesus away to the high priest in whose presence all the chief priests and elders and scribes had assembled. The chief priests and the whole council were trying to find some evidence against Jesus, which would warrant the death penalty. The moment daylight came the chief priests called together a meeting of elders, scribes and members of the whole council, bound Jesus and took him off and handed him over to Pilate.

It was about 9 a.m. when they nailed him to the cross. At midday darkness spread over the whole countryside and lasted until 3 p.m., at which time Jesus cried out in a loud voice, "My God, my God, why have you forsaken me?" Jesus let out a great cry, and died. The curtain of the Temple sanctuary was split in two from top to the bottom. And when **the centurion who stood in front of Jesus saw how <u>he died</u>**, he said, "This man was certainly a son of God!" [**Mark 14:43-65; 15:1-39** J.B. Phillips New Testament (PHILLIPS)]

Because it was the day to prepare for the Passover, the Jews wanted to avoid the bodies being left on the crosses over the Sabbath (for that was a particularly important Sabbath. They requested Pilate to have the men's legs broken and the bodies removed. So the soldiers broke the legs of the first man and of the other who was crucified with Jesus. But when they came to him, **they saw that he was already dead** and they did not break his legs. But **one of the soldiers pierced his side with a spear**, and at once there was an outrush of blood and water. The man who saw this is our witness: his evidence is true.

Joseph, who came from Arimathaea and was a disciple of Jesus, though secretly for fear of the Jews, requested Pilate that he might take Jesus' body, and Pilate gave him permission. He took his body down. Nicodemus, the man who had come to him at the beginning by night, also arrived bringing a mixture of myrrh and aloes, weighing about one hundred pounds. So they took his body and wound it with linen strips with the spices, according to the Jewish custom of preparing a body for burial. In the place where he was crucified, there was a garden containing a new tomb in which nobody had yet been laid. Because it was the preparation day and because the tomb was conveniently near, they laid Jesus in this tomb.

However, on the first day of the week Mary of Magdala arrived at the tomb very early in the morning, while it was still dark, and noticed the stone had been taken away from the tomb. Peter and the other disciple set off at once for the tomb, the two of them running together. The other disciple ran faster than Peter and was the first to arrive at the tomb. He stooped and looked inside and noticed the linen cloths lying there but did not go in himself. Hard on his heels came Simon Peter and went straight into the tomb. He noticed the linen cloths were lying there, and the handkerchief, which had been round Jesus's head, was not lying with the linen cloths but was rolled up by itself, a little way apart.

Mary stood just outside the tomb and she was crying. As she cried, she looked into the tomb and saw two angels in white who sat, one at the head and the other at the foot of the place where Jesus' body had lain. "Why are you crying?" the angels asked. "Because they have taken away my Lord, and I don't know where they have put him!" she said. Then she turned and noticed Jesus standing there, without realizing it was Jesus. "Why are you crying?" Jesus asked. "Who are you looking for?" Supposing he was the gardener, she said, "Oh, sir, if you have carried him away, please tell me where you have put him and I will take him away." **Jesus said to her, "Mary!"** At this she turned right round and said to him, in Hebrew, "Master!"

That evening, the disciples had met with the doors locked for fear of the Jews. Jesus came and stood right in the middle of them and said, "Peace be with you!" Then he showed them his hands and his side, and when they saw the Lord, the disciples were overjoyed. Jesus said to them again, "Yes, peace be with you! Just as the Father sent me, so I am now going to send you."

However, one of the twelve, Thomas (called the Twin), was not with them when Jesus came. The other disciples kept telling him, "We have seen the Lord", but he replied, "Unless I see in his own hands the mark of the nails, and put my finger where the nails were, and put my hand into his side, I will never believe!" Just over a week later, the disciples were indoors again and Thomas was with them. The doors were shut, but Jesus came and stood in the middle of them and said, "Peace be with you!" Then he said to Thomas, "Put your fingers here—look, here are my hands. Take my hand and put it in my side. You must not doubt, but believe." "My Lord and my God!" cried Thomas. "Is it because you have seen me that you believe?" Jesus said to him. "Happy are those who have never seen me and yet have believed!" **[John 19:31-20:29** J.B. Phillips New Testament (PHILLIPS)]

If this were a fabrication, written decades later, why would they have such amounts of doubt embedded within the account? The apostles themselves refused to believe, until the proof mounted to such a point that they had to accept the truth of the evidence. In addition, if they were fabricating the account in oral and written testimony, why would they have women be the first people that Jesus appeared to, as women could not be witnesses? Moreover, women were not treated as equals in that culture, so a fabricated story would have had Jesus appearing to the men first.

The Empty Tomb and the Report of the Guard

Matthew 28:11-13 English Standard Version (ESV)

¹¹ While they were going, behold, some of the guard went into the city and told the chief priests all that had taken place. ¹² And when they had assembled with the elders and taken counsel, they gave a sufficient sum of money to the soldiers ¹³ and said, "Tell people, 'His disciples came by night and stole him away while we were asleep.'

A stone was rolled in front of the tomb; guards were placed to protect it from exactly what happened, an empty tomb. When the apostles were traveling and speaking about the death, resurrection and ascension, not one Jewish leader challenged the fact, the tomb was empty and Jesus was missing, even though they had assigned a guard to prevent this from happening. Rather, those leaders had bribed the guards into lying, "Tell people, 'His disciples came by night and stole him away while we were asleep.'" –Matthew 28:13.

About a hundred years after Jesus' death, in a second-century Christian apologetic text, Justin Martyr wrote a work called *Dialogue With Trypho*. In this, he said: "You [the Jews] have sent chosen and ordained men throughout all the world to proclaim that a godless and lawless heresy had sprung from one Jesus, a Galilæan deceiver, whom we crucified, but his disciples stole him by night from the tomb, where he was laid."[72]

Most scholars believe that Trypho, a Jew was a fictitious character that Justin cited as a literary device to have the reasoned conversation the Christians were/are the true people of God. Justin defended Christianity against Judaism. No Jew ever challenged or called Justin a liar, which they would have done had it not been true they bribed the guards and lied about the disciples stealing the body. Therefore, the tomb was empty.

Luke the Physician

Colossians 4:14 Updated American Standard Version (UASV)

¹⁴ Luke the **beloved physician** greets you, as does Demas.

Luke 1:1-3 Updated American Standard Version (UASV)

¹ Inasmuch as **many** have undertaken to **compile an account** of the things accomplished among us, ² just as they were handed down to us by **those who from the beginning <u>were eyewitnesses</u>** and servants of the word, ³ it seemed good to me also, having **followed all things accurately from the beginning**, to write an orderly account for you, most excellent Theophilus, ⁴ so **that you may know fully the certainty** of the things that you have been taught orally.

Luke wrote both the Gospel of Luke, and the book of Acts. When he says he investigated everything carefully, this is no idle statement. "Sir William Ramsay, an atheist and the son of atheists, tried to disprove the Bible. He was a wealthy person who graduated from the prestigious University of Oxford. Like the [archaeologist] Albright, Ramsay studied under the famous liberal German historical school in the mid-nineteenth

---

[72]*Dialogue With Trypho*, by Justin Martyr, chap. CVIII (published in *The Ante-Nicene Fathers*, Vol. 1, p. 253).

century. Esteemed for its scholarship, this school also taught that the New Testament was not a historical document. As an anti-Semitic move, this would totally eradicate the Nation of Israel from history."

"With this premise, Ramsay devoted his whole life to archaeology and determined that he would disprove the Bible."

He set out for the Holy Land and decided to disprove the book of Acts. After 25 or more years (he had released book after book during this time), he was incredibly impressed by the accuracy of Luke in his writings finally declaring that 'Luke is a historian of the first rank; not merely are his statements of fact trustworthy' . . . 'this author should be placed along with the very greatest of historians' . . . 'Luke's history is unsurpassed in respect of its trustworthiness.'[73]

"Luke's accuracy is demonstrated by the fact that he names key historical figures in the correct time sequence as well as correct titles to government officials in various areas: Thessalonica, politarchs; Ephesus, temple wardens; Cyprus, proconsul; and Malta, the first man of the island. The two books, the Gospel of Luke and book of Acts, which Luke has authored remain accurate documents of history. Ramsay stated, 'This author [Luke] should be placed along with the very greatest of historians."

"Finally, in one of his books Ramsay shocked the entire intellectual world by declaring himself to be a Christian. Numerous other archaeologists have had similar experiences. Having set out to show the Bible false, they themselves have been proven false and, as a consequence, have accepted Christ as Lord."

"In an outstanding academic career, Ramsay was honored with doctorates from nine universities and eventually knighted for his contributions to modern scholarship. Several of his works on New Testament history are considered classics. When confronted with the evidence of years of travel and study, Sir William Ramsay learned what many others before him and since have been forced to acknowledge: When we objectively examine the evidence for the Bible's accuracy and veracity, the only conclusion we can reach is that the Bible is true."[74]

---

[73]*The Bearing of Recent Discovery on the Trustworthiness of the New Testament*, by Sir W. M. Ramsay, 1915, p. 222.

[74] Archaeology Verifies the Bible as God's Word, http://christiantrumpetsounding.com/Archaeology/Archaeology%20Bklt/Archaeology%2 (accessed November 14, 2015).

Later Archaeologists Confirm Ramsay

New Testament	Higher Criticism	Archaeology Verifies the Bible
Luke 3:1 In Luke's announcement of Jesus' public ministry (Luke 3:1), he mentions, **"Lysanius tetrarch of Abilene."**	Scholars questioned Luke's credibility since the only Lysanius known for centuries was a ruler of Chalcis who ruled from 40-36 B.C.	However, an inscription dating to be in the time of Tiberius, who ruled from 14-37 A.D., was found recording a temple dedication which names **Lysanius as the "tetrarch of Abila"** near Damascus. This matches well with Luke's account.
Acts 18:12-17 In Acts 18:12-17, Paul was brought before Gallio, the **proconsul of Achaea.**		At Delphi an inscription of a letter from Emperor Claudius was discovered. In it he states, "Lucius Junios Gallio, my friend, and the **proconsul of Achaia . . ."** Historians date the inscription to 52 A.D., which corresponds to the time of the apostle's stay in 51.
Acts 19:22 and Romans 16:23 In Acts 19:22 and Romans 16:23, **Erastus**, a coworker of Paul, is named the **Corinthian city treasurer.**		Archaeologists excavating a Corinthian theatre in 1928 discovered an inscription. It reads, **"Erastus in return for his aedilship** laid the pavement at his own expense." The pavement was laid in 50 A.D. The designation of treasurer describes the work of a Corinthian aedile.
Acts 28:7 In Acts 28:7, Luke gives Plubius, the chief man on the island of Malta, the title, **"first man of the island."**	Scholars questioned this strange title and deemed it unhistorical.	Inscriptions have recently been discovered on the island that indeed gives **Plubius the title of "first man."**

"In all, Luke names thirty-two countries, fifty-four cities, and nine islands without error."

Now that we know Luke was not only a physician, but also one of the greatest historians of his time, let us consider his account. Luke, after decades of investigations took him tens of thousands of miles by sea and land, comes to one conclusion; Jesus was resurrected from the dead. (Luke 24:1-52; Acts 1:3) Luke had reason to completely trust his evidence, because he traveled with the Apostle Paul who was one whom Jesus appeared to after his ascension to heaven, and who was an enemy of Christians at the time. Moreover, Luke was there when Paul performed a number of miracles. – Acts 14:8-10; 20:7-12; 28:8-9.

Eyewitnesses to the Resurrected Jesus

Paul, an enemy of Christians, who had approved of the stoning of Stephen, and sought to arrest as many Christians as possible, wrote after the risen Jesus' appearance to him,

1 Corinthians 15:3-8 English Standard Version (ESV)

³ For I delivered to you as of first importance what I also received: that Christ died for our sins in accordance with the Scriptures, ⁴ that he was buried, that he was raised on the third day in accordance with the Scriptures, ⁵ and that he appeared to Cephas, then to the twelve. ⁶ Then he appeared to more than five hundred brothers at one time, most of whom are still alive, though some have fallen asleep. ⁷ Then he appeared to James, then to all the apostles. ⁸ Last of all, as to one untimely born, he appeared also to me.

The apostle Peter said and wrote,

Acts 2:23-24 English Standard Version (ESV)

²³ this Jesus, delivered up according to the definite plan and foreknowledge of God, you crucified and killed by the hands of lawless men. ²⁴ God raised him up, losing the pangs of death, because it was not possible for him to be held by it.

1 Peter 1:3 English Standard Version (ESV)

³ Blessed be the God and Father of our Lord Jesus Christ! According to his great mercy, he has caused us to be born again to a living hope through the resurrection of Jesus Christ from the dead,

Many of those whom Luke and Paul speak of were alive when Paul penned his letter, and Luke wrote his books. Many were close friends of Jesus up unto his execution, and were there to see the soldier pierce Jesus' side, seeing the blood and water flow out. They saw Jesus alive later, before his ascension. Everyone who spoke openly of what they saw subjected themselves to the wrath of the Jews, who had no problem executing Christians. Moreover, they could make the lives of these people intolerable, which they would be forced to endure, the rest of their lives. Why would one place themselves in such a situation, if they never saw Jesus?

Historical Confirmation of Jesus

Jewish historian Josephus (37 C.E. - 100 C.E.) recorded the history of the Jewish people in Palestine from 70 C.E. to 100 C.E. In his work *Jewish Antiquities*, he states,

> Now there was about this time, Jesus, a wise man, if it be lawful to call him a man, for he was a doer of wonderful works, a teacher of such men as receive the truth with pleasure. He drew over to him both many of the Jews and many of the gentiles. He was the Christ and when Pilate, at the suggestion of the principal men amongst us, had condemned him to the cross, those that loved him at the first did not forsake him. For he appeared alive again the third day, as the divine prophets had foretold these and ten thousand other wonderful things concerning him; and the tribe of Christians, so named from him, are not extinct to this day.[75]

Publius (or Gaius) Cornelius Tacitus (56 C.E. - 117 C.E.) was a senator and a historian of the Roman Empire. The works of Tacitus are the most reliable source for the history of his era. Tacitus says,

> To get rid of the report, Nero fastened the guilt and inflicted the most exquisite tortures on a class hated for their abominations, called Christians by the populace. Christus [Christ], from whom the name had its origin, suffered the extreme penalty during the reign of Tiberius at the hands of one of our procurators, Pontius Pilatus, and a most mischievous superstition, thus checked for the moment, again broke out not only in Judæa, the first source of the evil, but even in Rome,

---

[75] *Antiquities of the Jews* (Book XVIII, chap. 3, par. 3)

where all things hideous and shameful from every part of the world find their centre and become popular. Accordingly, an arrest was first made of all who pleaded guilty; then, upon their information, an immense multitude was convicted, not so much of the crime of firing the city, as of hatred against mankind. Mockery of every sort was added to their deaths. Covered with the skins of beasts, they were torn by dogs and perished, or were nailed to crosses, or were doomed to the flames and burnt, to serve as a nightly illumination, when daylight had expired.[76]

Pliny the Younger (61 C.E. - 113 C.E.), as governor of Bithynia, wrote to Emperor Trajan inquiring how best to deal with the early Christians,

In the meanwhile, the method I have observed towards those who have been denounced to me as Christians is this: I interrogated them whether they were Christians; if they confessed it I repeated the question twice again, adding the threat of capital punishment; if they still persevered, I ordered them to be executed. For whatever the nature of their creed might be, I could at least feel no doubt that contumacy and inflexible obstinacy deserved chastisement. There were others also possessed with the same infatuation, but being citizens of Rome, I directed them to be carried thither.[77]

Many more early secular witnesses could be brought to the witness stand, evidencing that Jesus Christ was a historical person, who was a divine person, executed by the Roman Empire, resurrected and ascended back to heaven. Therefore, unbelievers, who believe that Jesus Christ and first-century Christianity have no foundation in provable facts, need to set aside these false ideas and reconsider the Bible as the Word of God. – John 17:17; Psalm 103:15; Isaiah 40:8; 1 Peter 1:25.

Miracles Are a Reality

One of the great apologists of our time has penned a book that deals with the logic, reasonableness, evidence of Jesus resurrection. If you wish

---

[76] Ab excessu divi Augusti (Annals, Book 15, paragraph 44) Translated by A. J. Church and W. J. Brodribb.

[77] Pliny Book 10, Letter 96 (English) - VROMA, http://www.vroma.org/%7Ehwalker/Pliny/Pliny10-096-E.html (accessed November 14, 2015).

to cover this at length, read **The Case for the Resurrection of Jesus** by Habermas, Gary R. and Licona, Michael R. (Sept. 25, 2004). Since we know that Jesus' resurrection is reality, we know that miracles are possible. The same power that raised Jesus from the dead:

- Brought about an earth-wide global deluge where one family survived on an ark;
- Split the Red Sea so hundreds of thousands could walk through;
- Enabled Elijah and Elisha resurrecting people from the dead;
- Enabled Jesus to resurrect numerous people;
- Enabled Peter and John to resurrect and heal;
- Enabled Paul to resurrect and heal; and
- Enabled first century Christians to speak languages they never learned, to bring about a larger, faster evangelism, and far more!

Review Question

- Why do many doubt the miracles of the Bible?
- What are three points of David Hume that he used to reject miracles? What responses can we provide for each of Hume's points?
- What is the best-attested miracle in the Bible?
- How accurate was Luke the physician and Gospel writer as an historian?
- How can the Bible background, culture and historical setting help us the Gospel accounts is true?
- How man eyewitnesses were there who personally saw the resurrected Jesus Christ.
- What secular evidence exists that supports the historicity of Jesus Christ?

CHAPTER 4 Is the Genesis Creation of the World a Myth and Legend?

Genesis 1:1 Updated American Standard Version (UASV)

¹ In the beginning, God created the heavens and the earth.

Over the past 200 years, the scientific community and the Bible scholars of Christianity have engaged in battle. Scientists believe they have proved the Genesis account as being nothing more than a myth or legend, being no different from the Ancient Near Eastern Text of the Enuma Elish ("Epic of Creation"). The latter is a story from the eleventh century BCE, which tells of a cosmic conflict between the gods. The young Marduk kills the wicked Tiamat, the mother goddess of the ocean. Marduk then creates the universe out of Tiamat's remains. Because many people have abandoned the belief in a literal creation account of Genesis, one would surmise the atheistic scientific community has won. Sadly, even some Bible scholars have abandoned the creation account found in Genesis.

It is important we resolve this issue, or we may suffer spiritual shipwreck, falling away from the faith. The entire Bible and its writers view the Genesis account as historically true. Therefore, Genesis is much more than a beginning. It is the foundation upon which all Scripture stands. If it were proven to be nothing more than a myth or legend, it would be next to impossible to take any portion of Scripture as being true and the inspired, inerrant Word of God. Read Genesis chapter one and then we will compare it with creation stories of ancient societies. Are we to believe that Moses, the author of Genesis, simply borrowed from these other accounts? The facts are simple, Moses' accounts are the true history, while these secular myths and legends are stories that developed over time.

The Creation of the World

Genesis 1 Updated American Standard Version (UASV)

1 In the beginning God created the heavens and the earth.

² Now the earth was without form and empty; and darkness was upon the face of the watery deep: and the Spirit of God was moving over the surface of the waters.

First Creation Day

³ And God said, "Let there be light," and there was light. ⁴ And God saw that the light was good; and God separated the light from the darkness. ⁵And God began calling the light Day, and the darkness he called Night. And there came to be evening and there came to be morning, the first day.

Second Creation Day

⁶ And God went on to say, "Let there be an expanse in the middle of the waters, and let there be a separation between the waters and the waters." ⁷And God proceeded to make the expanse, and make a separation between the waters, which were under the expanse and between the waters, which were above the expanse: and it came to be so. ⁸ And God called the expanse Heaven. And there was evening and there was morning, the second day.

Third Creation Day

⁹ And God said, "Let the waters under the heavens be gathered together into one place, and let the dry land appear." And it was so. ¹⁰ God called the dry land Earth, and the waters that were gathered together he called Seas. And God saw that it was good.

¹¹ And God said, "Let the earth sprout vegetation, plants yielding seed, and fruit trees bearing fruit in which is their seed, each according to its kind, on the earth." And it was so. ¹² The earth brought forth vegetation, plants yielding seed according to their own kinds, and trees bearing fruit in which is their seed, each according to its kind. And God saw that it was good. ¹³ And there was evening and there was morning, the third day.

Fourth Creation Day

¹⁴ And God said, "Let there be lights in the expanse of the heavens to separate the day from the night. And let them be for signs and for seasons, and for days and years, ¹⁵ and let them be lights in the expanse of the heavens to give light upon the earth." And it was so. ¹⁶ And God made the two great lights, the greater light to rule the day and the lesser light to rule the night, and the stars. ¹⁷ And God set them in the expanse of the heavens to give light on the earth, ¹⁸ to rule over the day and over the night, and to separate the light from the darkness. And God saw that it was good. ¹⁹ And there was evening and there was morning, the fourth day.

Fifth Creation Day

20 And God said, "Let the waters swarm with swarms of living creatures, and let birds fly above the earth across the expanse of the heavens." **21** So God created the great sea creatures and every living creature that moves, with which the waters swarm, according to their kinds, and every winged bird according to its kind. And God saw that it was good. **22** And God blessed them, saying, "Be fruitful and multiply and fill the waters in the seas, and let birds multiply on the earth." **23** And there was evening and there was morning, the fifth day.

Sixth Creation Day

24 And God said, "Let the earth bring forth living creatures according to their kinds, livestock and creeping things and beasts of the earth according to their kinds." And it was so. **25** And God made the beasts of the earth according to their kinds and the livestock according to their kinds, and everything that creeps on the ground according to its kind. And God saw that it was good.

26 Then God said, "Let us make man in our image,[78] after our likeness. And let them have dominion over the fish of the sea and over the birds of the heavens and over the livestock and over all the earth and over every creeping thing that creeps on the earth."

27 So God created man in his own image,
in the image of God he created him;
male and female he created them.

28 And God blessed them. And God said to them, "Be fruitful and multiply and fill the earth and subdue it, and have dominion over the fish of the sea and over the birds of the heavens and over every living thing that moves on the earth." **29** And God said, "Behold, I have given you every plant yielding seed that is on the face of all the earth, and every tree with seed in its fruit. You shall have them for food. **30** And to every beast of the earth and to every bird of the heavens and to everything that creeps on the earth, everything that has the breath of life, I have given every green plant for food." And it was so. **31** And God saw everything

---

[78] "This speaks of the creation of Adam in terms that are uniquely personal. It establishes a personal relationship between God and man that does not exist with any other aspect of creation. It is the very thing that makes humanity different from every other created animal. It explains why the Bible places so much stress on God's hands-on creation of Adam." MacArthur, John (2005-05-09). *The MacArthur Bible Commentary* (Kindle Locations 1925-1927). Thomas Nelson. Kindle Edition.

that he had made, and behold, it was very good. And there was evening and there was morning, the sixth day.

Ancient Creation Stories[79]

As we discussed in our opening paragraph, the main creation story comes from the Ancient Near Eastern Text of the Enuma Elish, "Epic of Creation."

> One of the best-known of the ancient texts, Enuma Elish gets its title from the first words of the text, often translated "When on high." This text, dated to the end of the second millennium BC, is a hymn commemorating the elevation of Marduk to the head of the pantheon. It includes some of the most detailed information about divine conflict and about cosmology available from ancient Mesopotamia. The first tablet opens with a cosmogony [study of the origin of the universe] / theogony [origin of gods] and introduces Tiamat in conflict with the gods and the slaying of Apsu, interwoven with the account of Marduk's birth. The conflict escalates in tablet two as Tiamat and the rebels threaten the gods. Marduk is finally selected as the champion of the gods with the understanding that if he wins he will be elevated to the head of the pantheon. All the negotiations and preparations come to a climax in tablet four as Marduk defeats Tiamat and lays out the cosmos [universe] using Tiamat's corpse. Establishing the functions of the cosmos continues into tablet six and concludes with the creation of people from the blood of Tiamat's partner, Kingu, and the building of Babylon and a temple for Marduk. Tablet seven draws the piece to a conclusion as the fifty names of Marduk are proclaimed to name his attributes, delineate his jurisdiction, and identify his prerogatives.[80]

---

[79] A myth is s traditional story about heroes or supernatural beings, often attempting to explain the origins of natural phenomena or aspects of human behavior. "It is generally understood that myths are stories in which the gods are the main characters. Since most people do not believe that "the gods" exist, they consider these stories fanciful and fictional."—John H. Walton. *Ancient Near Eastern Thought and the Old Testament: Introducing the Conceptual World of the Hebrew Bible* (Kindle Locations 367-368). Kindle Edition.

[80] John H. Walton. *Ancient Near Eastern Thought and the Old Testament: Introducing the Conceptual World of the Hebrew Bible* (Kindle Locations 410-417). Kindle Edition.

Genesis 1:3-31 gives the reader an outline of the six creative days and the basic events and creative activities on those days. Genesis 1:1-2 informs the reader of the creation of the heavens and the earth. God proceeded to prepare the earth for human beings. On the first creative day, God said, "'Let there be light,' and there was light." On the second creative day, he formed the expanse above the earth, with water both above and beneath the expanse. The third creative day he formed the dry ground, as well as vegetation and fruit trees. After that, on the fourth day, the sun, moon and stars were now discernible so too served "as signs and for seasons and for days and years." On the fifth day, God caused the waters to "swarm with living creatures, and let birds fly above the earth across the expanse of the sky." Then, God brought forth the land animals and mankind on the sixth creative day.

The question that begs to be answered is: 'Does it seem reasonable the Genesis creation account is based on the above mentioned creation story?' The comparison of these two accounts ends with some similarities. The creative acts in both accounts are in a similar sequence: firmament, dry land, celestial luminaries, and humans. Both accounts start with a watery chaos and Genesis ends with God at rest and Enuma Elish with the gods at rest. These similarities are not because Moses borrowed from the Ancient Near East, but because they are both based on an actual historical account. The Genesis account is God revealing the true historical events to us, while other creation accounts are an embellishment of those historical events. While we have not read the complete Enuma Elish account, there are numerous differences as well. The almighty God of the Genesis account is nothing like the terrified, quarreling, and vulgar gods of *Enuma Elish*. There is no evidence the Genesis account is dependent on such stories as the Enuma Elish account, but rather the other Ancient Near Eastern stories are based on the Genesis account, which they have simply embellished, leaving only remnants of similarities.

Old Testament Archaeologist Alfred J Hoerth writes, "Archaeologists cannot excavate remains of creation, but from texts like these [Enuma Elish], they know what other ancient cultures had to say about first things. Archaeology does not show that while the biblical account may not be as complete as some might wish,[81] it owes nothing to other ancient cultures

---

[81]The Genesis creation account, in fact, the Bible was not written as a science textbook. If God had written exactly how he created the universes, formed the earth to be inhabited, and brought about animal and human life, (1) how many thousands of pages would that have taken, (2) and no one would have understood the science of it for 3,500 years or more, (3) and it would have altered human history.

or their myths. The complete Enuma Elish reveals many dissimilarities with Genesis. The omnipotent God in Genesis is very unlike the frightened, feuding, and foul gods of the epic. Necessarily there are similarities, but the Genesis account shows no dependence. The fledgling Hebrew nation should have been thankful when God brought them out from the "bewildering variety" of opinions on their origin and, through Moses, told the story as it happened. Viewed only as a creation story, Genesis is not unique, but viewed in comparison with these other stories, Genesis is Lucid and complete." (Hoerth 1998, 187)

Review Question

- Does it seem reasonable the Genesis creation account is based on the above mentioned creation story?

CHAPTER 5 Science and the Bible

Has anyone ever noticed when science and the Bible are at odds with each other, it is automatically assumed the Bible is wrong and science is right? Bible scholars will look for natural ways for the Bible to agree with science. **Yet,** when science grows over the years, it discovers the Bible was right all along. Scientists and liberal scholars bury their heads in the sand as though science did not end up being wrong, while the Bible had been right for thousands of years. Does modern science make you feel unsure about the trustworthiness of Scripture?

Job 26:7 English Standard Version (ESV)

⁷ He stretches out the north over the void
and **hangs the earth on nothing**.

Isaiah 40:22 English Standard Version (ESV)

²² It is he who sits above the **circle of the earth**,
and its inhabitants are like grasshoppers;
who stretches out the heavens like a curtain,
and spreads them like a tent to dwell in;

Isaiah 40:18 English Standard Version (ESV)

¹⁸ To whom then will you liken God,
or what likeness compare with him?

While the Bible is not a scientific textbook, it is accurate when speaks on those subjects. While it is true the earth is not a perfect circle, is the precise dimension what the author intended to convey? First, we must understand the level the Bible intends to be exact in what is written. If Jim told a friend that 650 graduated with him from high school in 1984, it is not challenged, because it is clear he is using estimated numbers and does not mean to be precise. This is how God's Word operates, as well.

Acts 2:41 English Standard Version (ESV)

[41] So those who received his word were baptized, and there were added that day about three thousand souls.

Numbers within the Bible are often used with approximations. This is a frequent practice even today, in written works and verbal conversation. While Bible writers had no Google Earth, or had not been able to see the earth from the moon, they were accurate with their descriptions, unlike other myths and legends.

In The Beginning

According to atheists, "the universe is as it is, mysteriously, and it just happens to permit life," explains Paul Davies. "Had it been different," atheists say, "we would not be here to argue about it. The universe may or may not have a deep underlying unity, but there is no design, purpose, or point to it all—at least none that would make sense to us." "The advantage of this position," notes Davies, "is that it is easy to hold—easy to the point of being a cop-out," or a convenient way to avoid facing the issue.

In his book Evolution: A Theory in Crisis, molecular biologist Michael Denton concluded the theory of evolution "is more like a principle of medieval astrology than a serious . . . scientific theory." He also referred to Darwinian evolution as one of the greatest myths of our time.

The appeal to luck as the first cause does smack of myth. Imagine this: An archaeologist sees a rough stone that is roughly square. He may attribute that shape to chance, which would be reasonable. However, later he finds a stone that is perfectly formed in the shape of a human bust, down to the finest details. Does he attribute this item to chance? No. His logical mind says, "Someone made this." Using similar reasoning, the Bible states: "Every house is constructed by someone, but he that constructed all things is God." (Heb. 3:4) Do you agree with that statement?

"The more we get to know about our universe," writes Lennox, "the more the hypothesis there is a Creator God, who designed the universe for a purpose, gains in credibility as the best explanation of why we are here."[82]

For example, to avoid extremes of temperature, the earth must orbit at the correct distance from the sun. In other solar systems, planets have been detected that orbit sun like stars and are considered being in the "habitable zone"—meaning, they are capable of sustaining liquid water. But even these so-called habitable planets may still not be suitable for human life. They must also rotate at the right speed and be the right size.

If the earth were slightly smaller and lighter, the force of gravity would be weaker and much of the earth's precious atmosphere would escape into space. This truth can be seen in the case of the moon and the two planets Mercury and Mars. Being smaller and weighing less than the earth, they have little or no atmosphere. However, what if the earth were slightly bigger and heavier than it is? Then the earth's gravitation would be stronger, and light gases, such as hydrogen and helium, would take longer to escape from the atmosphere. "More importantly," explains the science textbook *Environment of Life*, "The delicate balance between the gases of the atmosphere would be upset."

On the other hand, consider just oxygen, which fuels combustion. If its level were to increase by 1 percent, forest fires would break out more frequently. On the other hand, if the greenhouse gas carbon dioxide kept increasing, we would suffer the consequences of an overheated earth.

Earth's Orbit

Another ideal feature is the shape of earth's orbit. If the orbit were more elliptic, we would suffer unbearable extremes of temperature. Instead, the earth has a nearly circular orbit. The situation would change if a giant planet like Jupiter were to pass nearby. In recent years, scientists have uncovered evidence that some stars have large Jupiter-like planets orbiting close to them. Many of these Jupiter-like planets have eccentric orbits. Any earth-like planets in this kind of system would be in trouble.

Astronomer Geoffrey Marcy compared these external planet systems with the four planets Mercury, Venus, Earth, and Mars, which make up

---

[82] Universe - Wikiquote, https://en.wikiquote.org/wiki/Universe (accessed November 14, 2015).

our inner solar system. In an interview, Marcy exclaimed: "Look at how perfect this [arrangement] is. It's like a jewel. You've got circular orbits. They're all in the same plane. They're all going around in the same direction. . . . It's almost uncanny." Can this be explained by chance?

Our solar system has another marvelous feature. The giant planets Jupiter, Saturn, Uranus, and Neptune orbit the sun at a safe distance from us. Instead of being a threat, these planets fill a vital role. Astronomers have likened them to "celestial vacuum cleaners" because their gravity sucks in large meteors, which might otherwise endanger life on earth. Indeed, the earth has been well "founded." (Job 38:4) Both its size and its position in our solar system are just right, but that is not all. The earth has other unique features that are essential features for human life.

Oxygen and Photosynthesis

Oxygen atoms make up 63 percent of the weight of living organisms on earth. Oxygen in the upper atmosphere protects terrestrial plants and animals from the sun's ultraviolet rays. However, oxygen is quick to react with other elements, such as when it reacts with iron and causes rust. So, how does the atmosphere keep its 21-percent level of this highly reactive element?

The answer is photosynthesis—a marvelous process whereby earth's vegetation uses sunlight to make food. A by-product of photosynthesis is oxygen—more than a billion tons of which are released into the atmosphere each day. "Without photosynthesis," explains *The New Encyclopædia Britannica*, "not only would replenishment of the fundamental food supply halt but the Earth would eventually become devoid of oxygen."

Science textbooks use several pages to explain the step-by-step process called photosynthesis. Some steps are not yet fully understood. Evolutionists cannot explain how each step evolved from something simpler. Indeed, each step appears to be irreducibly complex. "There is no generally accepted view of the origin of the photosynthetic process," admits *The New Encyclopædia Britannica*. One evolutionist glossed over the problem by stating photosynthesis was "invented" by "a few pioneering cells."

That statement, though unscientific, reveals another amazing truth: Photosynthesis needs cell walls within which the process can safely take place, and the continuation of the process requires cell reproduction. Did all that just happen by chance in a few "pioneering cells"?

From Self-Reproducing Cell to Man

What are the chances atoms gathered together to form the simplest self-reproducing cell? In his book *A Guided Tour of the Living Cell*, Nobel Prize-winning scientist Christian de Duve admits: "If you equate the probability of the birth of a bacterial cell to that of the chance assembly of its component atoms, even eternity will not suffice to produce one for you."

Let us take a giant leap from one bacterial cell to the billions of specialized nerve cells that comprise the human brain. Scientists describe the human brain as the most complicated physical structure in the known universe. It is truly unique. For example, large sections of the human brain are called association areas. These areas analyze and interpret information that comes from the sensory part of the brain. One of the association areas behind your forehead enables you to contemplate the universe's marvels. Can chance processes really explain the existence of such association areas? "Equivalents of significant parts of these areas are not found in any other animal," admits evolutionist Dr. Sherwin Nuland in his book *The Wisdom of the Body*.

Scientists have proved the human brain processes information at a much faster rate than the most powerful computer. Bear in mind that modern computer technology has resulted from decades of human effort. What about the superior human brain? Two scientists, John Barrow and Frank Tipler, admit the following in their book *The Anthropic Cosmological Principle*: "There has developed a general consensus among evolutionists that the evolution of intelligent life, comparable in information-processing ability to that of Homo sapiens, is so improbable that it is unlikely to have occurred on any other planet in the entire visible universe." Our existence, these scientists conclude, is "an extremely fortuitous accident."[83]

---

[83] Transcript: Doctrine of Creation and Evolution (part 19 ..., http://www.reasonablefaith.org/defenders-2-podcast/transcript/s9-19 (accessed November 14, 2015).

Did It All Happen by Chance?

What is your conclusion? Could the universe with all its wonders really have come about by chance? Do you not agree every piece of grand music must have a composer and the instruments must be finely tuned for it to sound good? What about our awesome universe? "We live in a very finely tuned universe," observes mathematician and astronomer David Block. His conclusion? "Our universe is a home. Designed, I believe, by the hand of God."

If that is your conclusion, then surely you will agree with the Bible's description of the Creator, Jehovah: "He is the Maker of the earth by his power, the One firmly establishing the productive land by his wisdom, and the One who by his understanding stretched out the heavens." (Jere. 51:15)

Review Question

- Is the Bible truly at odds with science when it touches on those subjects?
- How does the intricacy of the universe, our solar system and earth evidence design?

CHAPTER 6 Why has God Permitted Wickedness and Suffering?

The big issue that drove me to Agnostcism [Dr. Bart D. Ehrman is now an atheist] has to do not with the Bible, but with the pain and suffering in the world. I eventually found it impossible to explain the evil so rampant among us--whether in terms of genocides (which continue), unspeakable human cruelty, war disease, hurricanes, tsunamis, mudslides, the starvation of millions of innocent children, you name it--if there was a good and loving God who was actively involved in this world. **Misquoting Jesus (p. 248)**

As you will see with this chapter, Ehrman starts with the wrong premise. **Point One,** he begins with, "If God is a God of love, who has the power to fix anything, how can there have been such horrific pain and suffering in imperfection over the last 6,000 years?" **Point Two,** he also starts with the premise "God is responsible for everything that happens." If one starts with the wrong premise, there is no doubt he will reach the wrong conclusion(s). **Point One** is dealt with below, but Ehrman is looking through the binoculars from the wrong end, the big side through the small. When you do that, you get a narrow, focused outlook. God looks through the binoculars the right way, and can see the big picture. Ehrman can only see a fraction and a moment of time, 70 years – 80 years, while God sees everything that has happened the for more than 6,000 years in great detail, and he can see what the outcome would be if he had handled things in different ways.

Point Two, people often misunderstand suffering and evil. God is responsible for everything, but not always directly. If he started the human race, and we end up with what we now have, he is essentially responsible. Likewise, people who have a child are responsible for their child committing murder 21 years into his life because they procreated and gave birth to the child. The mother and father are **in**directly responsible. King David commits adultery with Bathsheba and has her husband Uriah killed to cover it up, and impregnates Bathsheba, but the adulterine child, who remains nameless, died. Is God responsible for the death of that child? We can answer yes and no to that question. He is responsible in two ways: **(1)** He created humankind, so there would have been no affair, murder, adulterine child if he had not. **(2)** He did not step in and save the child, when he had the power to do so. However, he is not directly responsible, because he did not make King David and Bathsheba commit the acts that led to the child being born, nor did he bring an illness on the adulterine child. He just did not step in to save the child at a time that had a high rate of infant deaths.

The reason why people think God does not care about us is the words of religious leaders. When a tragedy strikes, what do pastors and Bible scholars often say? When the terrorist attacks occurred on September 11, 2001, with thousands dying in the Twin Towers of the World Trade Center in New York City, many ministers said: "It was God's will. God must have had some good reason for doing this." When religious leaders make these comments, or similar ones, they are blaming God for bad things that happen. Yet, the disciple James wrote, "Let no one say when he is tempted, 'I am being tempted by God,' for God cannot be tempted with evil, and he himself tempts no one." (James 1:13) God never directly causes what is bad. Indeed, "Far be it from God that he should do wickedness, and from the Almighty that he should do wrong." (Job 34:10)

Human history has been inundated with pain and suffering on an unprecedented scale, much of which they have brought on themselves. The question that has plagues people is, "Why would a loving God allow it to start, and worse, why allow it to go on for over 6,000 years?" Many apologist scholars have struggled to answer this question because they overanalyze it opposed to looking for the answer in God's Word. Therefore, to answer this question we must go back to Adam and Eve at the time of the first sin. Many have read this account, but I will list the texts as a refresher.

Genesis 2:17 English Standard Version (ESV)

[17] but of the tree of the knowledge of good and evil you shall not eat, for in the day that you eat of it <u>you shall surely die</u>."

As you can see, humankind's continued existence in a paradise with perfection was dependent upon obedience, his continued acceptance of God as his sovereign.

Genesis 3:1-5 English Standard Version (ESV)

[1] Now the serpent was more crafty than any other beast of the field that the LORD God had made. He said to the woman, "Did God actually say, 'You shall not eat of any tree in the garden'?" [2] And the woman said to the serpent, "We may eat of the fruit of the trees in the garden, [3] but God said, 'You shall not eat of the fruit of the tree that is in the midst of the garden, neither shall you touch it, lest you die.'" [4] But the serpent said to the woman, "<u>You will not surely die</u>. [5]For God knows that when you eat of it your eyes will be opened, and you will be like God, knowing good and evil."

Later Bible texts establish Satan using a serpent as his mouthpiece, like a ventriloquist would a dummy. Note that Satan contradicts the clear statement made to Adam in Genesis 2:17, "You will not surely die." Backing up a little, we see Satan ask an inferential question, "Did God actually say, 'You shall not eat of any tree in the garden'?" First, he overstates what he knows to be true, not "any tree," just one tree. Second, Satan infers, "I can't believe that God would say . . . how dare he say such.' Notice too that Eve has been told so thoroughly about the tree that she even goes beyond what Adam told her, not just that you "do not eat from it,' no, 'you do not even touch it!' Then, Satan lied and slandered God as a liar by saying "they would not die." To make matters worse, he infers God is withholding good from them, and they would be better off to rebel, being like God, "knowing good and bad." This latter point is not knowledge of good and bad. It is the self-sovereignty of choosing good and bad for oneself and created creatures acting in a rebellious manner. What was symbolized by the tree is well expressed in a footnote on Genesis 2:17, in *The Jerusalem Bible* (1966):

This knowledge is a privilege which God reserves to himself and which man, by sinning, is to lay hands on, 3:5, 22. Hence it does not mean omniscience, which fallen man does not possess; nor is it moral discrimination, for unfallen man already had it and God could not refuse it to a rational being. It is the power of deciding for himself what is good and what is evil and of acting accordingly, a claim to complete moral independence by which man refuses to recognize his status as a created being. The first sin was an attack on God's sovereignty, a sin of pride.

The Issues at Hand

(1) Satan called God a liar and said he was not to be trusted, as to the issue of life or death.

(2) Satan's challenge questioned the right and legitimacy of God's rightful place as the Universal Sovereign.

(3) Satan suggested people would remain obedient to God only as long as their submission to God benefitted them.

(4) Satan said humans could walk on their own, with no need for dependence on God.

(5) Satan argued man could be like God, choosing for himself what is right and wrong.

(6) Satan claimed God's way of ruling was not in the best interests of humans, and they could do better without God.

Job 1:6-11 English Standard Version (ESV)

⁶ Now there was a day when the sons of God came to present themselves before the LORD, and Satan also came among them. ⁷ The LORD said to Satan, "From where have you come?" Satan answered the LORD and said, "From-going to and fro on the earth, and from walking up and down on it." ⁸ And the LORD said to Satan, "Have you considered my servant Job, that there is none like him on the earth, a blameless and upright man, who fears God and turns away from evil?" ⁹ Then Satan answered the LORD and said, "<u>Does Job fear God for no reason</u>? ¹⁰ Have you not put a hedge around him and his house and all that he has, on every side? You have blessed the work of his hands, and his possessions have increased in the land. ¹¹ But <u>stretch out your hand and touch all that he has, and he will curse you to your face</u>."

Job 2:4-5 English Standard Version (ESV)

⁴ Then Satan answered the LORD and said, "Skin for skin! All that <u>a man</u> has he will give for his life. ⁵ But stretch out your hand and touch his bone and his flesh, and he will curse you to your face."

This general reference to "a man," as opposed to specifically naming Job, suggests all men and women will only obey God when things are good, but when the slightest difficulty arises, he will not obey. If you faced intense trials, would you prove your love for your heavenly Father and show you preferred his rule to that of any other?

God Settles the Issues

Satan did not challenge one thing: the power of God. Satan did not suggest God was unable to destroy him as an accuser of God's creatures. He challenged God's way of ruling, not his right to rule. Therefore, this moral issue must be resolved.

An illustration of how God chose to deal with the problem can be demonstrated in human terms. A neighbor down the street slandered a man who had a son and a daughter. The slanderer said this other man was not a good father, that he withheld good from his children, and was overbearing to the point of being abusive. The slanderer stated the children would be better off without the father. He further argued the children had no real love for their father, and only obeyed him because he provided food and shelter. How should the father deal with these false and slanderous accusations? If he went down the street and pummeled the slanderer, it would only validate the lies, making neighbors believe he is telling the truth.

The answer lies within his family, they can serve only as his witnesses. (Prov. 27:11; Isa. 43:10) If the children stay obedient and grow to be successful adults, turning out to be loving, caring, honest people with spotless character, it proves the accusations were false. If the children accept the lies, rebel, and grow up to be despicable people, it just validates they would have been better off by staying with the father. So, God chose to deal with the issues. The issues that were raised must be settled beyond all reasonable doubt.

If God had destroyed the rebellious three: Satan, Adam, and Eve, he would not have resolved the issues of whether man could walk on his own, if he would be better off without his Creator, God's rulership were not best, and God were hiding good from man. In addition, there was an audience of untold billions of angelic creatures watching this. If God destroyed without settling things, these spirit creatures would be following God out of dreadful fear, not love, fear of displeasing God. Moreover, say he did destroy them, and started over and ten thousand years later, now with billions of humans now on earth, the issues were raised again. God would be forced to destroy billions of people again, and again, and again throughout time until he settled these issues.

God has allowed time to pass and the issues to be resolved. Man thought he was better off without God and could walk on his own. In addition, man has attempted every rulership imaginable, and one must ask, "Have they proven themselves better than rulership under the sovereignty of their Creator?" (Prov. 1:30-33; Isa. 59:4, 8) Sadly, the issues must be taken to the brink of destroying man (Rev. 11:18), otherwise, the argument would be that if given enough time, they could have changed things. If a man goes up to the point of destroying himself and Armageddon comes at the last minute, it would set case law, solve the issue, and the Bible would serve as the example forever. If the issues of God's sovereignty or the loyalty of his creatures, angelic or human, is ever questioned again, the Holy Bible will serve as a law established based on previous verdicts of not guilty.

What Have Been the Results?

(1) God does not cause evil and suffering. He does not cause injustices. (Rom. 9:14)

(2) The fact God has allowed evil, pain, and suffering has proved that independence from God has not brought about a better world. (Jere. 8:5, 6, 9)

(3) God's permission of evil, pain, and suffering has also proved that Satan has not been able to turn all humans away from God. (Ex. 9:16; 1 Sam. 12:22; Heb. 12:1)

(4) The fact God has permitted evil, pain, and suffering to continue has provided proof that only God, the Creator, has the capability and the right to rule over humans for their eternal blessing and happiness. (Eccles. 8:9)

(5) Satan has been the god of this world since the sin in Eden, over 6,000 years, and how has that worked out for man, and what has been the result of man's desire for independence from God and his rule? (Matt. 4:8-9; John 16:11; 2 Cor. 4:3-4; 1 John 5:19; Psalm 127:1)

Satan's impact on the earth's activities has carried with it conflict, evil, and death, and his rulership has been by means of deception, power, and his own self-interest. He has demonstrated himself an unfit ruler of everything. Therefore, God is now vindicated in putting an end to this corrupted rebel, along with all who have shared in his evil deeds. – Romans 16:20.

God has tolerated evil, sickness, pain, suffering, and death until our day in order to settle all the issues raised by Satan. We are self-centered in thinking this has only pained us. Imagine you are holding a rope on a sinking ship that 20 other men, women, and children are clinging to, when your child loses her grip and falls into the ocean. You can either hold the rope, saving 20 people, or you can let go and attempt to rescue your daughter. God has been watching the suffering of billions from the day of Adam and Eve's sin. Moreover, it has been his great love for us, which causes him to cling to the rope of issues, saving us from a future of repeated problems. He will not allow evil to remain forever. He has set a fixed time (Acts 17.31) when he will end this wicked system of Satan's rule.

Daniel 11:27 Holman Christian Standard Bible (HCSB)

[27] The two kings, whose hearts are bent on evil, will speak lies at the same table but to no avail, for still the end will come <u>at the appointed time</u>.

Unlike what many people may think (the world that lies in the hands of Satan), being obedient to God is not difficult. We simply must set aside our pride and accept the wisdom of God is so far greater than our own, and accept that he has worked for the good of obedient humans because he loves each one of us.

Matthew 7:21 Holman Christian Standard Bible (HCSB)

[21] "Not everyone who says to Me, 'Lord, Lord!' will enter the kingdom of heaven, but [only] the one who does the will of My Father in heaven.

1 John 2:15-17 Holman Christian Standard Bible (HCSB)

[15] Do not love the world or the things that belong to the world. If anyone loves the world, love for the Father is not in him. Because everything that belongs to the world, [16] the lust of the flesh, the lust of the eyes, and the pride in one's lifestyle, is not from the Father, but is from the world. [17] And the world with its lust is passing away, but the one who does God's will remains forever.

As Christians, there is a love we must not have. We must "not love the world or anything in it." Instead, we must keep ourselves from becoming infected by the corruption of unrighteous human society that is alienated from God. We must not breathe in its mental disposition or be moved by its sinful dominant attitude. (Eph. 2:1, 2; James 1:27) If we demonstrate the views of the world that oppose God, "the love of the Father" would not be in us. – James 4:4.

Review Question

- How is it that Bart D. Ehrman starts with the wrong premise?
- What issues did Satan raise in the Garden of Eden and in heaven with God?
- How did God settle the issues Satan had raised?
- What has been the results?

CHAPTER 7 Why is Life So Unfair?

On December 14, 2012, 20-year-old Adam Lanza fatally shot twenty children and six adult staff members in a mass murder at Sandy Hook Elementary School, in the village of Sandy Hook in Newtown, Connecticut. Before driving to the school, Lanza shot and killed his mother Nancy at their Newtown home. As first responders arrived, he committed suicide by shooting himself in the head.[84]

Parents, who sent their children to school that morning, never expected that by the end of the day, Adam Lanza would have murdered them. Worse still, there were signs that, if paid attention to, things may have not turned out the way they did. These parents are certainly, what comes to mind when we think of life being unfair.

Unfairness the World Over

The world is full of these type of accounts the world over. We have social depravities everywhere we look. In the United States, there are hundreds of thousands living in homeless shelters, under bridges, eating at soup kitchens, and many have young children with them as well. On the

---

[84] http://en.wikipedia.org/wiki/Sandy_Hook_Elementary_School_shooting

other hand, the United States throws away more food than any other country. Sadly, the hungry in the United States, while truly unfair, rates very low when one considers the inhumane conditions of other countries. In some countries, like Mexico, you have a millionaire living in a mansion, with a poor person living in a shack next door, and a person living in a car, living next door to him. Almost two billion people live in such hopeless poverty and inhuman conditions that those in the Western part of the world could never relate.

A slum is a run-down area of a city. It can also be called shantytown, favela, skid row, barrio and ghetto.

Slums are characterized by urban decay, unemployment and high rates of poverty.

A slum in India.

Poverty is defined as a state of want; lacking means; inadequacy. Poverty "brings hunger, disease, high infant mortality, homelessness, and even war." Poverty "falls on the more vulnerable groups in society, such as women, the elderly, minority groups, and children." About 1 billion people around the world live on less than $1 a day.[85]

---

[85] ttp://prezi.com/8duqy_es2rmu/inadequate-living-conditions-around-the-world/

God's View of Fairness

Leviticus 19:15 English Standard Version (ESV)

¹⁵ "You shall do no injustice in court. You shall not be partial to the poor or defer to the great, but in righteousness shall you judge your neighbor.

The New American Commentary (Leviticus) says, "Even though those who are disadvantaged are to be treated properly, no special favors are to be given to the poor in judicial settings (19:15; see Exod 23:3). All proceedings are to be characterized by justice, just as God is just (Job 36:3; Pss 85:10; 89:14; 97:2; 119:42; Isa 42:6; 45:18, 19; Jer 11:20; Hos 2:19)."[86] The irony is, one of the charges Satan made against God was that he is unfair. In addition, he said God was not rightly exercising his sovereignty. Then, he was believing that God was going to fairly hear his case and deal with his rebellion in a fair and just way. In other words, he believed God would allow him to live if Satan could prove the charges he had raised. Thus, Satan's charge of God being unfair was self-defeating in

---

[86] (Rooker, Leviticus: The New American Commentary 2001, p. 258)

that he depended on him to be fair in hearing the issues. God is just and impartial.

Deuteronomy 32:4 English Standard Version (ESV)

4 "The Rock, his work is perfect,
   for all his ways are justice.
A God of faithfulness and without iniquity,
   just and upright is he.

"This word [**rock**], representing the stability and permanence of God, was placed at the beginning of the verse for emphasis and was followed by a series of phrases which elaborated the attributes of God as the rock of Israel. It is one of the principal themes in this song (see vv. 15, 18, 30, 31), emphasizing the unchanging nature of God in contrast to the fickle nature of the people."[87] All of God's actions are perfect in that he expresses his attributes of justice, wisdom, love, and power in perfect balance.

Acts 10:34-35 English Standard Version (ESV)

34 So Peter opened his mouth and said: "Truly I understand that God shows no partiality, 35 but in every nation anyone who fears him and does what is right is acceptable to him.

Kenneth O. Gangel writes, "Cornelius and his family already were worshipers of God and thus had some prior preparation for the gospel. Peter could have assumed such knowledge on their part and not have to start by first introducing the basic monotheistic message of faith in God as he did when preaching to pagan Gentiles. Peter's sermon at Cornelius's basically followed the pattern of his prior sermons to the Jews but with several significant differences. One is found at the very outset, where he stressed that God shows no favoritism, accepts people from every nation, and that Jesus is "Lord of all." This emphasis on the universal gospel is particularly suited to a message to Gentiles. Peter's vision had led him to this basic insight that God does not discriminate between persons, that there are no divisions between "clean" and "unclean" people from the divine perspective. The Greek word used for favoritism (v. 34) is constructed on a Hebrew idiom meaning *to lift a face*.[88] Peter saw that

---

[87] MacArthur, John (2005-05-09). *The MacArthur Bible Commentary* (Kindle Locations 9334-9337). Thomas Nelson. Kindle Edition.

[88] For God's judgment on the basis of one's conduct, see also Gen 4:7; Rom 2:6; Rev 20:12f. For God's impartiality cf. Eph 6:9; Col 3:25, Jas 2:1, 9; 1 Pet 1:17; Rev 22:12. The idiom "lifting a face" pictures God as an oriental monarch lifting the face of a petitioner. To

God does not discriminate on the basis of race or ethnic background, looking up to some and down on others. But God does discriminate between those whose behavior is acceptable and those whose attitude is not acceptable. Those who reverence God and practice what is right are acceptable to him (v. 35; cf. Luke 8:21)." (Polhill 2001, p. 261)

From Where Does Unfairness Stem?

Genesis 2:17 Updated American Standard Version (UASV)

¹⁷ "but from the tree of the knowledge of good and evil you shall not eat, for in the day that you eat from it you shall surely die."

"The tree of the knowledge of good and evil," resulted in man's failure to respect God's decree and his sovereignty, which brought man's fall.

Genesis 3:4-5 Updated American Standard Version (UASV)

⁴ And the serpent **[Satan the Devil]** said to the woman, "You shall not surely die. ⁵ For God knows that when you eat of it your eyes will be opened, and you will be like God, knowing good and evil." knowing good and evil.

⁶ So when the woman saw that the tree was good for food, and that it was a delight to the eyes, and that the tree was to be desirable to make one wise, and she took of its fruit and ate, then she also gave some to her husband when with her, and he ate.

Satan the Devil, a very powerful angelic spirit person rebelled against God, seeking glory and power for himself. He use the serpent hanging from the tree, like a ventriloquist uses a dummy to project his voice to deceive Eve and inevitably cause Adam to rebel.

Genesis 3:24 Updated American Standard Version (UASV)

²⁴ So he drove the man out, and at the east of the garden of Eden he placed the cherubim and a flaming sword that turned every way to guard the way to the tree of life.

The New American Commentary (Genesis) says, "Such imagery effectively depicts the excommunication of the man and woman from the presence of God. Later Israel was all too aware that an audience with

---

lift the petitioner's face is to receive him or her with favor (cf. Esth 4:11; 5:2, where the custom is different but the import is the same).

God was the exclusive privilege of Aaron's lineage and only at the invitation of God once a year. Our parents squandered what men and women have longed to regain ever since. However, not all is lost since God initiates for Israel a new way into his presence but at the costly price of innocent blood. In spite of man's inability to obtain life through the garden's tree, the tabernacle revealed at Sinai enabled Israel to live with God, though imperfectly. The means and extent of access to God's presence was altered because of sin, but divine mercy overtook the wayward man and woman. For their future generations provision was afforded through Israel. This all, however, only foreshadowed the perfect and final passage into the presence of God by the very body of Jesus Christ, whose blood cleanses us so that we might know life through his death (Heb. 9:6–14)." (Mathews 2001, p. 258)

John 8:44 English Standard Version (ESV)

⁴⁴ You are of your father the devil, and your will is to do your father's desires. He was a murderer from the beginning, and does not stand in the truth, because there is no truth in him. When he lies, he speaks out of his own character, for he is a liar and the father of lies.

John MacArthur writes, "Jesus' words refer to the fall when Satan tempted Adam and Eve and successfully killed their spiritual life (Gen. 2:17; 3:17–24; Rom. 5:12; Heb. 2:14)."[89]

Revelation 12:9 English Standard Version (ESV)

⁹ And the great dragon was thrown down, that ancient serpent, who is called the devil and Satan, the deceiver of the whole world, he was thrown down to the earth, and his angels were thrown down with him.

The MacArthur Bible Commentary says, "Satan and his demons were cast out of heaven at the time of their original rebellion, but still have access to it (cf. Job 1:6; 2:1). That access will then be denied, and they will be forever barred from heaven. Devil and Satan. Cf. 20:2. Devil comes from a Greek verb meaning "to slander" or "to falsely accuse." He is a malignant liar (John 8:44; 1 John 3:8). His accusations against believers (v. 10) are unsuccessful because of Christ our Advocate (1 John 2:1). Satan, meaning "adversary," or "enemy," appears especially in Job and the Gospels. deceives the whole world. As he has throughout human history,

---

[89] MacArthur, John (2005-05-09). *The MacArthur Bible Commentary* (Kindle Locations 47425-47426). Thomas Nelson. Kindle Edition.

Satan will deceive people during the Tribulation (cf. 13:14; 20:3; John 8:44). After his temporary release from the bottomless pit at the end of the Millennium, he will briefly resume his deceitful ways (20:8, 10)."[90]

Unfairness in the Last Days

Revelation 12:12 English Standard Version (ESV)

[12] Therefore, rejoice, O heavens and you who dwell in them! But woe to you, O earth and sea, for the devil has come down to you in great wrath, because he knows that his time is short!"

The Holman New Testament Commentary (Revelation) says, "Satan's overthrow means that his accusations can never again ascend to the throne of God. This is great news for all the holy angels. It is cause for **you who dwell in** the heavens to **rejoice**. What brings heavenly joy causes **woe to the earth and the sea**. More terrors await them from the sea beast and from the land beast that the dragon will call up. The dragon is **filled with fury**, for he has never before been so utterly defeated. He recognizes this as a sign: **his time is short** to damage God and his people, so he must act quickly with renewed energy. (Easley 1998, p. 213)

Daniel 12:4 English Standard Version (ESV)

[4] But you, Daniel, shut up the words and seal the book, until the time of the end. Many shall run to and fro, and knowledge shall increase."

The angel "Gabriel therefore was instructing Daniel to preserve "the words of the scroll," not merely this final vision146 but the whole book147 for those who will live at "the time of the end" when the message will be needed. This future generation will undergo the horrors of the tribulation ("time of distress") and will need the precious promises contained in the Book of Daniel—that God will be victorious over the kingdoms of this world and that the suffering will last for only a brief time—to sustain them." (Miller 1994, p. 321)

2 Timothy 3:1-5 English Standard Version (ESV)

[1] But understand this, that in the last days there will come times of difficulty. [2] For people will be lovers of self, lovers of money, proud, arrogant, abusive, disobedient to their parents, ungrateful,

---

[90] MacArthur, John (2005-05-09). The MacArthur Bible Commentary (Kindle Locations 67207-67213). Thomas Nelson. Kindle Edition.

unholy, **³** heartless, unappeasable, slanderous, without self-control, brutal, not loving good, **⁴** treacherous, reckless, swollen with conceit, lovers of pleasure rather than lovers of God, **⁵** having the appearance of godliness, but denying its power. Avoid such people.

The MacArthur Bible Commentary says, "**3:1 the last days**. This phrase refers to this age, the time since the first coming of the Lord Jesus. See note on 1 Timothy 4:1. perilous times. Perilous is used to describe the savage nature of two demon-possessed men (Matt. 8:28). The word for times had to do with epochs, rather than clock or calendar time. Such savage, dangerous eras or epochs will increase in frequency and severity as the return of Christ approaches (v. 13). The church age is fraught with these dangerous movements accumulating strength as the end nears. Cf. Matthew 7:15; 24:11, 12, 24; 2 Peter 2:1, 2. **3:2–4** This list of attributes characterizing the leaders of the dangerous seasons is a description of unbelievers similar to the Lord's in Mark 7:21, 22. **3:5 having a form of godliness but denying its power.** Form refers to the outward shape or appearance. Like the unbelieving scribes and Pharisees, false teachers and their followers are concerned with mere external appearances (cf. Matt. 23:25; Titus 1:16). Their outward form of Christianity and virtue makes these individuals all the more dangerous."[91]

Unfairness Removed

Romans 16:20 English Standard Version (ESV)

²⁰ The God of peace will soon crush Satan under your feet. The grace of our Lord Jesus Christ be with you.

Do Not Love the World

1 John 2:15-17 English Standard Version (ESV)

¹⁵ Do not love the world or the things in the world. If anyone loves the world, the love of the Father is not in him. **¹⁶** For all that is in the world, the desires of the flesh and the desires of the eyes and pride of life, is not from the Father but is from the world. **¹⁷** And the world is passing away along with its desires, but whoever does the will of God abides forever.

---

[91] MacArthur, John (2005-05-09). The MacArthur Bible Commentary (Kindle Locations 60742-60751). Thomas Nelson. Kindle Edition.

The End of the Age

Matthew 24:1-3 English Standard Version (ESV)

¹ Jesus left the temple and was going away, when his disciples came to point out to him the buildings of the temple. ² But he answered them, "You see all these, do you not? Truly, I say to you, there will not be left here one stone upon another that will not be thrown down." ³ As he sat on the Mount of Olives, the disciples came to him privately, saying, "Tell us, when will these things be, and what will be the sign of your coming and of the end of the age?"

Here in verse three, we have Jesus and the disciples taking a seat on the Mount of Olives, looking down on the temple below. The temple compound was the ninth wonder of the ancient world. Jesus had just told the disciples that this marvel was going to be so devastated in a coming destruction, "there will not be left here one stone upon another that will not be thrown down." Looking down, the disciples asked Jesus what they thought to be but one question, not knowing the answer that Jesus would give, showed it to be three separate questions. Of course, the initial question **(1)** was their wondering when the destruction that Jesus spoke of was coming. There second portion of that question was **(2)** what will be the sign of your coming. The third portion of the question was **(3)** the end of the age.[92] Herein, we will focus on questions **(2)** and **(3)**. In short, **(1)** the destruction of Jerusalem took place in 70 C.E., just 37-years after the death, resurrection, and ascension of Christ.

> They ask these questions about the destruction of Jerusalem and the temple, his own second coming (... [*parousia*], presence, common in the papyri for the visit of the emperor), and the end of the world. Did they think that they were all to take place simultaneously? There is no way to answer. At any rate Jesus treats all three in this great eschatological discourse, the most difficult problem in the Synoptic Gospels. ... It is sufficient for our purpose to think of Jesus as using the destruction of the temple and of Jerusalem which did happen in that generation in a.d. 70, as also a symbol of his own second coming and of the end of the world (... [*sunteleias tou aiōnos*]) or consummation of the age. In a painting the artist by skilful perspective may give on the same surface the inside of a room, the fields outside the window, and the sky far beyond. Certainly in this discourse Jesus blends in apocalyptic language the background of his death on the cross, the coming destruction of Jerusalem, his own second coming and the end of the world. He now touches one, now the other. It is not easy for us to separate clearly the various items.[93]

In "what will be the sign of your **coming**," the Greek word behind "coming" (*parousia*) needs a little more in-depth explaining.

> *Parousia* ... lit., "a presence," *para*, "with," and *ousia*, "being" (from *eimi*, "to be"), denotes both an "arrival" and a consequent "presence with." For instance, in a papyrus letter a lady speaks of the necessity of her parousia in a place in order to attend to matters relating to her property there. Paul speaks

---

[92] Whether one sees this as two questions or three questions is not that big of a difference. If it is two questions; then, the coming/presence of Christ and the end of the age are being treated as one event. However, if there are three; then, the coming/presence of Christ and the end of the age are being treated as two events. Either way, you have Christ's coming/presence and the end of the age. If the Greek word *parousia* carries the sense of both the arrival of Christ and his presence for a time before the end of the age, as explained by Vine's Expository Dictionary, this seems to better support it being a three part question. How long that interval is between the arrival, the presence and the conclusion, no one can truly know.

[93] A.T. Robertson, *Word Pictures in the New Testament* (Nashville, TN: Broadman Press, 1933), Mt 24:3.

of his *parousia* in Philippi, Phil. 2:12 (in contrast to his *apousia*, "his absence"; see absence). Other words denote "the arrival" (see *eisodos* and *eleusis*, above). *Parousia* is used to describe the presence of Christ with His disciples on the Mount of Transfiguration, 2 Pet. 1:16. When used of the return of Christ, at the rapture of the church, it signifies, not merely His momentary "coming" for His saints, but His presence with them from that moment until His revelation and manifestation to the world. In some passages the word gives prominence to the beginning of that period, the course of the period being implied, 1 Cor. 15:23; 1 Thess. 4:15; 5:23; 2 Thess. 2:1; Jas. 5:7-8; 2 Pet. 3:4. In some, the course is prominent, Matt. 24:3, 37; 1 Thess. 3:13; 1 John 2:28; in others the conclusion of the period, Matt. 24:27; 2 Thess. 2:8.[94]

"What will be the sign of your coming" As we can see from the context of Matthew 24 and Vine's *Expository Dictionary*, parousia, describes not only the arrival of Christ, but his presence as well. This does not give us the sense of a coming and some swift departure. Rather, the presence aspect is a period of time that we cannot know the exact length of, so it does no good even to speculate by adding adjectives, like a "lengthy" or "short" presence.

"the end of the age" What is meant by the Greek word *aion*, which is translated "age." It refers to a certain period of time, an epoch, or age.

> *aion* (αἰών, 165), "an age, era" (to be connected with *aei*, "ever," rather than with *ao*, "to breathe"), signifies a period of indefinite duration, or time viewed in relation to what takes place in the period.[95]

What period of time is being referred to here? If we look at God's use of Moses to help in the Exodus of his people from Egypt, and Moses penning of the Mosaic Law, we would say that from the Exodus to the sacrifice ransom death of Christ was an "age" (period of time or epoch)

---

[94] The reader should be aware that the Greek word parousia does mean presence, the word is derived from para (with) and ousia (being). However, it does not denote the idea of invisible as the Jehovah Witnesses attest to. See W. E. Vine, Merrill F. Unger, and William White Jr., *Vine's Complete Expository Dictionary of Old and New Testament Words* (Nashville, TN: T. Nelson, 1996), 111.

[95] W. E. Vine, Merrill F. Unger, and William White Jr., *Vine's Complete Expository Dictionary of Old and New Testament Words* (Nashville, TN: T. Nelson, 1996), 19.

where the Israelite nation was the only way to God. Then, Jesus entered humanity into another age by his ransom sacrifice, which runs up unto his second coming/presence and the end of this age of Christianity.

Jesus answers this two or three-part question throughout the rest of Matthew 24 and chapter 25. Matthew gives us Jesus' presentation of the events that lead to Jesus coming and presence, to set up his kingdom to rule **over** the earth for a thousand years. Most will be shocked by my saying "over" the earth, as almost all translations render Revelation 5:10 as "and you have made them a kingdom and priests to our God, and they shall reign **on** the earth."

epí [2093] is in the genitive and can range from: "on, upon; over; at, by; before, in the presence of; when, under, at the time of;"[96] Below you are going to find a list of the genitive epi within Revelation that has a similar construction.

If we are to establish that some translations are choosing a rendering because it suits their doctrine, we must compare how they render the same thing elsewhere. I do believe that the English is a problem in trying to say, "They shall reign **on** the earth." First, because this is not a location issue: i.e., "where." The genitive *epi* is dealing not with where, but with authority over, which is expressed by having it over ... not on ...

Please also take special note that the context of all of these epi genitives that follow the active indicative verb and then are followed by the genitive definite article and noun are dealing with authority.

The verb "to reign" is properly used of kings and queens, and here implies complete power over the world and its inhabitants. So another way of expressing this is "and they shall rule over the world and its inhabitants" or "they shall have power over ...."[97]

Revelation 5:9-10 has a high level of theological content. It either says that Jesus and his co-rulers are going to over the earth, or on the

---

[96] William D. Mounce, Mounce's Complete Expository Dictionary of Old & New Testament Words (Grand Rapids, MI: Zondervan, 2006), 1150.

[97] Bratcher, Robert G.; Hatton, Howard: A Handbook on the Revelation to John. New York: United Bible Societies, 1993 (UBS Handbook Series; Helps for Translators), S. 105

earth. It is theological bias to have several cases of similar context and the same grammatical construction, rendering the verses the same every time, yet to then render one verse contrary to the others, simply because it aligns with one's theology. Please see Revelation 2:26; 6:8; 9:11; 11:6; 13:7; 14:18; 16:9; 17:18, and then look at Revelation **5:10**. Nowhere in Scripture does it say that Jesus is going to rule over the earth.

Signs of the End of the Age

Matthew 24:4 New American Standard Bible (NASB)

⁴ And Jesus answered and said to them, "See to it that no one misleads you.

Jesus' disciples, like any other Jew of the day, would have seen the destruction of Jerusalem in 70 C.E., the first century Jewish historian, Josephus, tells us 1,100,000 Jews were killed in the destruction of Jerusalem, with another 97,000 taken captive. (War VI. 9.3)[98] Therefore, here in advance (33 C.E.), Jesus wanted his disciples to be on the watch, to not be misled, as though the destruction of Jerusalem (66-70 C.E.) also meant "the end of the age."

Matthew 24:5 English Standard Version (ESV)

⁵ For many will come in my name, saying, 'I am the Christ,' and they will lead many astray.

Yes, this would be one of the ways that many coming in Jesus' name would have led the disciples astray, claiming to be the Christ (Hebrew *Messiah*), namely the "anointed one." Therefore, it would not be Christians alone, who would be filling this role as false christs/messiahs/anointed ones.

> "From Josephus it appears that in the first century before the destruction of the Temple [in 70 C.E.] a number of Messiahs arose promising relief from the Roman yoke, and finding ready followers ... Thus about 44, Josephus reports, a certain impostor, Theudas, who claimed to be a prophet, appeared and urged the people to follow him with their belongings to the Jordan, which he would divide for them. According to Acts v. 36 (which seems to refer to a different date), he secured about

---

[98] Flavius Josephus and William Whiston, *The Works of Josephus: Complete and Unabridged* (Peabody: Hendrickson, 1987).

400 followers. Cuspius Fadus sent a troop of horsemen after him and his band, slew many of them, and took captive others, together with their leader, beheading the latter ... Another, an Egyptian, is said to have gathered together 30,000 adherents, whom he summoned to the Mount of Olives, opposite Jerusalem, promising that at his command the walls of Jerusalem would fall down, and that he and his followers would enter and possess themselves of the city. But Felix, the procurator (c. 55-60), met the throng with his soldiery. The prophet escaped, but those with him were killed or taken, and the multitude dispersed. Another, whom Josephus styles an impostor, promised the people "deliverance and freedom from their miseries" if they would follow him to the wilderness. Both leader and followers were killed by the troops of Festus, the procurator (60-62; "Ant." xx. 8, § 10). Even when Jerusalem was already in process of destruction by the Romans, a prophet, according to Josephus suborned by the defenders to keep the people from deserting announced that God commanded them to come to the Temple, there to receive miraculous signs of their deliverance. Those who came met death in the flames.

Unlike these Messiahs, who expected their people's deliverance to be achieved through divine intervention, Menahem, the son of Judas the Galilean and grandson of Hezekiah, the leader of the Zealots, who had troubled Herod, was a warrior. When the war broke out he attacked Masada with his band, armed his followers with the weapons stored there, and proceeded to Jerusalem, where he captured the fortress Antonia, overpowering the troops of Agrippa II. Emboldened by his success, he behaved as a king, and claimed the leadership of all the troops. Thereby he aroused the enmity of Eleazar, another Zealot leader, and met death as a result of a conspiracy against him (ib. ii. 17, § 9). He is probably identical with the Menahem b. Hezekiah mentioned in Sanh. 98b, and called, with reference to Lam. i. 17, "the comforter ["menaḥem"] that should relieve" (comp. Hamburger, "R. B. T." Supplement, iii. 80). With the destruction of the Temple the appearance of Messiahs ceased for a time. Sixty years later a politico-Messianic movement of large proportions took place with Bar Kokba at its head. This leader of the revolt against Rome was hailed as Messiah-king by Akiba, who referred to him. *The Jewish*

Encyclopedia lists 28 false Messiahs between the years 132 C.E. and 1744 C.E.[99]

Matthew 24:6 English Standard Version (ESV)

⁶ And you will hear of wars and rumors of wars. See that you are not alarmed, for this must take place, but the end is not yet.

There have been religious leaders that have been misled by the two Great Wars of the 20th century, World War I and II, associating each of them with the "end of the age." The First Jewish–Roman War (66–73 C.E.),[100] at times called The Great Revolt, could have misled the disciples into thinking that the end was imminent. Therefore, Jesus tells them that they should not be alarmed, and that the end is not yet. This counsel of Jesus has had to be applied from First Jewish–Roman War to the two Great Wars of the 20th century, every time a war came along, which seems to be an end all for humanity. Nevertheless, this one sign alone is not enough to signal the end, because imperfect humans are prone to war.

Matthew 24:7 English Standard Version (ESV)

⁷ For nation will rise against nation, and kingdom against kingdom, and there will be famines and earthquakes in various places.

Here Jesus expounds on his previous comments about war, because the conflicts of humankind have been so pervasive that there was a need for a reference book, *Dictionary of Wars* by George C. Kohn. Therefore, while we should take note of current events, wars, rumors of wars and even kingdom against kingdom is not enough alone to suppose that the end is here. Therefore, Jesus adds yet another two signs, famines and earthquakes. These two have been a part of humankind's history. Of course, the impact is going to be far greater with seven billion living people on earth, as opposed to a hundred million in 100 C.E. Nevertheless, these are just the beginning. It seems that a war between the Islamic state and Christian nations is inevitable.

Matthew 24:8 English Standard Version (ESV)

⁸ All these are but the beginning of the birth pains.

---

[99] Vol. X, pp. 252-255.

[100] The Second Jewish–Roman War (132–135 C.E.) Simon Bar Kokba, who claimed to be the long awaited Messiah, led a revolt against Roman Emperor Hadrian (76-139), for setting up a shrine to Jupiter (supreme Roman god), on the temple site in Jerusalem, as well as outlawing circumcision and instruction of the Law in public.

Wars, rumors of wars, kingdoms again kingdom, famines and earthquakes are just the beginning of the things to come. However, they are not the goal post that the end is imminent. Such tragedies being merely a "beginning of the birth pains," the end was "not yet." Men likely cannot appreciate this verse, because the woman only knows the pain of giving birth to a child. It is the most natural thing in her life and yet the most painful. Therefore, consider that what comes after this metaphorical concept is going to be far more painful for humankind. These pains will grow in severity until the birth of the end of the age, and the return of Jesus. Nevertheless, like any other birth that has finally reached the end, the joy of a newborn child makes one forget the prior pains. This is true after the tribulation, the joys from the Kingdom will outweigh the previous pains.

Matthew 24:9 English Standard Version (ESV)

⁹ "Then they will deliver you up to tribulation and put you to death, and you will be hated by all nations for my name's sake.

Verse 9 of the new section, 9-12, begins with "then" (Greek *tote*), which brings the reader into another section of signs, offering us more of the lines in the fingerprint, the full picture that we are in the time of to the end. "Then" can have the meaning coming *after, or at the same time*, or it could mean simply *therefore*. It would seem that "then" is best understood as meaning 'at the same time,' because these signs, as well as those that we covered in 4-7, and those coming in verse 10 are of a composite sign. Meaning, you are looking for a time when they are all happening, and on a worldwide scale.

Who are "they" that deliver Christians up to tribulation? It would those Christians of verse 5, who were led astray, abandoning the Christian faith. The last 30 years, this has truly seen the abandonment of Christianity, as well as much tribulation for those that have remained faithful. What I am primarily referring to is liberal Christianity (80 percent of Christianity), who has abandoned the biblical truth, for the lie, so they can maintain a good relationship with the world, and progressivism. Christianity has never been more hated than it is today. Sadly, conservative Christians have been deeply opposed and persecuted by liberal Christianity, atheists, not to mention Islam and other religions.

Verse 9 says they will deliver you over (ESV), or hand you over (HCSB), to tribulation. If one is handed over, he must first be seized and then delivered to those, who are seeking to do him harm, even death. Why are the Christians hated so? Former Christians and liberal Christians hate the stand that conservative Christians take by truly living by God's Word, in a world that is anything but. Radical Islam is simply trying to impose themselves on everyone who stands in their way of dominating the world. Thus, being handed over is a result for one's true faith in Jesus Christ.

Matthew 24:10 English Standard Version (ESV)

¹⁰ And then many will fall away and betray one another and hate one another.

While early Christianity suffered horrible deaths through being martyred for simply being a Christian, the hatred today is just as vile by those that slaughter Christians around the world. Nevertheless, persecution through social media, news media, and by way of lawsuits, and protests in the streets, has become the new form of persecution in the Western world. Many have fallen away from Jesus, becoming apostates toward their former brothers and sisters, loathing their very existence.

Matthew 24:11 English Standard Version (ESV)

¹¹ And many false prophets will arise and lead many astray.

What is a prophet? The primary meaning is one who proclaims the word of God, a spokesperson for God. Therefore, a false prophet would be a spokesperson giving the impression that he is a spokesman for God, but really he is far from it. These ones are very subtle and deceptive in their ability to present themselves as a person representing God. Some modern day examples would be, Jim Bakker, Kenneth Copeland, Benny Hinn, T.D. Jakes, Joyce Meyer, Juanita Bynum, Creflo Dollar, Eddie Long, Pat Robertson, and Joel Olsteen. Of course, these are just some of the televangelists, who are false prophets, with tens of millions of followers. Other false prophet religious leaders have tens of millions of followers as well. Then, there are charismatic Christian denominations that numbered over 500 million followers. These ones claim gifts of God (faith healing, speaking in tongues, etc.), which clearly are anything but. The true Christians are falling away in great numbers, being led astray by these false prophets, and those who have not, need to remain awake!

Matthew 24:12 English Standard Version (ESV)

¹² And because lawlessness will be increased, the love of many will grow cold.

The world we live in is overflowing with murders, rapes, armed robberies and assaults, not to mention war. It has grown so pervasive that many have grown callused to seeing the newspapers, websites and television news filled with one heinous crime, one after another. In looking at just one city in the United States, in 2012, 532 people were murdered in the city of Chicago, with a population of 2.7 million. However, in San Pedro Sula of the country Honduras, 1,143 people were murdered with only a population of 719,447. Statistics from the United Nations report 250,000 cases of rape or attempted rape annually. However, it must be kept in mind that because of the savagery of the times, in "many parts of the world, rape is very rarely reported, due to the extreme social stigma cast on women who have been raped, or the fear of being disowned by their families, or subjected to violence, including honor killings."[101]

Verse 12 says that the love of "the love of many will **grow cold**," and indeed it has. There are atrocious crimes against individuals, groups, nations, which would cripple the mind of anyone living decades ago. However, because of seeing it every day, all day long, the world has grown hardened to the lawlessness that exists around them. Christians carry the hope of salvation in their heart, which Jesus addresses next.

Matthew 24:13 English Standard Version (ESV)

13 But the one who endures to the end will be saved.

What are we to endure? We are to endure while we maintain our walk with God through false Christs who will lead many astray, the wars, and the natural disasters. We are to endure while we maintain our walk with God through the loss of many of our spiritual brothers and sisters who fall away, the betrayal of former Christians, and the hatred of humankind who is alienated from God. We are to endure while we maintain our walk with God through false prophets that have arisen and lead many astray, the increase of the lawlessness in this world, and the love of humanity growing colder. Yes, each of us, who survives to the end of the Christian era, to the return of Christ, will be saved from Jesus' destruction of the wicked. However, we are not to simply sit around, we have a work to accomplish that is the last sign of the end of the age.

Matthew 24:14 English Standard Version (ESV)

14 And this gospel of the kingdom will be proclaimed throughout the whole world as a testimony to all nations, and then the end will come.

---

[101] http://en.wikipedia.org/wiki/Rape_statistics

This is the last of the signs that Jesus gave that should concern us, as it is directly related to the end of the age, and the return of Christ, namely **'the gospel of the kingdom being proclaimed throughout the whole world.'** Jesus makes it very clear what he meant by "the whole world," by then saying "all nations" (Gk., *ethnos*). What Jesus meant here was more directed toward all races, not so much the "nations" that we know the world to be divided into today. Therefore, Jesus speaking of the whole world was a reference to **"a body of persons united by kinship, culture, and common traditions, *nation, people*."**[102] Today, while for the most part, nations are made up of different races, the world is also becoming a melting pot.

In the phrase "**testimony** to all nations," we find the Greek word *martyrion*, which was a legal term of "**that which serves as testimony or proof, *testimony, proof*.**"[103] The testimony here that is to be shared by Christ's disciples has to with Jesus and the kingdom. Evidence, proof, testimony has the ability to overcome the false reasoning of those in the world, to win them over, as well as convict those who refuse to see the evidence for what it is. Elsewhere Jesus said very clearly,

Matthew 11:15	**Matthew 13:9**	**Matthew 13:43**
English Standard Version (ESV)	English Standard Version (ESV)	English Standard Version (ESV)
¹⁵ He who has ears to hear, let him hear.	⁹ He who has ears, let him hear."	⁴³ Then the righteous will shine like the sun in the kingdom of their Father. He who has ears, let him hear.

No One Knows That Day and Hour

Matthew 24:36 English Standard Version (ESV)

³⁶ "But concerning that day and hour no one knows, not even the angels of heaven, nor the Son, but the Father only.

---

[102] William Arndt, Frederick W. Danker, and Walter Bauer, *A Greek-English Lexicon of the New Testament and Other Early Christian Literature* (Chicago: University of Chicago Press, 2000), 276.

[103] IBID, 619.

While none of us can know the precise time of Jesus' return, we do know that we are to be busy in the work that he has given us. Regardless of the time left, how will you use it? Here is how we should use our time before Christ's return. We should **live as though it is tomorrow**, but **plan as though it is 50-years away**. What do we mean by this? We live as though Christ is returning tomorrow, by walking with God, having a righteous standing before him. We plan as though it is 50-years away by living a life that makes strategies for a long-term evangelism that fulfills our end of the great commission. (Matt 24:14; 28:19-20; Ac 1:8)

Our sinful nature would not do well if we knew the exact day and hour. We do badly enough when we simply think Christ's return is close. You have had religions that have set dates for Christ's return, or are constantly saying, 'the end is near!' The ones who set actual dates for Christ's return: quit their jobs, sell their homes, take all their money out of the bank, and take their kids out of school, either (1) to have a good time before the end, or (2) to spend the last couple years yelling from the rooftops that "the end is coming!"

Those who are constantly saying, 'the end is near,' are similar, in that they do not take job promotions, because it would cut into their evangelism, they do not allow their children to have university educations or plan careers, because to them the end is near. Nevertheless, these groups are at least concerned about their evangelism, but fail to realize, we do not know when the end is coming.

We need to find a way in the time that remains, be it 5 years, 50 years, or 500 years, to encourage and foster "sincere brotherly love," and to display "obedience to the truth." What do we need to be obedient to? **(1)** We need to clean up the household of Christianity. **(2)** We need to then, carry out the great commission that Jesus assigned, to preach, to teach, and to make disciples! (Matt 24:14; 28:19-20; Ac 1:8) It is our assignment, in the time remaining, to assist God in helping those with a receptive heart, to accept the good news of the kingdom. Yes, we are offering those of the world, the hope of getting on the path of salvation, an opportunity at everlasting life. Just because we do not know the day or the hour, does not mean that we should be less urgent about this assignment. Remember Jesus' illustration,

Matthew 24:43 English Standard Version (ESV)

[43] But know this, that if the master of the house had known in what part of the night the thief was coming, he would have stayed awake and would not have let his house be broken into.

Moreover, remember Jesus' question,

Luke 18:8 English Standard Version (ESV)

⁸ I tell you, he will give justice to them speedily. Nevertheless, when the Son of Man comes, will he find faith on earth?"

If we were to consider the chaos within Christianity today, the 41,000 different denominations of Christianity, all believing differently, could we honestly say that Jesus would truly find the faith?

Fairness Restored

Isaiah 2:1-4 Updated American Standard Version (UASV)

¹ The word that Isaiah the son of Amoz saw concerning Judah and Jerusalem.

² It will come to pass in the latter days
that the mountain of the house of Jehovah
will be established on the top of the mountains,
 and will be lifted up above the hills;
and all the nations will stream to it,
³   and many peoples will come, and say:
"Come, let us go up to the mountain of Jehovah,
 to the house of the God of Jacob,
that he may teach us concerning his ways
 and that we may walk in his paths."
For the law[104] will go forth from Zion,
 and the word of Jehovah from Jerusalem.
⁴ He will judge between the nations,
 and will correct matters for many peoples;
and they shall beat their swords into plowshares,
 and their spears into pruning hooks;
nation shall not lift up sword against nation,
 neither shall they learn war anymore.

On these verses, Trent C. Butler writes, "**2:1**. This section begins with another introduction much like Isaiah 1:1, but this one only introduces the following sermons, not the entire book. What follows is a vision, what Isaiah ... saw. Interestingly, the first part of this vision also appears in Micah 4:1–5. The form of this sermon sounds like a call to worship

---

[104] Or *instruction* or *teaching*

introduced by a prophetic announcement of salvation. Apparently Isaiah and his younger contemporary Micah both used the same call to worship from the Jerusalem temple to speak to God's people. This would mean that God used the temple hymnody as a source for his inspired word."

"**2:2.** While the destruction of Jerusalem dominated chapter 1, the city's function as the center of salvation for all nations introduces this section. The last days are still within world history with separate nations acting. Israel used the same language as her Near Eastern neighbors in talking about the national temple as the highest mountain on earth where the deity fights battles for his people (cp. Pss. 46; 48). The prophet Isaiah applied this language to the temple in Jerusalem even though Jerusalem was obviously not the highest of the mountains Israel could see. Jerusalem would be high and lifted up because God was at work there, causing his purpose for the world to be realized in historical events. The emphasis is not on the height of Jerusalem. The emphasis is on the unheard-of foreign nations coming to Jerusalem to worship. God's hope always encompasses the world, not just one small nation (see Gen. 12:1–4)."

"**2:3–4.** The prophet, as he often did, took up the popular theology of the people's hymnody and subtly shifted it from present to future tense. Only in the last days would Zion occupy such an exalted position. God would no longer battle the nations. Jerusalem could no longer glory in the hope that nations would march to her with large gifts and tribute for her victorious king. The prophetic hope is that God's word will become the world's weapon. Military academies and weapons will vanish. People will learn to live according to God's ways. They will obey his teachings. Nations will come to Jerusalem, not because a victorious king forces them to, but because they are attracted to Jerusalem by the God who lives there and the wisdom he gives there. No longer will they have to fight to settle their differences. In Jerusalem God will be the great Mediator who settles all human disputes without battle. Military weapons will become obsolete. The world's only war will be on poverty and hunger."[105]

Isaiah 11:3-5 Updated American Standard Version (UASV)

³ And he will delight in the fear of Jehovah,
And he will not judge by what his eyes see,
   Nor make a decision by what his ears hear;
⁴ But with righteousness he shall judge the poor,

---

[105] Anders, Max; Butler, Trent (2002-04-01). Holman Old Testament Commentary - Isaiah (p. 29-30). B&H Publishing.

And decide with fairness for the meek of the earth;[106]
And he shall strike the earth with the rod of his mouth,
And with the breath of his lips he shall kill the wicked.
⁵ Righteousness shall be the belt of his waist,
And faithfulness the belt of his loins.

On these verses, Trent C. Butler writes, "The wise king would enter the royal courtroom to judge his nation correctly. As judge, the king would be empowered with the breath of his lips, the same word translated "Spirit" in verse 2. By this he would protect the poor from the wicked, establishing the economic justice so central to prophetic preaching. The new age established by the new king would bring righteousness, a dominant theme for Isaiah. Coupled with faithfulness, this clothed the king for his royal reign."[107]

Isaiah 42:1 English Standard Version (ESV)

¹ Behold my servant, whom I uphold,
 my chosen, in whom my soul delights;
I have put my Spirit upon him;
 he will bring forth justice to the nations.

On this verse, Trent C. Butler writes, "This is the first of four "Servant Songs" in Isaiah 40-55 (49:1–6; 50:4–9; 52:13–53:12). Here God formally presented the servant to an audience, although both the name of the servant and the nature of the audience remain mysteriously unclear. We do not have to find answers to all our questions about the servant. We need to understand that he is God's chosen one, God takes great delight in him, and God upholds or supports him."

"The servant's mission surprised Israel and it surprises us. His mission was not to deliver Israel from captivity and exile. The mission was for the nations. The servant gained power for his mission from the divine Spirit just as earlier rulers and prophets had. (For Spirit of God, see "Deeper Discoveries," chs. 62-64.) The servant's task was to bring justice to the nations. (For justice, see "Deeper Discoveries," ch. 1.) Justice involves a much broader meaning than the English term. In verse 4 it stands parallel to Torah, law or teaching. It is the verdict handed down by a judge (2

---

[106] "The Messiah will reverse Israel's earlier dealings with the underprivileged (3:14, 15; 10:2)." – MacArthur, John (2005-05-09). The MacArthur Bible Commentary (Kindle Locations 27444-27445). Thomas Nelson. Kindle Edition.

[107] Anders, Max; Butler, Trent (2002-04-01). Holman Old Testament Commentary - Isaiah (p. 83). B&H Publishing.

Kgs. 25:6); the whole court process (Isa. 3:14); the gracious and merciful judgment of God (Isa. 30:18); or the natural right and order claimed by a person or group of persons (Exod. 23:6)."

"In our text, the term for the servant's mission apparently encompasses a broad meaning. It refers to the natural world order and the rights expected by the nations of the earth within that order. God restores that order with its natural rights through his gracious and merciful judgment on the basis of his law or teaching."[108]

Isaiah 35:3-7 English Standard Version (ESV)

³ Strengthen the weak hands,
   and make firm the feeble knees.
⁴ Say to those who have an anxious heart,
   "Be strong; fear not!
Behold, your God
   will come with vengeance,
with the recompense of God.
   He will come and save you."

⁵ Then the eyes of the blind shall be opened,
   and the ears of the deaf unstopped;
⁶ then shall the lame man leap like a deer,
   and the tongue of the mute sing for joy.
For waters break forth in the wilderness,
   and streams in the desert;
⁷ the burning sand shall become a pool,
   and the thirsty ground springs of water;
in the haunt of jackals, where they lie down,
   the grass shall become reeds and rushes.

On these verses, Trent C. Butler writes, "The revelation of God's glory provided the background for a new prophetic commission (vv. 3-4; cp. ch. 6). If God could change the dry wasteland so radically, how much more he could do so for humanity! The prophet was called to encourage the weak and feeble. Their reason for fear would vanish. God would come in vengeance. The divine appearance would destroy the enemy (34:8) but bring salvation to the people of God. Such salvation is not

---

[108] Anders, Max; Butler, Trent (2002-04-01). Holman Old Testament Commentary - Isaiah (p. 232). B&H Publishing.

limited to a spiritual realm. The sick and disabled would find all their reasons for having an inferiority complex destroyed."[109]

Isaiah 65:20-23 English Standard Version (ESV)

[20] No more shall there be in it
   an infant who lives but a few days,
   or an old man who does not fill out his days,
for the young man shall die a hundred years old,
   and the sinner a hundred years old shall be accursed.
[21] They shall build houses and inhabit them;
   they shall plant vineyards and eat their fruit.
[22] They shall not build and another inhabit;
   they shall not plant and another eat;
for like the days of a tree shall the days of my people be,
   and my chosen shall long enjoy the work of their hands.
[23] They shall not labor in vain
   or bear children for calamity,
for they shall be the offspring of the blessed of the Lord,
   and their descendants with them.

On these verses, Trent C. Butler writes, "The injustices of life would disappear. Long life would be the rule for God's people, death at a hundred being like an infant's death that could only be explained as the death of a sinner. All of God's people would live to a ripe old age and enjoy the fruits of their life. The age of Messiah would clearly have dawned (cp. 11:6–9). No longer would people lose their property and crops to foreign invaders. Each of God's faithful people would enjoy the works of their hands. Labor would be rewarded in the field and in the birth place. Every newborn would escape the "horror of sudden disaster" (author's translation; NIV, misfortune). Curses would disappear. Every generation would be blessed by God."[110]

Psalm 37:7-11 English Standard Version (ESV)

[7] Be still before the Lord and wait patiently for him;
   fret not yourself over the one who prospers in his way,
   over the man who carries out evil devices!

---

[109] Anders, Max; Butler, Trent (2002-04-01). Holman Old Testament Commentary - Isaiah (p. 191). B&H Publishing.

[110] Anders, Max; Butler, Trent (2002-04-01). Holman Old Testament Commentary - Isaiah (p. 374). B&H Publishing.

⁸ Refrain from anger, and forsake wrath!
   Fret not yourself; it tends only to evil.
⁹ For the evildoers shall be cut off,
   but those who wait for the Lord shall inherit the land.
¹⁰ In just a little while, the wicked will be no more;
   though you look carefully at his place, he will not be there.
¹¹ But the meek shall inherit the land
   and delight themselves in abundant peace.

On these verses, Stephen J. Lawson wrote, "David repeated his original advice: Do not fret when men succeed. He returned to the earlier thought of verse 2—sinners who seem to flourish for a season will eventually be destroyed (Eccl. 3:16–17). To point this out, he used a series of contrasts between the godly and the ungodly. **Refrain from anger**, he declared, because these **evil men** in the final day would be cut off and die before entering eternity damned. **But those who hope in the LORD**—the meek—**will inherit the land** (cp. Matt. 5:5). This indicated the fullness of God's blessing."[111]

Revelation 21:3-4 English Standard Version (ESV)

³ And I heard a loud voice from the throne saying, "Behold, the dwelling place of God is with man. He will dwell with them, and they will be his people, and God himself will be with them as their God. ⁴ He will wipe away every tear from their eyes, and death shall be no more, neither shall there be mourning, nor crying, nor pain anymore, for the former things have passed away."

On these verses, Kendell Easley wrote, "For the third and final time John hears **a loud voice from the throne** (16:17; 19:5). The word for **dwelling** is traditionally translated "tabernacle" or "tent." When the Israelites had lived in the wilderness after the exodus, God's presence was evident through the tent (Exod. 40:34). Part of the reward for Israel's obedience to God was, "I will put my dwelling place [tabernacle] among you, and I will not abhor you. I will walk among you and be your God, and you will be my people" (Lev. 26:11–12). Israel's disobedience, of course, led finally to the destruction of the temple."

"The permanent remedy began when God became enfleshed in Jesus: "The Word became flesh and made his dwelling among us" (John 1:14). A form of the same verb translated "made his dwelling" in John

---

[111] Anders, Max; Lawson, Steven (2004-01-01). Holman Old Testament Commentary - Psalms: 11 (p. 199). B&H Publishing.

1:14 is now used by the heavenly voice: **he will live with them**. Here, then, is the final eternal fulfillment of Leviticus 26."

"**They will be his people, and God himself will be with them and be their God** is a divine promise often made, particularly in context of the new covenant (Jer. 31:33; 32:38; Ezek. 37:27; 2 Cor. 6:16). In eternity, it will find full completion in its most glorious sense. One striking note here is that the word translated "people," while often singular in Revelation (for example, 18:4), here is plural, literally "peoples." This points to the great ethnic diversity of those in heaven."

"The great multitude who came out of the Great Tribulation received the pledge of many blessings including the final removal of any cause for **tears** (7:15–17). Now this promise extends to every citizen-saint of the New Jerusalem. The picture of God himself gently taking a handkerchief and wiping away all tears is overwhelming. It pictures the removal of four more enemies:

• **death**—destroyed and sent to the fiery lake (20:14; 1 Cor. 15:26)

• **mourning**—caused by death and sin, but also ironically the eternal experience of those who loved the prostitute (18:8)

• **crying**—one result of the prostitute's cruelty to the saints (18:24)

• **pain**—the first penalty inflicted on mankind at the Fall is finally lifted at last (Gen. 3:16)"

"All these belonged to **the old order of things** where sin and death were present. The last thought could also be translated, "The former things are gone." No greater statement of the end of one kind of existence and the beginning of a new one can be found in Scripture." (Easley 1998, p. 395)

Resurrection of Life and Judgment

John 5:28-29 English Standard Version (ESV)

²⁸ Do not marvel at this, for an hour is coming when all who are in the tombs will hear his voice ²⁹ and come out, those who have done good to the resurrection of life, and those who have done evil to the resurrection of judgment.

When Jesus returns, he will bring many angels, and wipe out the wicked. However, the righteous will not be destroyed, and the righteous prior to Jesus first coming back in the first century, will receive a resurrection. The unrighteous, which had never had the opportunity to know God, will also be resurrected for a chance to hear the Good News, and then, they will be judged on what they do during the millennial reign of Christ. (Acts 24:15) Therefore, the punishment for sin is death, the punishment for those, who "keep on sinning deliberately after receiving the knowledge of the truth, there no longer remains a sacrifice for sins," i.e., eternal death. However, "there will be a resurrection of both the just and the unjust [i.e., those who never heard the Good News]." – Acts 24:15

In death, Scripture show us as being unable to praise God. The Psalmist tells us, "For in death there is no remembrance of you; in Sheol [gravedom] who will give you praise?" (Psa. 6:5) Isaiah the prophet writes, "For Sheol [gravedom] cannot thank you [God], death cannot praise you; those who go down to the pit cannot hope for your faithfulness. 'It is the living who give thanks to you, as I do today; a father tells his sons about your faithfulness.'" – Isaiah 38:18-19.

Passing Over from Death to Life

John 5:24 English Standard Version (ESV)

24 Truly, truly, I say to you, whoever hears my word and believes him who sent me has eternal life. He does not come into judgment, but has passed from death to life.

Regeneration is God restoring and renewing somebody morally or spiritually, where the Christian receives a new quality of life. This one goes from the road of death over to the path of life. (John 5:24) Here he becomes a new person, with a new personality, having removed the old person. (Eph. 4:20-24) **This does not mean** that the imperfection is gone, and the sinful desires are removed, but that he now has the mind of Christ, the Spirit and the Word of God to gain control over his thinking and his fleshly desires. Therefore, if one has truly experienced a conversion it will be evident by the changes in one's new personality from the old personality, his life, and his actions. If this is the case, he will be fulfilling the words of Jesus, "let your light shine before others, so that they may see your good works and give glory to your Father who is in heaven." (Matt. 5:16)

Can we see one as truly a man of faith, a committed Christian, who attends the meetings, but never carries out any personal study, never shares the gospel with another, never helps his spiritual brothers or sisters (physically, materially, mentally, or spiritually), nor helps his neighbor, or any of the other things one would find within a man of faith? James had something to say about this back in chapter 1:26-27, "If anyone thinks he is religious and does not bridle his tongue but deceives his heart, this person's religion is worthless. Religion that is pure and undefiled before God, the Father, is this: to visit orphans and widows in their affliction, and to keep oneself unstained from the world." One who does not possess real faith, will not help the poor, he will not separate himself from worldly pursuits, he will favor those that he can benefit from (the powerful and wealthy), and ignore those than he cannot make gains from (orphans and widows), he will not know the love of God, nor his mercy. (Jas. 2:8, 9, 13)

Titus 3:5 Lexham English Bible (LEB)

⁵ he saved us, not by deeds of righteousness that we have done, but because of his mercy, **through the washing of regeneration** and renewal by the Holy Spirit,

The Greek word *polingenesia* means to a renewal or rebirth of a new life in Christ, by the Holy Spirit. Jesus told Nicodemus, "unless someone is born of ... Spirit, he is not able to enter into the kingdom of God." (John 3:5). At the moment a person is converted, he is regenerated or renewed, passing over from death to life eternal. Jesus explains this at John 5:24, "the one who hears my word and who believes the one who sent me has eternal life, and does not come into judgment, but has passed from death into life." The principal feature of rebirth of a new life in Christ, by the Holy Spirit, regeneration, is the passing over from death to life eternal.

At that point, the Spirit dwells within this newly regenerated one. From the time of Adam and Eve, God has desired to dwell with man. God fellowshipped with Adam in the Garden of Eden. After Adam's rebellion, he chose faithful men, to walk with him in their life course, to communicate with them. Enoch, Noah, and Abraham walked with God. In the Hebrew language the tabernacle is called *mishkan* meaning "dwelling place." In both the tabernacle and the temple, God was represented as dwelling with the people in the Most Holy. He also dwelt with the people through the Son, "And the Word became flesh and dwelt among us, and we have seen his glory, glory as of the only Son from the Father, full of grace and truth." (John 1:14) After Jesus' ascension, God dwelt among the Christians, by way of the Holy Spirit, in the body of each individual Christian, which begins at conversion.

Review Questions

- What are the living conditions for most of the earth?
- What is God's view of fairness?
- From where does this unfairness stem?
- How is this unfairness to unfold in the last days?
- Who will remove this unfairness?
- What did Jesus say about the end of the age?
- What are some of the signs of the end of the age?
- How should we deal with the fact that we do not know the day and hour?
- What is the resurrection of life and judgment?
- What does it mean to pass over from death to life?

CHAPTER 8 Does God Step in and Solve Our Every Problem Because We are Faithful?

Praising God as the Grand Savior

Psalm 42 depicts for us the circumstances of a Levite, one of the offspring's of Korah, who found himself in exile. His inspired words can be very beneficial to us in preserving thankfulness for friendship with fellow Christians and continuing steadfastly while going through hostile conditions.

Thirsting for God as a Deer Thirsts for Water

The psalmist stated,

Psalm 42:1-2 English Standard Version (ESV)

¹ As a deer pants for flowing streams,
  so pants my soul for you, O God.
² My soul thirsts for God,
  for the living God.
When shall I come and appear before God?

A female deer cannot survive long without water. If water is low, the deer will risk its life going out of cover to get at the lifesaving water, even though she knows that the prey could attack at any moment. Like the deer that longs for water because it is a matter of life or death, the psalmist longed for God. The word "pants" in the Hebrew means "to have a keen, consuming desire for." His driving passion was not for people, possessions, or prosperity but for God."[112]

The Bible lands are a dry country, where the vegetation wastes away rapidly throughout the dry season, and water is a very valuable commodity, as it is limited in the extreme. That is why the Psalmist says that he was a 'soul thirsting for God.' He had been going without his essential spiritual needs being satisfied, that is the freedom of going to the sanctuary; therefore, he asks when he might again "appear before God."

He had been confined because of persecution, which prevented him from having contact with his fellow believers, which resulted in intense sadness, unhappiness and hopelessness, as verse three indicates.

Psalm 42:3 English Standard Version (ESV)

³ My tears have been my food
  day and night,
while they say to me all the day long,
  "Where is your God?"

Because of this hostile situation, the Psalmist was depressed to the point of being unable to eat. Therefore, his 'tears were his food.' Yes, "day and night" tears would roll down his cheeks into his mouth. His isolation and distress were not enough, as his enemies aggravated his wounds by provoking, ridiculing, in a hurtful or mocking way, as they

---

[112] Anders, Max; Lawson, Steven (2004-01-01). *Holman Old Testament Commentary - Psalms: 11* (p. 224). B&H Publishing.

would say all day long, "Where is your God?" He needed to find a way to reassure himself during this time of difficulty, to not be overrun by sorrow and heartache.

Why am I in Despair?

Psalm 42:4-6 English Standard Version (ESV)

4 These things I remember,
    as I pour out my soul:
how I would go with the throng
    and lead them in procession to the house of God
with glad shouts and songs of praise,
    a multitude keeping festival.

5 Why are you cast down, O my soul,
    and why are you in turmoil within me?
Hope in God; for I shall again praise him,
    my salvation 6 and my God.

My soul is cast down within me;
    therefore I remember you
from the land of Jordan and of Hermon,
    from Mount Mizar.

Here we find the Psalmist not living in the moment of suffering, but rather remembering a time before he was in exile. He 'pours out his soul,' reaching the depths of his inner self with such passion, as he reminisces within about the former days. The Levite recalls in his mind what life was like when he was in his land, as he lived and worshiped with his brother and sister Israelites, as they walked "to the house of God," to celebrate the festival. Initially, these memories did not bring joy, but the pain of knowing they were a thing of the past, deeply missed.

Then, he asked himself, "Why are you cast down, O my soul and why are you in turmoil within me"? At that moment, he realized that his hope of salvation was not in himself, but in God. Therefore, the sweet memories truly brought him relief! He knew that if he patiently waited, God would act in his behalf. He then knew that his unfavorable conditions were not going to define his faith that, in time God would aid him in his time of need. When that moment would happen, he would "praise him" for 'his salvation' and being 'his God.' He might have been far removed from the sanctuary, but the Psalmist kept his God at the forefront of his mind.

If we ever find ourselves in difficult times, unrelenting times, we need to follow the pattern set by the Psalmist. We need to remember that God is well aware of our circumstances, and he will not forsake us. We must realize that the issues that were raised by Satan in the Garden of Eden, the sovereignty of God, the rightfulness of his rulership, and the issues raised by Satan to God in the book of Job, the loyalty of God's creatures, are greater than we are.

Proverbs 3:25-26 Lexham English Bible (LEB)

[25] Do not be afraid of sudden panic,
   or the storm of wickedness that will come.
[26] [Jehovah] will be your confidence
   and guard your foot from capture.

Before delving into the rest of Psalm 42, let us take a moment to establish what these verses do not mean. Should we understand that these verses or any others in Scripture teach that because we are wisely walking with God that he will miraculously step in to protect each servant personally from difficult times, diseases, mental disorders, injury or death? No. These sorts of miracles are the extreme exception to the rule. Of the 4,000 plus years of Bible history, from Adam to Jesus, with tens of millions of people living and dying, we have but a few dozen miracles that we know of in Scripture. Even in Bible times, miracles were not typical, far from it. Hundreds of years may pass with no historical record of a miracle happening at all.

If we are wisely walking with God, we can be confident that bodily disease, mental disorders, injury or early death is far less likely than if we were not. Moreover, we can draw on the resurrection hope. Does God miraculously move events to save us out of difficult times or miraculously heal us? Yes, he certainly can, but it is an extreme exception to the rule. He miraculously heals those who are going to play a significant role in his settling of the issues that were raised in the Garden of Eden.

What God's Word teaches us is this, that if we walk by using discernment and exercising sound judgment from Scripture, unless unexpected events befall us, we can be sure that we will not stumble into the difficulties that the world of humankind alienated from God faces every day. Conversely, the wicked do not have this protection as they reject the Word of God as foolish. In other words, Christians live by the moral values of Scripture, which gives them an advantage over those who do not. Therefore, God answers our prayers by our faithfully acting in behalf of those prayers, by applying Scripture in a balanced manner. If we have not taken in a deep understanding of God's Word, how can we have the Spirit inspired wisdom, the very knowledge of God to guide and direct us in our ways? Just because we are not being rescued when we feel that we should, this does not mean that we have lost faith, or that God is displeased. Even though the Psalmist had no doubt that Jehovah God was coming to his aid, he still experienced grief.

Psalm 42:7 English Standard Version (ESV)

⁷ Deep calls to deep
  at the roar of your waterfalls;
all your breakers and your waves
  have gone over me.

Yes, the Psalmist's surroundings of his exile were very beautiful; however, they brought him back to the reality of his difficulty! Verse 7 may very well be describing the snow on Mount Hermon when it melts. Marvelous waterfalls are fashioned, which pour into the Jordan, causing it to increase in size. It is as though one wave is speaking to another wave. This extraordinary spectacle of power brought to the Psalmist's mind that he had been consumed by distress as if being overcome by a flood. Nevertheless, his faith in God does not waiver.

Psalm 42:8 English Standard Version (ESV)

⁸ By day [Jehovah][113] commands his steadfast love,
  and at night his song is with me,
  a prayer to the God of my life.

There is no doubt in the Psalmist's mind that Jehovah God will engulf him with his steadfast love, freeing him of anxiety. This will empower him to praise God in song and to offer a prayer of thanks 'to the God of his life.'

The Korahite Levite thinks,

Psalm 42:9-10 English Standard Version (ESV)

⁹ I say to God, my rock:
  "Why have you forgotten me?
Why do I go mourning

---

[113] Translations take liberties with God's personal name, by removing it and replacing it with the title LORD in all caps. There is no rational reason, or Scriptural grounds for doing so. In fact, Scripture shows just the opposite.—See the American Standard Version Isaiah 42:8; Malachi 3:16; Micah 4:5; Proverbs 18:10; Joel 2:32; Ezekiel 36:23; Exodus 9:16; Malachi 1:11; Psalm 8:1;148:3.

> because of the oppression of the enemy?"
> ¹⁰ As with a deadly wound in my bones,
>   my adversaries taunt me,
> while they say to me all the day long,
>   "Where is your God?"

Then, it seems that the Psalmist slips, even though he views God as 'his rock,' a place of protection from one's enemies. Yes, he now asks, "Why have you forgotten me?" Yes, the Psalmist was allowed to remain in his circumstances of sadness, feeling depressed, as his enemies took pleasure in what appeared to be a victory. The psalmist speaks of himself as being criticized in an unbearable way. So malicious was the mockery and disdain that it could be likened 'as with a deadly wound in his bones.' However, the Levite again comes to himself with self-talk, challenging his irrational thinking with rational thinking.

Wait for God

Psalm 42:11 English Standard Version (ESV)

> ¹¹ Why are you cast down, O my soul,
>   and why are you in turmoil within me?
> Hope in God; for I shall again praise him,
>   my salvation and my God.

It is not the troubles of the Psalmist, which actually caused him to feel bad. It is what he told himself that contributed to how he felt. Self-talk is what we tell ourselves in our thoughts. In fact, self-talk is the words we tell ourselves about people, self, experiences, life in general, God, the future, the past, the present; it is specifically all the words we say to ourselves all the time. Destructive self-talk, even subconsciously, can be very harmful to our mood: causing mood slumps, our self-worth plummeting, our body feeling sluggish, our will to accomplish even the smallest of things is not to be realized and our actions defeat us.

Intense negative thinking of the Psalmist led to his feeling forsaken, resulting in painful emotions, and depressive state. However, his thoughts based on a good mood were entirely different from those based on his being upset. Negative thoughts that flooded his mind were the actual contributors of his self-defeating emotions. These very thoughts were what kept the Psalmist sluggish and contributed to his feeling abandoned. Therefore, his thinking was also the key to his relief.

Every time the Psalmist felt down because of his irrational self-talk, he attempted to locate the corresponding negative thought he had to this feeling. It was those thoughts that created his feelings of low self-worth. By offsetting them and replacing them with rational thoughts, he actually changed his mood. The negative thoughts that move through his mind did so with no effort, and were the easiest course to follow, because imperfect human tendencies gave him that way of thinking, a pattern of thinking. However, the Psalmist challenged those irrational thoughts of being forsaken with rational ones, saying that he would hope in God and that he would continue to praise him as in the end God is his salvation, even if that salvation comes in the form of a resurrection.

The centerpiece to it all is our Christlike mine. Our moods, behaviors and body responses result from the way we view things (fleshly or spiritual). It is a proven fact that we cannot experience any event in any way, shape, or form unless we have processed it with our mind first. No event can depress us; it is our perception of that event that will contribute to intense sadness, even depression. If we are only sad over an event, our thoughts will be rational, but if we are depressed or anxious over an event, our thinking will be bent and irrational, distorted and utterly wrong.

If we are to remain rational in our thinking, we need to grasp the fact that God does not always step in when we believe he should, nor is he obligated to do so. As was stated earlier, he has greater issues that need resolving, which have eternal effects for the whole of humankind. There is far more times that when God does not step in, meaning that our relief may come in the hope of the resurrection. However, for his servants that apply his Word in a balanced manner, fully, God is acting in their best interest by way of his inspired, inerrant Word.

Review Questions

- Christian leaders and charismatic Christians overly attributed actions to God, what impact has it had?
- Does God always step in and solve faithful Christian's problems? Explain.

CHAPTER 9 Bible Difficulties Explained

IT SEEMS THAT the charge that the Bible contradicts itself has been made more and more in the last 20 years. Generally, those making such claims are merely repeating what they have heard, because most have not even read the Bible, let alone done an in-depth study of it. I do not wish, however, to set aside all concerns as though they have no merit. There are many who raise legitimate questions that seem, on the surface anyway, to be about well-founded contradiction. Sadly, these issues have caused many to lose their faith in God's Word, the Bible. The purpose of this books is, to help its readers to be able to defend the Bible against Bible critics (1 Pet. 3:15), to contend for the faith (Jude 1:3), and help those, who have begun to doubt. – Jude 1:22-23.

Before we begin explaining things, let us jump right in, getting our feet wet, and deal with two major Bible difficulties, so we can see that there are reasonable, logical answers. After that, we will delve deeper into explaining Bible difficulties.

Is God permitting Human Sacrifice at Judges 11:30-31?

Judges 11:29-34, 37-41 English Standard Version (ESV)

²⁹ Then the Spirit of the Lord was upon Jephthah, and he passed through Gilead and Manasseh and passed on to Mizpah of Gilead, and from Mizpah of Gilead he passed on to the Ammonites. ³⁰ And Jephthah **made a vow** to the Lord and said, "If you will give the Ammonites into my hand, ³¹ then **whatever**[114] comes out from the doors of my house to meet me when I return in peace from the Ammonites shall be the Lord's, and I will offer it up for a burnt offering." ³² So Jephthah crossed over to the Ammonites to fight against them, and the Lord gave them into his hand. ³³ And he struck them from Aroer to the neighborhood of Minnith, twenty cities, and as far as Abel-keramim, with a great blow. So the Ammonites were subdued before the people of Israel.

³⁴ Then Jephthah came to his home at Mizpah. And behold, **his daughter came out** to meet him with tambourines and with dances. She was his only child; besides her he had neither son nor daughter.

---

[114] Whoever

37 So she said to her father, "Let this thing be done for me: leave me alone two months, that I may go up and down on the mountains and weep for my virginity, I and my companions." **38** So he said, "Go." Then he sent her away for two months, and she departed, **she and her companions, and wept for her virginity** on the mountains. **39** And at the end of two months, she returned to her father, who **did with her according to his vow that he had made.** She had never known a man [been intimate with a man], and it became a custom in Israel **40** that the daughters of Israel went year by year to **lament [or commemorate] the daughter** of Jephthah the Gileadite four days in the year.

It is true; to infer that having the idea of an animal sacrifice would really have not been an impressive vow, which the context requires. Human sacrifice would be repugnant, if we are talking about taking a life. Jephthah had no sons, so he likely knew it was the daughter, who would come to greet him.

First, the text does not say he killed his daughter. The idea of some that he did kill her is concluded only by an inference. While it is not good policy to interpret backward, using Paul on Judges, he does say humans are to be **"as a living sacrifice."** Therefore, Jephthah could have offered his daughter at the temple, "as a living sacrifice" in service, like Samuel.

This is not to be taken dismissively, because under Jewish backgrounds, it is no small thing to offer a **perpetual virginity** as a sacrifice. This would mean Jephthah's lineage would not be carried on, the family name, was no more.

Second, the context says she went out to weep for two months, not mourn her death. It says, "she left with her friends and **mourned her virginity**."

If she was facing impending death, she could have married, and spent that last two months as a married woman. There would be absolutely no reason for her to mourn her virginity, if she were not facing perpetual virginity. – Exodus 38:8; 1 Samuel 2:22

Third, it was completely forbidden to offer a human sacrifice. – Leviticus 18:21; 20:2-5; Deuteronomy 12:31; 18:10

Imagine an Israelite believing that he could please God with a human sacrifice that was intended to offer up a human life. To do so would have been a rejection of Jehovah's Sovereignty (the very person you are asking for help), and a rejection of the Law that made them a special people. Worse still, this interpretation would have us believe that Jehovah knew this was coming, allowed the vow, and then aided this type of man to succeed over his enemies.

The last point is simple enough. If such a man as one who would make such a vow, in gross violation of the law, and then carry it out; there is no way he would be mentioned by Paul in Hebrews chapter 11.

There is no way God would have granted and helped in Jephthah's initial success knowing the vow that was coming, because both Jehovah and Jephthah would be as bad as the Canaanites. There is no way that God would accept such a vow and then go on to help Jephthah with his enemies yet again. Then, to allow such a vow to be carried out, to then put Jephthah on the wall of star witnesses for God in Hebrews chapter 11.

Does Isaiah 45:7 mean that God Is the Author of Evil?

Isaiah 45:7 King James Version (KJV)

7 I form the light, and create darkness: I make peace, and **create evil**: I the Lord do all these things.

Isaiah 45:7 English Standard Version (ESV)

7 I form light and create darkness,

I make well-being and **create calamity**,

I am the Lord, who does all these things.[115]

Encarta Dictionary: (Evil) (1) morally bad: profoundly immoral or wrong (2) deliberately causing great harm, pain, or upset

QUESTION: Is this view of evil always the case? No, as you will see below.

Some apologetic authors try to say, 'we are not understanding Isaiah 45:7 correctly, because there are other verses that say God is not evil (1 John 1:5), cannot look approvingly on evil (Hab. 1:13), and cannot be tempted by evil. (Jam. 1:13)' Well, while all of these things are Scripturally true, the question at hand is not: Is God evil, can God approvingly look on evil, or can God be tempted with evil? Those questions are not relevant to the one at hand, as God cannot be those things, and at the same time, he can be the yes to our question. The question is, is God the author, the creator of evil?

---

[115] See Jeremiah 18:11, Lamentations 3:18, and Amos 3:6

We would hardly argue that God was **not just** in his bringing "calamity" or "evil" down on Adam and Eve. Thus, we have Isaiah 45:7 saying that God is the creator of "calamity" or "evil."

Let us begin simple, without trying to be philosophical. When God removed Adam and Eve from the Garden of Eden, he sentenced them and humanity to sickness, old age, and death. (Rom. 5:8; i.e., enforce penalty for sin), which was to bring "calamity" or "evil" upon humankind. Therefore, as we can "evil" does not always mean wrongdoing. Other examples of God bringing "calamity" or "evil" are Noah and the flood, the Ten Plagues of Egypt, and the destruction of the Canaanites. These acts of evil were not acts of wrongdoing. Rather, they were righteous and just, because God, the Creator of all things, was administering justice to wrongdoers, to sinners. He warned the perfect first couple what the penalty was for sin. He warned the people for a hundred years by Noah's preaching. He warned the Canaanites centuries before.

Nevertheless, there are times, when God extends mercy, refraining from the execution of his righteous judgment to one worthy of calamity. For example, he warned Nineveh, the city of blood, and they repented, so he pardoned them. (Jon 3:10) God has made it a practice to warn persons of the results of sin, giving them undeservedly many opportunities to change their ways. – Ezekiel 33:11.

God cannot sin; it is impossible for him to do so. So, when did he create evil? Without getting into the eternity of his knowing what he was going to do, and when, let us just say, evil did not exist when he was the only person in existence. We might say the idea of evil existed because he knew what he was going to do. However, the moment he created creatures (spirit and human), the potential for evil came into existence because both have a free will to sin. Evil became a reality the moment Satan entertained the idea of causing Adam to sin, to get humanity for himself, and then acted on it.

God has the right and is just to bring calamity of or evil down on anyone that is an unrepentant sinner. God did not even have to give us the underserved kindness of offering us his Son. God is the author or agent of evil regardless of the source books that claim otherwise. If he had never created free will beings, evil would have never gone from the idea of evil to the potential of evil, to the existence of evil. However, God felt that it was better to get the sinful state out of angel and human existence, recover, and then any who would sin thereafter, he would be justified in handing out evil or calamity to just that person or angel alone.

Who among us would argue that he should have created humans and angels like robots, automatons with no free will? The moment he chose the free will, he moved evil from an idea to a potential, and Satan moved it to a reality. God has a moral nature that does not bring about evil and sin when he is the only person in existence. However, the moment he created beings in his image, who had the potential to sin, he brought about evil. The moment we have a moral code of good and evil that is placed upon one's with free will; then, we have evil.

In English, the very comprehensive Hebrew word ra' is variously translated as "bad," "downcast (sad, NASB)," "ugly," "evil," "grievous (distressing, NASB)," "sore," "selfish (stingy, HCSB)," and "envious," depending upon the context. (Gen 2:9; 40:7; 41:3; Ex 33:4; Deut. 6:22; 28:35; Pro 23:6; 28:22)

Evil as an adjective **describes** the **quality of** a class of people, places, or things, or of a specific person, place, or thing

Evil as a noun, **defines** the **nature** of a class of people, places, or things, or of a specific person, place, or thing (e.g., the evil one, evil eye).

We can agree that "evil" is a thing. Create means to bring something into existence, be it people, places, or things, as well something abstract, for lack of a better word at the moment. We would agree that when God was alone evil was not a reality, it did not exist? We would agree that the moment that God created free will creatures (angels and humans), creating humans in his image, with his moral nature, he also brought the potential for evil into existence, and it was realized by Satan?

Inerrancy: Can the Bible Be trusted?

If the Bible is the Word of God, it should be in complete agreement throughout; there should be no contradictions. Yet, the rational mind must ask, why is it that some passages appear to be contradictions when compared with others? For example, Numbers 25:9 tells us that 24,000 died from the scourge, whereas at 1 Corinthians 10:8, the apostle Paul says it was 23,000. This would seem to be a clear error. Before addressing such matters, let us first look at some background information.

Full inerrancy in this book means that the original writings are fully without error in all that they state, as are the words. The words were not dictated (automaton), but the intended meaning is inspired, as are the words that convey that meaning. The Author allowed the writer to use his style of writing, yet controlled the meaning to the extent of not allowing the writer to choose a wrong word, which would not convey the intended meaning. Other more liberal-minded persons hold with *partial inerrancy*, which claims that as far as faith is concerned, this portion of God's Word is without error, but that there are historical, geographical, and scientific errors.

There are several different levels of inerrancy. *Absolute Inerrancy* is the belief that the Bible is fully true and exact in every way; including not only relationships and doctrine, but also science and history. In other words, all information is completely exact. *Full Inerrancy* is the belief that the Bible was not written as a science or historical textbook, but is phenomenological, in that it is written from the human perspective. In other words, speaking of such things as the sun rising, the four corners of the earth, or the rounding off of number approximations are all from a human perspective. *Limited Inerrancy* is the belief that the Bible is meant only as a reflection of God's purposes and will, so the science and history is the understanding of the author's day, and is limited. Thus, the Bible is susceptible to errors in these areas. *Inerrancy of Purpose* is the belief that it is only inerrant in the purpose of bringing its readers to a saving faith. The Bible is not about facts, but about persons and relationships, thus, it is subject to error. *Inspired: Not Inerrant* is the belief that its authors are human and thus subject to human error. It should be noted that this author holds the position of full inerrancy.

For many today, the Bible is nothing more than a book written by men. The Bible critic believes the Bible to be full of myths and legends, contradictions, and geographical, historical, and scientific errors. University professor Gerald A. Larue had this to say, "The views of the writers as expressed in the Bible reflect the ideas, beliefs, and concepts current in their own times and are limited by the extent of knowledge in those times."[116] On the other hand, the Bible's authors claim that their writings were inspired of God, as Holy Spirit moved them along. We will discover shortly that the Bible critics have much to say, but it is inflated or empty.

2 Timothy 3:16-17 Updated American Standard Version (UASV)

[16] All Scripture is inspired by God and profitable for teaching, for reproof, for correction, for training in righteousness; [17] so that the man of God may be fully competent, equipped for every good work.

2 Peter 1:21 Updated American Standard Version (UASV)

---

[116] Gerald Larue, "The Bible as a Political Weapon," *Free Inquiry* (Summer 1983): 39.

²¹ for no prophecy was ever produced by the will of man, but men carried along by the Holy Spirit spoke from God.

The question remains as to whether the Bible is a book written by imperfect men and full of errors, or is written by imperfect men, but inspired of God. If the Bible is just another book by imperfect man, there is no hope for humankind. If it is inspired of God and without error, although penned by imperfect men, we have the hope of everything that it offers: a rich happy life now by applying counsel that lies within and the real life that is to come, everlasting life. This author contends that the Bible is inspired of God and free of human error, although written by imperfect humans.

Before we take on the critics who seem to sift the Scriptures looking for problematic verses, let us take a moment to reflect on how we should approach these alleged problem texts. The critic's argument goes something like this: 'If God does not err and the Bible is the Word of God, then the Bible should not have one single error or contradiction, yet it is full of errors and contradictions.' If the Bible is riddled with nothing but contradictions and errors as the critics would have us believe, why, out of 31,173 verses in the Bible, should there be only 2-3 thousand Bible difficulties that are called into question, this being less than ten percent of the whole?

First, let it be said that it is every Christian's obligation to get a deeper understanding of God's Word, just as the apostle Paul told Timothy:

1 Timothy 4:15-16 Updated American Standard Version (UASV)

¹⁵ Practice these things, be absorbed in them, so that your progress will be evident to all. **¹⁶** Pay close attention to yourself and to your teaching; persevere in these things, for as you do this you will ensure salvation both for yourself and for those who hear you.

Paul also told the Corinthians:

2 Corinthians 10:4-5 Updated American Standard Version (UASV)

⁴ For the weapons of our warfare are not of the flesh[117] but powerful to God for destroying strongholds.[118] **⁵** We are destroying speculations and

---

[117] That is *merely human*

[118] That is *tearing down false arguments*

every lofty thing raised up against the knowledge of God, and we are taking every thought captive to the obedience of Christ,

Paul also told the Philippians:

Philippians 1:7 Updated American Standard Version (UASV)

⁷ It is right for me to feel thus about you all, because I hold you in my heart, for you are all partakers with me of grace, both in my imprisonment and in the defense and confirmation of the gospel.

In being able to defend against the modern-day critic, one has to be able to reason from the Scriptures and overturn the critic's argument(s) with mildness. If someone were to approach us about an alleged error or contradiction, what should we do? We should be frank and honest. If we do not have an answer, we should admit such. If the text in question gives the appearance of difficulty, we should admit this as well. If we are unsure as to how we should answer, we can simply say that we will look into it and get back with them, returning with a reasonable answer.

However, do not express disbelief and doubt to your critics, because they will be emboldened in their disbelief. It will put them on the offense and you on the defense. With great confidence, you can express that there is an answer. The Bible has withstood the test of 2,000 years of persecution and is the most printed book of all time, currently being translated into 2,287 languages. If these critical questions were so threatening, the Bible would not be the book that it is.

When you are pursuing the text in question, be unwavering in purpose, or resolved to find an answer. In some cases, it may take hours of digging to find the solution. Consider this: as you resolve these difficulties, you are also building your faith that God's Word is inerrant. Moreover, you will want to do preventative maintenance in your personal study. As you are doing your Bible reading, take note of these surface discrepancies and resolve them as you work your way through the Bible. Make this a part of your prayers as well. I recommend the following program. At the end of this chapter I list several books that deal with difficult passages. As you read your Bible from Genesis to Revelation, do not attempt it in one year; make it a four-year program. Use a good exegetical commentary like *The New International Commentary of the Old and New Testament* (NICOT/NICNT) or *The New American Commentary* set, and *The Big Book of Bible Difficulties* by Norman L. Geisler, as well as *The Encyclopedia of Bible Difficulties* by Gleason Archer.

You should be aware that the originally written books were penned by men under inspiration. In fact, we do not have those originals, what textual scholars call autographs, but we do have thousands of copies. The copyists, however, were not inspired; therefore, as one might expect, throughout the first 1,400 years of copying, thousands of errors were transmitted into the texts that were being copied by imperfect hands that were not under inspiration when copying. Yet, the next 450 years saw a restoration of the text by textual scholars from around the world. Therefore, while many of our best literal translations today may not be inspired, they are a mirror-like reflection of the autographs by way of textual criticism.[119] Therefore, the fallacy could be with the copyist error that has simply not been weeded out. In addition, you must keep in mind that God's Word is without error, but our interpretation and understanding of that Word is not.

In this chapter, we are not going to take the space that we will in later chapters that are dedicated to one difficulty. Here, in short, we will address a number of them. Before looking at a few examples, it should be noted that the Bible is made up of 66 smaller books that were hand-written over a period of 1,600 years, having some 40 writers of various trades such as shepherd, king, priest, tax collector, governor, physician, copyist, fisherman, and tentmaker. Therefore, it should not surprise us that some difficulties are encountered as we casually read through the Bible. Yet, if one were to take a deeper look, one would find that these difficulties are easily explained. Let us take a few pages to examine some passages that have been under attack.

Again, our objective here is not to be exhaustive, not even close. What we are looking to do is cover a few alleged contradictions and a couple of alleged mistakes. This is to give you, the reader, a small sampling of the reasonable answers that you will find in the recommended books at the end of the chapter. Remember, your Bible is a sword that you must use both offensively and defensively. One must wonder how long a warrior of ancient times would last who was not expertly trained in the use of his weapon. Let us look at a few scriptures that support our need to learn our Bible well so will be able to defend what we believe to be true.

---

[119] Textual criticism is the study of copies of any written work of which the autograph (original) is unknown, with the purpose of ascertaining the original text. Harold J. Green, Introduction to New Testament Textual Criticism (Peabody, MA: Hendrickson, 1995), 1.

When "false apostles, deceitful workmen, disguising themselves as apostles of Christ" were causing trouble in the congregation in Corinth, the apostle Paul wrote that under such circumstances, we are to *tear down their arguments* and *take every thought captive*. (2 Corinthians 10:4, 5; 11:13–15) All who present critical arguments against God's Word, or contrary to it, can have their arguments overturned by the Christian who is able and ready to defend that Word in mildness. – 2 Timothy 2:24–26.

1 Peter 3:15 Updated American Standard Version (UASV)

¹⁵ but sanctify Christ as Lord in your hearts, always being prepared to make a defense[120] to anyone who asks you for a reason for the hope that is in you; yet do it with gentleness and respect;

Peter says that we need to be prepared to make a *defense*. The Greek word behind the English 'defense' is *apologia*, which is actually a legal term that refers to the defense of a defendant in court. Our English apologetics is just what Peter spoke of, having the ability to give a reason to any who may challenge us, or to answer those who are not challenging us but who have honest questions that deserve to be answered.

2 Timothy 2:24-25 Updated American Standard Version (UASV)

²⁴ For a slave of the Lord does not need to fight, but needs to be kind to all, qualified to teach, showing restraint when wronged ²⁵ with gentleness correcting those who are in opposition, if perhaps God may grant them repentance leading to accurate knowledge[121] of the truth,

Look at the Greek word (*epignosis*) behind the English "knowledge" in the above. "It is more intensive than *gnosis* (1108), knowledge, because it expresses a more thorough participation in the acquiring of knowledge on the part of the learner."[122] The requirement of all of the Lord's servants is that they be able to teach, but not in a quarrelsome way, and in a way to correct his opponents with mildness. Why? Because the purpose of it all is that by God, and through the Christian teacher, one may come to repentance and begin taking in an accurate knowledge of the truth.

---

[120] Or *argument*; or *explanation*

[121] *Epignosis* is a strengthened or intensified form of *gnosis* (*epi*, meaning "additional"), meaning, "true," "real," "full," "complete" or "accurate," depending upon the context. Paul and Peter alone use *epignosis*.

[122] Spiros Zodhiates, *The Complete Word Study Dictionary: New Testament*, Electronic ed. (Chattanooga, TN: AMG Publishers, 2000, c1992, c1993), S. G1922.

Inerrancy: Practical Principles to Overcoming Bible Difficulties

Below are several ways of looking at the Bible that enable the reader to see he is not dealing with an error or a contradiction, but rather a Bible difficulty.

Different Points of View

At times, you may have two different writers who are writing from two different points of view.

Numbers 35:14 New International Version (NIV)

¹⁴ Give three on this side of the Jordan and three in Canaan as cities of refuge.

Joshua 22:4 New International Version (NIV)

⁴ Now that the Lord your God has given them rest as he promised, return to your homes in the land that Moses the servant of the Lord gave you on the other side of the Jordan.

Here we see that Moses is speaking about the east side of the Jordan when he says "on this side of the Jordan." Joshua, on the other hand, is also speaking about the east side of the Jordan when he says "on the other side of the Jordan." So, who is correct? Both are. When Moses was penning Numbers the Israelites had not yet crossed the Jordan River, so the east side was "this side," the side he was on. On the other hand, when Joshua penned his book, the Israelites had crossed the Jordan, so the east side was just as he had said, "on the other side of the Jordan." Thus, we should not assume that two different writers are writing from the same perspective.

A Careful Reading

At times, it may simply be a case of needing to slow down and carefully read the account, considering exactly what is being said. Many times, we are reading the Bible as if we are reading a novel, which will hamper any serious growth in knowledge and understanding.

Joshua 18:28 New American Standard Bible (NASB)

²⁸ and Zelah, Haeleph and the Jebusite (that is, Jerusalem), Gibeah, Kiriath; fourteen cities with their villages. This is the inheritance of the sons of Benjamin according to their families.

Judges 1:21 New International Version (NIV)

²¹ The Benjamites, however, did not drive out the Jebusites, who were living in Jerusalem; to this day the Jebusites live there with the Benjamites.

Joshua 15:63 New International Version (NIV)

⁶³ Judah could not dislodge the Jebusites, who were living in Jerusalem; to this day the Jebusites live there with the people of Judah.

Judges 1:8-9 New American Standard Bible (NASB)

⁸ Then the sons of Judah fought against Jerusalem and captured it and struck it with the edge of the sword and set the city on fire. ⁹ Afterward the sons of Judah went down to fight against the Canaanites living in the hill country and in the Negev and in the lowland.

2 Samuel 5:5-9 New American Standard Bible (NASB)

⁵ At Hebron he reigned over Judah seven years and six months, and in Jerusalem he reigned thirty-three years over all Israel and Judah.

⁶ Now the king and his men went toJerusalem against the Jebusites, the inhabitants of the land, and they said to David, "You shall not come in here, but the blind and lame will turn you away"; thinking, "David cannot enter here." ⁷ Nevertheless, David captured the stronghold of Zion, that is the city of David. ⁸ David said on that day, "Whoever would strike the Jebusites, let him reach the lame and the blind, who are hated by David's soul, through the water tunnel." Therefore they say, "The blind or the lame shall not come into the house." ⁹ So David lived in the stronghold and called it the city of David. And David built all around from the Millo and inward.

There is no doubt that even the advanced Bible reader of many years can come away confused because the above accounts seem to be contradictory. In Joshua 18:28 and Judges 1:21, we see that Jerusalem was an inheritance of the tribe of Benjamin, yet the Benjamites were unable to conquer Jerusalem. But in Joshua 15:63 we see that the tribe of Judah could not conquer them either, with the reading giving the impression that it was a part of their inheritance. In Judges 1:8, however, Judah was eventually able to conquer Jerusalem and burn it with fire. Yet, to add even more to the confusion, we find at 2 Samuel 5:5–8 that David is said to have conquered Jerusalem hundreds of years later.

Now that we have the particulars, let us look at it more clearly. The boundary between Benjamin's inheritances ran right through the middle of Jerusalem. Joshua 8:28 is correct, in that what would later be called the "city of David" was in the territory of Benjamin, but it also in part crossed over the line into the territory of Judah, causing both tribes to go to war against this Jebusite city. It is also true that the tribe of Benjamin was unable to conquer the city and that the tribe of Judah eventually did. However, if you look at Judges 1:9 again, you will see that Judah did not finish the job entirely and moved on to conquer other areas. This allowed the remaining ones to regroup and form a resistance that neither Benjamin nor Judah could overcome, so these Jebusites remained until the time of David, hundreds of years later.

Intended Meaning of Writer

First, the Bible student needs to understand the level that the Bible intends to be exact in what is written. If Jim told a friend that 650 graduated with him from high school in 1984, it is not challenged, because it is all too clear that he is using rounded numbers and is not meaning to be exactly precise. This is how God's Word operates as well. Sometimes it means to be exact, at other times, it is simply rounding numbers, in other cases, the intention of the writer is a general reference, to give readers of that time and succeeding generations some perspective. Did Samuel, the author of judges, intend to pen a book on the chronology of Judges, or was his focus on the falling away, oppression, and the rescue by a judge, repeatedly. Now, it would seem that Jeremiah, the author of 1 Kings was more interested in giving his readers an exact number of years.

Acts 2:41 English Standard Version (ESV)

[41] So those who received his word were baptized, and there were added that day about three thousand souls.

As you can see here, numbers within the Bible are often used with approximations. This is a frequent practice even today, in both written works and verbal conversation.

Acts 7:2-3 English Standard Version (ESV)

[2] And Stephen said:

"Brothers and fathers, hear me. The God of glory appeared to our father Abraham when he was in Mesopotamia, before he lived in Haran, [3] and said to him, 'Go out from your land and from your kindred and go into the land that I will show you.'

If you were to check the Hebrew Scriptures at Genesis 12:1, you would find that what is claimed to have been said by God to Abraham is not quoted word-for-word; it is simply a paraphrase. This is a normal practice within Scripture and in writing in general.

Numbers 34:15 English Standard Version (ESV)

¹⁵ The two tribes and the half-tribe have received their inheritance beyond the Jordan east of Jericho, toward the sunrise."

Just as you would read in today's local newspaper, the Bible writer has written from the human standpoint, how it appeared to him. The Bible also speaks of "to the end of the earth" (Psalm 46:9), "from the four corners of the earth" (Isa 11:12), and "the four winds of the earth" (Revelation 7:1). These phrases are still used today.

Unexplained Does Not mean Unexplainable

Considering that there are 31,173 verses in the Bible, encompassing 66 books written by about 40 writers, ranging from shepherds, to kings, an army general, fishermen, tax collector, a physician and on and on, and being penned over a 1,600 year period, one does find a few hundred Bible difficulties (about one percent). However, 99 percent of those are explainable. Yet no one wants to be so arrogant to say that he can explain them all. It has nothing to do with the inadequacy of God's Word, but is based on human understanding. In many cases, science or archaeology and the field of custom and culture of ancient peoples has helped explain difficulties in hundreds of passages. Therefore, there may be less than one percent left to be answered, yet our knowledge of God's Word continues to grow.

Guilty Until Proven Innocent

This is exactly the perception that the critic has of God's Word. The legal principle of being "innocent until proven guilty" afforded mankind in courts of justice is withheld from the very Word of God. What is ironic here is that this policy has contributed to these Bible critics looking foolish over and over again when something comes to light that vindicates the portion of Scripture they are challenging.

Daniel 5:1 English Standard Version (ESV)

¹ King Belshazzar made a great feast for a thousand of his lords and drank wine in front of the thousand.

Bible critics had long claimed that Belshazzar was not known outside of the book Daniel; therefore, they argue that Daniel was mistaken. Yet it hardly seems prudent to argue error from absence of outside evidence. Just because archaeology had not discovered such a person did not mean that Daniel was wrong, or that such a person did not exist. In 1854, some small clay cylinders were discovered in modern-day southern Iraq, which would have been the city of Ur in ancient Babylonia. The cuneiform documents were a prayer of King Nabonidus for "Bel-sar-ussur, my eldest son." These tablets also showed that this "Bel-sar-ussur" had secretaries as well as a household staff. Other tablets were discovered a short time later that showed that the kingship was entrusted to this eldest son as a coregent while his father was away.

He entrusted the 'Camp' to his oldest (son), the firstborn [Belshazzar], the troops everywhere in the country he ordered under his (command). He let (everything) go, entrusted the kingship to him and, himself, he [Nabonidus] started out for a long journey, the (military) forces of Akkad marching with him; he turned towards Tema (deep) in the west."[123]

Ignoring Literary Styles

The Bible is a diverse book when it comes to literary styles: narrative, poetic, prophetic, and apocalyptic; also containing parables, metaphors, similes, hyperbole, and other figures of speech. Too often, these alleged errors are the result of a reader taking a figure of speech as literal, or reading a parable as though it is a narrative.

Matthew 24:35 English Standard Version (ESV)

[35] Heaven and earth will pass away, but my words will not pass away.

If some do not recognize that they are dealing with a figure of speech, they are bound to come away with the wrong meaning. Some have concluded from Matthew 24:35 that Jesus was speaking of an eventual destruction of the earth. This is hardly the case, as his listeners would not have understood it that way based on their understanding of the Old Testament. They would have understood that he was simply being emphatic about the words he spoke, using hyperbole. What he was conveying is that his words are more enduring than heaven and earth,

---

[123] J. Pritchard, ed., *Ancient Near Eastern Texts* (1974), 313.

and with heaven and earth being understood as eternal, this merely conveyed even more so that Jesus' words could be trusted.

Two Accounts of the Same Incident

If you were to speak to officers that take accident reports for their police department, you would find that there is cohesion in the accounts, but each person has merely witnessed aspects that have stood out to them. We will see that this is the case as well with the examples below, which is the same account in two different gospels:

Matthew 8:5 English Standard Version (ESV)

⁵ When he had entered Capernaum, a centurion came forward to him, appealing to him,

Luke 7:3 English Standard Version (ESV)

³ When the centurion heard about Jesus, he sent to him elders of the Jews, asking him to come and heal his servant.

Immediately we see the problem of whether the centurion or the elders of the Jews spoke with Jesus. The solution is not really hidden from us. Which of the two accounts is the more detailed account? You are correct if you said Luke. The centurion sent the elders of the Jews to represent him to Jesus, so; that whatever response Jesus might give, it would be as though he were addressing the centurion; therefore, Matthew gave his readers the basic thought, not seeing the need of mentioning the elders of the Jews aspect. This is how a representative was viewed in the first century, just as some countries see ambassadors today as being the very person they represent. Therefore, both Matthew and Luke are correct.

Man's Fallible Interpretations

Inspiration by God is infallible, without error. Imperfect man and his interpretations over the centuries, as bad as many of them have been, should not cast a shadow over God's inspired Word. The entire Word of God has one meaning and one meaning only for every penned word, which is what God willed to be conveyed by the human writer he chose to use.

The Autograph Alone Is Inspired and Inerrant

It has been argued by conservative scholars that only the autograph manuscripts were inspired and inerrant, not the copying of those manuscripts over the next 3,000 years for the Old Testament and 1,500 years for the New Testament. While I would agree with this position as well, it should be noted that we do not possess the autographs, so to argue that they are inerrant is to speak of nonexistent documents. However, it should be further understood that through the science of textual criticism, we can establish a mirror reflection of the autograph manuscripts. B. F. Westcott, F. J. A. Hort, F. F. Bruce, and many other textual scholars would agree with Norman L Geisler's assessment: "The New Testament, then, has not only survived in more manuscripts than any other book from antiquity, but it has survived in a purer form than any other great book—*a form that is 99.5 percent pure.*"[124]

An example of a copyist error can be found in Luke's genealogy of Jesus at Luke 3:35–37. In verse 37 you will find a Cainan, and in verse 36 you will find a second Cainan between Arphaxad (Arpachshad) and Shelah. As one can see from most footnotes in different study Bibles, the Cainan in verse 36 is seen as a scribal error, and is not found in the Hebrew Old Testament, the Samaritan Pentateuch, or the Aramaic Targums, but is found in the Greek Septuagint. (Genesis 10:24; 11:12, 13; 1 Chronicles 1:18, but not 1 Chronicles 1:24) It seems quite unlikely that it was in the earlier copies of the Septuagint, because the first-century Jewish historian Josephus lists Shelah next as the son of Arphaxad, and Josephus normally followed the Septuagint.[125] So one might ask why this second Cainan is found in the translations at all if this is the case? The manuscripts that do contain this second Cainan are some of the best manuscripts that are used in establishing the original text: 01 B L A^1 33 (Kainam); A 038 044 0102 A^{13} (Kainan).

Look at the Context

Many alleged inconsistencies disappear by simply looking at the context. Taking words out of context can distort their meaning. *Merriam-Webster's Collegiate Dictionary* defines context as "the parts of a discourse

---

[124] Norman L. Geisler and William E. Nix: *A General Introduction to the Bible* (Chicago, Moody Press, 1980), 367. (Emphasis is mine.)

[125] *Jewish Antiquities*, I, 146 [vi, 4].

that surround a word or passage and can throw light on its meaning."[126] Context can also be "the circumstances or events that form the environment within which something exists or takes place." If we were to look in a thesaurus for a synonym, we would find "background" for this second meaning. At 2 Timothy 2:15, the apostle Paul brings home the point of why context is so important: "Do your best to present yourself to God as one approved, a worker who has no need to be ashamed, rightly handling the word of truth." A Christian soldier can wield his weapons ("the sword of the Spirit") effectively in warfare only if he has practiced and has learned to use them well.

Ephesians 2:8-9 English Standard Version (ESV)

⁸ For by grace you have been saved through faith. And this is not your own doing; it is the gift of God, ⁹ not a result of works, so that no one may boast.

James 2:26 English Standard Version (ESV)

²⁶ For as the body apart from the spirit is dead, so also faith apart from works is dead.

So, which is it? Is salvation possible by faith alone as Paul wrote to the Ephesians, or is faith dead without works as James wrote to his readers? As our subtitle brings out, let us look at the context. In the letter to the Ephesians, the apostle Paul is speaking to the Jewish Christians who were looking to the works of the Mosaic Law as a means to salvation, a righteous standing before God. Paul was telling these legalistic Jewish Christians that this is not so. In fact, this would invalidate Christ's ransom, because there would have been no need for it if one could achieve salvation by meticulously keeping the Mosaic Law. (Rom. 5:18) But James was writing to those in a congregation who were concerned with their status before other men, who were looking for prominent positions within the congregation, and not taking care of those that were in need. (Jam. 2:14–17) So, James is merely addressing those who call themselves Christian, but in name only. No person could truly be a Christian and not possess some good works, such as feeding the poor, helping the elderly. This type of work was an evident demonstration of one's Christian personality. Paul was in perfect harmony with James on this. – Romans 10:10; 1 Corinthians 15:58; Ephesians 5:15, 21–33; 6:15; 1 Timothy 4:16; 2 Timothy 4:5; Hebrews 10:23-25.

---

[126] Merriam-Webster, Inc: *Merriam-Webster's Collegiate Dictionary*. Eleventh ed. (Springfield, Mass.: Merriam-Webster, Inc. 2003).

Inerrancy: Are There Contradictions?

Below I will follow this pattern. I will list the critic's argument first, followed by the text of difficulty, and conclude with an answer to the critic. What should be kept at the forefront of our mind is this: one is simply looking for the best answer, not absoluteness. If there is a reasonable answer to a Bible difficulty, why are the critics able to set them aside with ease? Because they start with the premise that this is not the Word of God, but only a book by imperfect men and full of contradictions; thus, the bias toward errors has blinded their judgment.

Critic: The critic would argue that there was an Adam and Eve, and an Abel who was now dead, so, where did Cain get his wife? This is one of the most common questions by Bible critics.

Genesis 4:17 New English Translation (NET Bible)

¹⁷ Cain had marital relations with his wife, and she became pregnant and gave birth to Enoch. Cain was building a city, and he named the city after his son Enoch.

Answer: If one were to read a little further along, they would come to the realization that Adam had a son named Seth; it further adds that Adam "became father to sons *and daughters*." (Genesis 5:4) Adam lived for a total of 800 years after fathering Seth, giving him ample opportunity to father many more sons and daughters. So it could be that Cain married one of his sisters. If he waited until one of his brothers and sisters had a daughter, he could have married one of his nieces once she was old enough. In the beginning, humans were closer to perfection; this explains why they lived longer and why at that time there was little health risk of genetic defects in the case of children born to closely related parents, in contrast to how it is today. As time passed, genetic defects increased and life spans decreased. Adam lived to see 930 years. Yet Shem, who lived after the Flood, died at 600 years, while Shem's son Arpachshad only lived 438 years, dying before his father died. Abraham saw an even greater decrease in that he only lived 175 years, while his grandson Jacob was 147 years when he died. Thus, due to increasing imperfection, God prohibited the marriage of closely related people under the Mosaic Law because of the likelihood of genetic defects.—Leviticus 18:9.

Critic: If God is here hardening Pharaoh's heart, what exactly makes Pharaoh responsible for the decisions he makes?

Exodus 4:21 Revised Standard Version (RSV)

²¹ And the Lord said to Moses, "When you go back to Egypt, see that you do before Pharaoh all the miracles which I have put in your power; but I will harden his heart, so that he will not let the people go.

Answer: This is actually a prophecy. God knew that what he was about to do would contribute to a stubborn and obstinate Pharaoh, who was going to be unwilling to change or give up the Israelites so they could go off to worship their God. Therefore, this is not stating what God is going to do; it is prophesying that Pharaoh's heart will harden because of the actions of God. The fact is, Pharaoh allowed his own heart to harden because he was determined not to agree with Moses' wishes or accept Jehovah's request to let the people go. Moses tells us at Exodus 7:13 (ESV) that "Pharaoh's heart was hardened, and he would not listen to them, as the Lord had said." Again, at 8:15 we read, "When Pharaoh saw that there was a respite, he hardened his heart and would not listen to them, as the Lord had said."

Critic: The Israelites had just received the Ten Commandments, with one commandment being: "You shall not make for yourself a carved image, or any likeness of anything that is in heaven above, or that is in the earth beneath, or that is in the water under the earth." Therefore, how is the bronze serpent not a violation of this commandment?

Numbers 21:9 English Standard Version (ESV)

⁹ So Moses made a bronze serpent and set it on a pole. And if a serpent bit anyone, he would look at the bronze serpent and live.

Answer: First, an idol is "a representation or symbol of an object of worship; *broadly*: a false god."[127] Second, it should be noted that not all images are idols. The bronze serpent was not made for the purpose of worship, or for some passionate devotion or veneration. There were times, however, when images were created with absolutely no intention of it receiving devotion, veneration, or worship, yet were later made into objects of veneration. That is exactly what happened with the copper serpent that Moses had formed in the wilderness. Many centuries later, "in the third year of Hoshea son of Elah, king of Israel, Hezekiah the son of Ahaz, king of Judah, began to reign. He removed the high places and broke the pillars and cut down the Asherah. And he broke in pieces the

---

[127] Merriam-Webster, Inc: *Merriam-Webster's Collegiate Dictionary*. Eleventh ed. (Springfield, Mass.: Merriam-Webster, Inc., 2003).

bronze serpent that Moses had made; for until those days the people of Israel had made offerings to it (it was called Nehushtan)."—2 Kings 18:1, 4.

Critic: Deuteronomy 15:11 (NET) says: *"There will never cease to be some poor people in the land;* therefore, I am commanding you to make sure you open your hand to your fellow Israelites who are needy and poor in your land." Is this not a contradiction of Deuteronomy 15:4? Will there be no poor among the Israelites, or will there be poor among them? Which is it?

Deuteronomy 15:4 New English Translation (NET Bible)

⁴ However, there should not be any poor among you, for the Lord will surely bless you in the land that he is giving you as an inheritance,

Answer: If you look at the context, Deuteronomy 15:4 is stating that if the Israelites obey Jehovah's command to take care of the poor, "there should not be any poor among" them. Thus, for every poor person, there will be one to take care of that need. If an Israelite fell on hard times, there was to be a fellow Israelite ready to step in to help him through those hard times. Verse 11 stresses the truth of the imperfect world since the rebellion of Adam and inherited sin: there will always be poor among mankind, the Israelites being no different. However, the difference with God's people is that those who were well off were to offset conditions for those who fell on difficult times. This is not to be confused with the socialistic welfare systems in the world today. Those Jews were hardworking men, who labored from sunup to sundown to take care of their families. But if disease overtook their herd or unseasonal weather brought about failed crops, an Israelite could sell himself into the service of a fellow Israelite for a period of time; thereafter, he would be back on his feet. And many years down the road, he may very well do the same for another Israelite who fell on difficult times.

Critic: Joshua 11:23 says that Joshua took the land according to what God had spoken to Moses and handed it on to the nation of Israel as planned. However, in Joshua 13:1, God is telling Joshua that he has grown old and much of the Promised Land has yet to be taken possession of. How can both be true? Is this not a contradiction? Many times at first glance, what seems like a contradiction is no such thing at all. We just have to trust the Word of God and take the time to investigate further with good conservative study tools. Keep in mind, not all study tools are equal.

Joshua 11:23 English Standard Version (ESV)

²³ So Joshua took the whole land, according to all that the Lord had spoken to Moses. And Joshua gave it for an inheritance to Israel according to their tribal allotments. And the land had rest from war.

Joshua 13:1 English Standard Version (ESV)

13 Now Joshua was old and advanced in years, and the Lord said to him, "You are old and advanced in years, and there remains yet very much land to possess.

Answer: No, it is not a contradiction. When the Israelites were to take the land, it was to take place in two different stages: the nation as a whole was to go to war and defeat the 31 kings of this land; thereafter, each Israelite tribe was to take their part of the land based on their individual actions. (Joshua 17:14–18; 18:3) Joshua fulfilled his role, which is expressed in 11:23, while the individual tribes did not complete their campaigns, which is expressed in 13:1. Even though the individual tribes failed to live up to taking their portion, the remaining Canaanites posed no real threat. Joshua 21:44, *ASV*, reads: "Jehovah gave them rest round about."

Critic: The critic would point out that John 1:18 clearly says that "*no one has ever seen God*," while Exodus 24:10 explicitly states that Moses and Aaron, Nadab and Abihu, and seventy of the elders of Israel "*saw the God of Israel*." Worse still, God informs them in Exodus 33:20: "You cannot see my face, for man shall not see me and live." The critic with his knowing smile says, 'This is a blatant contradiction.'

John 1:18 New American Standard Bible (NASB)

¹⁸ No one has seen God at any time; the only begotten God who is in the bosom of the Father, He has explained *Him*.

Exodus 24:10 New American Standard Bible (NASB)

¹⁰ and they saw the God of Israel; and under His feet there appeared to be a pavement of sapphire, as clear as the sky itself.

Exodus 33:20 English Standard Version (ESV)

²⁰ But," he [God] said, "you cannot see my face, for man shall not see me and live."

Answer: Exodus 33:20 is one-hundred percent correct: No human could see Jehovah God and live. The apostle Paul at Colossians 1:15 tell us that Christ is the image of the invisible God, and the writer informs us at

Hebrews 1:3 that Jesus is the "exact representation of His nature." Yet if you were to read the account of Saul of Tarsus (the apostle Paul), you would see that a mere partial manifestation of Christ's glory blinded Saul – Acts 9:1–18.

When the Bible says that Moses and others have seen God, it is not speaking of *literally* seeing him, because first of all He is an invisible spirit person. It is a *manifestation* of his glory, which is an act of showing or demonstrating his presence, making himself perceptible to the human mind. In fact, it is generally an angelic representative that stands in his place and not him personally. Exodus 24:16 informs us that "the glory of the Lord dwelt on Mount Sinai," not the Lord himself personally. When texts such as Exodus 24:10 explicitly state that Moses and Aaron, Nadab and Abihu, and seventy of the elders of Israel "*saw the God of Israel*," it is this "glory of the Lord," an angelic representative. This is shown to be the case at Luke 2:9, which reads: "And *an angel of the Lord* appeared to them, and *the glory of the Lord shone around them* [the shepherds], and they were filled with fear."

Many Bible difficulties are cleared up elsewhere in Scripture; for example, in the New Testament you will find a text clarifying a difficulty from the Old Testament, such as Acts 7:53, which refers to those "who received the law *as delivered by angels* and did not keep it." Support comes from Paul at Galatians 3:19: "Why then the law? It was added because of transgressions, until the offspring should come to whom the promise had been made, and it was put in place through angels by an intermediary." The writer of Hebrews chimes in at 2:2 with "For since the message *declared by angels* proved to be reliable, and every transgression or disobedience received a just retribution. . . ." As we travel back to Exodus again, to 19:19 specifically, we find support that it was not God's own voice, which Moses heard; no, it was an angelic representative, for it reads: "Moses was speaking and God was answering him with a voice." Exodus 33:22–23 also helps us to appreciate that it was the back of these angelic representatives of Jehovah that Moses saw: "While my glory passes by . . . Then I will take away my hand, and you shall see my back, but my face shall not be seen."

Exodus 3:4 states: "God called to him out of the bush, 'Moses, Moses!' And he said, 'Here I am.'" Verse 6 informs us: "I am the God of your father, the God of Abraham, the God of Isaac, and the God of Jacob." Yet, in verse 2 we read: "And the angel of the Lord appeared to him in a flame of fire out of the midst of a bush." Here is another example of using God's Word to clear up what seems to be unclear or difficult to understand at first glance. Thus, while it speaks of the Lord making a direct appearance, it is really an angelic representative. Even today, we hear such comments, as 'the president of the United States is to visit the Middle East later this week.' However, later in the article it is made clear that he is not going personally, but it is one of his high-ranking representatives. Let us close with two examples, starting with,

Genesis 32:24-30 English Standard Version (ESV)

24 And Jacob was left alone. And a man wrestled with him until the breaking of the day. **25** When the man saw that he did not prevail against Jacob, he touched his hip socket, and Jacob's hip was put out of joint as he wrestled with him.**26** Then he said, "Let me go, for the day has broken." But Jacob said, "I will not let you go unless you bless me." **27** And he said to him, "What is your name?" And he said, "Jacob."**28** Then he said," Your name shall no longer be called Jacob, but Israel, for you have striven with God and with men, and have prevailed."**29** Then Jacob asked him, "Please tell me your name." But he said, "Why is it that you ask my name?" And there he blessed him. **30** So Jacob called the name of the place Peniel, saying, "For I have seen God face to face, and yet my life has been delivered."

It is all too obvious here that this man is simply a materialized angel in the form of a man, another angelic representative of Jehovah God. Moreover, the reader of this book should have taken in that the Israelites as a whole saw these angelic representatives, and spoke of them as though they were dealing directly with Jehovah God himself.

This proved to be the case in the second example found in the book of Judges where an angelic representative visited Manoah and his wife. Like the above mentioned account, Manoah and his wife treated this angelic representative as if he were Jehovah God himself: "And Manoah said to the angel of the Lord, 'What is your name, so that, when your words come true, we may honor you?' And the angel of the Lord said to him, 'Why do you ask my name, seeing it is wonderful?' Then Manoah knew that he was the angel of the Lord. And Manoah said to his wife, "We shall surely die, *for we have seen God.*" – Judges 13:3–22.

Inerrancy: Are There Mistakes?

I have addressed the alleged contradictions, so it would seem that our job is done here, right? Not hardly. Yes, there are just as many who claim that the Bible is full of mistakes.

Critic: Matthew 27:5 states that Judas hanged himself, whereas Acts 1:18 says that "falling headlong he burst open in the middle and all his bowels gushed out." Is this a contradiction? Did Matthew or Luke make a mistake?

Matthew 27:5 English Standard Version (ESV)

⁵ And throwing down the pieces of silver into the temple, he departed, and he went and hanged himself.

Acts 1:18 English Standard Version (ESV)

¹⁸ (Now this man acquired a field with the reward of his wickedness, and falling headlong he burst open in the middle and all his bowels gushed out.

Answer: Neither Matthew, nor Luke made a mistake. What you have is Matthew giving the reader the manner in which Judas committed suicide. On the other hand, Luke is giving the reader of Acts, the result of that suicide. Therefore, instead of a mistake, we have two texts that complement each other, really giving the reader the full picture. Judas came to a tree alongside a cliff that had rocks below. He tied the rope to a branch and the other end around his neck, and jumped over the edge of the cliff in an attempt at hanging himself. One of two things could have happened: (1) the limb broke plunging him to the rocks below, or (2) the rope broke with the same result, and he burst open onto the rocks below.

Critic: The apostle Paul made a mistake when he quotes how many people died.

Numbers 25:9 English Standard Version (ESV)

⁹ Nevertheless, those who died by the plague were twenty-four thousand.

1 Corinthians 10:8 English Standard Version (ESV)

⁸ We must not indulge in sexual immorality as some of them did, and twenty-three thousand fell in a single day.

Answer: We must keep in mind the above principle that we spoke of, the *Intended Meaning of the Writer*. We live in a far more precise age today, where specificity is highly important. However, we round large numbers off (even estimate) all the time: "there were 237,000 people in Time Square last night." The simplest answer is that the number of people slain was in between 23,000 and 24,000, and both writers rounded the number off. However, there is even another possibility, because the book of Numbers specifically speaks of "all the chiefs of the people" (25:4-5), which could account for the extra 1,000, which is mentioned in Numbers 24,000. Thus, you have the people killing the chiefs of the people and the plague killing the people. Therefore, both books are correct.

Critic: After 215 years in Egypt, the descendants of Jacob arrived at the Promised Land. As you recall they sinned against God and were sentenced to forty years in the wilderness. However, once they entered the Promised Land, they buried Joseph's bones "at Shechem, in the piece of land that *Jacob bought* from the sons of Hamor the father of Shechem," as stated at Joshua 24:32. Yet, when Stephen had to defend himself before the Jewish religious leaders, he said that Joseph was buried "in the tomb that *Abraham had bought* for a sum of silver from the sons of Hamor." Therefore, at once it appears that we have a mistake on the part of Stephen. If we have one mistake in the Bible, it can no longer be claimed that it is fully inerrant.

Acts 7:15-16 English Standard Version (ESV)

[15] And Jacob went down into Egypt, and he died, he and our fathers,[16] and they were carried back to Shechem and laid in the tomb that Abraham had bought for a sum of silver from the sons of Hamor in Shechem.

Genesis 23:17-18 English Standard Version (ESV)

[17] So the field of Ephron in Machpelah, which was to the east of Mamre, the field with the cave that was in it and all the trees that were in the field, throughout its whole area, was made over [18] to Abraham as a possession in the presence of the Hittites, before all who went in at the gate of his city.

Genesis 33:19 English Standard Version (ESV)

[19] And from the sons of Hamor, Shechem's father, he [Jacob] bought for a hundred pieces of money the piece of land on which he had pitched his tent.

Joshua 24:32 English Standard Version (ESV)

[32] As for the bones of Joseph, which the people of Israel brought up from Egypt, they buried them at Shechem, in the piece of land that Jacob bought from the sons of Hamor the father of Shechem for a hundred pieces of money. It became an inheritance of the descendants of Joseph.

Answer: If we look back to Genesis 12:6-7, we will find that Abraham's first stop after entering Canaan from Haran was Shechem. It is here that Jehovah told Abraham: "To your offspring I will give this land." At this point Abraham built an altar to Jehovah. It seems reasonable that Abraham would need to purchase this land that had not yet been given to his offspring. While it is true that the Old Testament does not mention this purchase, it is likely that Stephen would be aware of such by way of oral tradition. As Acts chapter seven demonstrates, Stephen had a wide-ranging knowledge of Old Testament history.

Later, Jacob would have had difficulty laying claim to the tract of land that his grandfather Abraham had purchased, because there would have been a new generation of inhabitants of Shechem. This would have been many years after Abraham moved further south and Isaac moved to Beersheba, and including Jacob's twenty years in Paddan-aram (Gen 28:6, 7). The simplest answer is that this land was not in use for about 120 years because of Abraham's extensive travels and Isaac's having moved away, leaving it unused; likely it was put to use by others. So, Jacob simply repurchased what Abraham had bought over a hundred years earlier. This is very similar to the time Isaac had to repurchase the well at Beersheba that Abraham had already purchased earlier. – Genesis 21:27–30; 26:26–32.

Genesis 33:18–20 tells us that 'Jacob bought this land for a hundred pieces of money, from the sons of Hamor.' This same transaction is also mentioned at Joshua 24:32, in reference to transporting Joseph's bones from Egypt, to be buried in Shechem.

We should also address the cave of Machpelah that Abraham had purchased in Hebron from Ephron the Hittite. The word "tomb" is not mentioned until Joshua 24:32, and is in reference to the tract of land in Shechem. Nowhere in the Old Testament does it say that Abraham bought a "tomb." The cave of Machpelah obtained by Abraham would eventually become a family tomb, receiving Sarah's body and, eventually, his own, and those of Isaac, Rebekah, Jacob, and Leah. (Genesis 23:14–19; 25:9; 49:30, 31; 50:13) Gleason L. Archer, Jr., concludes this Bible difficulty, saying:

The reference to a *mnema* ("tomb") in connection with Shechem must either have been proleptic [to anticipate] for the later use of that shechemite tract for Joseph's tomb (i.e., 'the tomb that Abraham bought' was intended to imply 'the tomb location that Abraham bought"); or else conceivably the dative relative pronoun *ho* was intended elliptically [omission] for *en to topo ho onesato Abraam* ("in the place that Abraham bought") as describing the location of the *mnema* near the Oak of Moreh right outside Shechem. Normally Greek would have used the relative-locative adverb *hou* to express 'in which' or 'where'; but this would have left *onesato* ("bought") without an object in its own clause, and so *ho* was much more suitable in this context. (Archer 1982, 379–81)

Another solution could be that Jacob is being viewed as a representative of Abraham, for he is the grandson of Abraham. This was quite appropriate in Biblical times, to attribute the purchase to Abraham as the Patriarchal family head.

Critic: 2 Samuel 24:1 says that God moved David to count the Israelites, while 1 Chronicles 21:1 Satan, or a resister did. This would seem to be a clear mistake on the part of one of these authors.

2 Samuel 24:1 English Standard Version (ESV)

¹ Again the anger of the Lord was kindled against Israel, and he incited David against them, saying, "Go, number Israel and Judah."

1 Chronicles 21:1 English Standard Version (ESV)

¹ Then Satan stood against Israel and incited David to number Israel.

Answer: In this period of David's reign, Jehovah was very displeased with Israel, and therefore he did not prevent Satan from bringing this sin on them. Often in Scripture, it is spoken of as though God did something when he allowed an event to take place. For example, it is said that God 'hardened Pharaoh's heart' (Exodus 4:21), when he actually allowed the Pharaoh's heart to harden.

Inerrancy: Are There Scientific Errors?

Many truths about God are beyond the scope of science. Science and the Bible are not at odds. In fact, we can thank modern day science, as it has helped us to better under the creation of God, from our solar system, to the universes, to the human body and mind. What we find is a level of order, precision, design and sophistication, which points to a Designer, the eyes of many Christians, to an Almighty God, with infinite intelligence and power. The apostle Paul makes this all too clear, when he writes, "For his invisible attributes, namely, his eternal power and divine nature, have been clearly perceived, ever since the creation of the world, in the things that have been made. So they are without excuse." – Romans 1:20.

Back in the seventeenth century, the world-renowned scientist Galileo proved beyond any doubt that the earth was not the center of the universe, nor did the sun orbit the earth. In fact, he proved it to be the other way around (no pun intended), with the earth revolving around the sun. However, he was brought up on charges of heresy by the Catholic Church and ordered to recant his position. Why? From the viewpoint of the Catholic Church, Galileo was contradicting God's Word, the Bible. As it turned out, Galileo and science were correct and the Church was wrong, for which it issued a formal apology in 1992. However, the point we wish to make here is that in all the controversy, the Bible was never in the wrong. It was a misinterpretation on the part of the Catholic Church, and not a fault with the Bible. One will find no place in the Bible that claims the sun orbits the earth. So where would the Church get such an idea? The Church got such an idea from Ptolemy (b. about 85 C.E.), an ancient astronomer, who argued for such an idea.

As it usually turns out, the so-called contradiction between science and God's Word lies at the feet of those who are interpreting Scripture incorrectly. To repeat the sentiments of Galileo when writing to a pupil–Galileo expressed the same sentiments: "Even though Scripture cannot err, its interpreters and expositors can, in various ways. One of these, very serious and very frequent, would be when they always want to stop at the purely literal sense."[128] I believe that today's scholars, in hindsight, would have no problem agreeing.

While the Bible is not a science textbook, it is scientifically accurate when it touches on matters of science.

The Circle of the Earth Hangs on Nothing

Isaiah 40:22 English Standard Version (ESV)

[22] It is he who sits above **the circle of the earth**,
and its inhabitants are like grasshoppers;
who stretches out the heavens like a curtain,
and spreads them like a tent to dwell in;

More than 2,500 years ago, the prophet Isaiah wrote that the earth is a circle or sphere. First, how would it be possible for Isaiah to know the earth is a circle or sphere, if not from inspiration? Scientific America writes, "As countless photos from space can attest, Earth is round–the "Blue Marble," as astronauts have affectionately dubbed it. Appearances, however, can be deceiving. Planet Earth is not, in fact, perfectly round."[129]

---

[128] Letter from Galileo to Benedetto Castelli, December 21, 1613.

[129] Charles Q. Choi (April 12, 2007). Scientific America. Strange but True: Earth Is Not Round. Retrieved Monday, August 03, 2015.

Scientifically speaking, the sun is not perfectly, absolutely 100 percent round but in everyday speech, this verse is both acceptable and accurate, when we keep in mind it is written from a human perspective, not from a scientific perspective. Moreover, Isaiah was not discussing astronomy; he was simply making an inspired observation that man came to realize once he was in space, looking back at the earth, it is round. See the section about title, "Intended Meaning of Writer."

Job 26:7 English Standard Version (ESV)

⁷ He stretches out the north over the void
and hangs the earth on nothing.

Here the author describes the earth as hanging upon nothing. Many have never heard of the Greek mathematician and astronomer Eratosthenes. He was born in about 276 B.C.E. and received some of his education in Athens, Greece. In 240 B.C., the "Greek astronomer, geographer, mathematician and librarian Eratosthenes calculates the Earth's circumference. His data was rough, but he wasn't far off."[130] While man very early on used their God given intelligence to arrive at some outstanding conclusion that were actually very accurate, we learn two points here. Eratosthenes was a very astute scientist, while Isaiah, who wrote some 500 years earlier, was no scientist at all. Moreover, Moses, who wrote the book of Job over 1,230 years before Eratosthenes, knew that the earth hung upon nothing.

How Is the Sun Standing Still Possible?

Joshua 10:13 English Standard Version (ESV)

¹³And the sun stood still, and the moon stopped, until the nation took vengeance on their enemies.

The Canaanites had besieged the Gibeonites, a group of people that gained Jehovah God's backing because they had faith in Him. In this battle, Jehovah helped the Israelites continue their attack by causing "the sun [to stand] still, and the moon stopped, until the nation took vengeance on their enemies." (Jos 10:1-14) Those who accept God as the creator of the universe and life can accept that he would know a way of stopping the earth from rotating. However, there are other ways of

---

http://www.scientificamerican.com/article/earth-is-not-round/

[130] Alfred, Randy (June 19, 2008). "June 19, 240 B.C.E: The Earth Is Round, and It's This Big". Wired. Retrieved Monday, August 03, 2015.

understanding this account. We must keep in mind that the Bible speaks from an earthly observer point of view, so it need not be that he stopped the rotation. It could have been a refraction of solar and lunar light rays, which would have produced the same effect.

Psalm 136:6 English Standard Version (ESV)

⁶to him who spread out the earth above the waters, for his steadfast love endures forever;

Hebrews 3:4 English Standard Version (ESV)

⁴(For every house is built by someone, but the builder of all things is God.)

2 Kings 20:8-11 English Standard Version (ESV)

⁸And Hezekiah said to Isaiah, "What shall be the sign that the LORD will heal me, and that I shall go up to the house of the LORD on the third day?" ⁹And Isaiah said, "This shall be the sign to you from the LORD, that the LORD will do the thing that he has promised: shall the shadow go forward ten steps, or go back ten steps?" ¹⁰And Hezekiah answered, "It is an easy thing for the shadow to lengthen ten steps. Rather let the shadow go back ten steps." ¹¹And Isaiah the prophet called to the LORD, and he brought the shadow back ten steps, by which it had gone down on the steps of Ahaz.

How is it that the stars fought on behalf of Barak?

Judges 5:20 English Standard Version (ESV)

²⁰ From heaven the stars fought, from their courses they fought against Sisera.

Judges 4:15 English Standard Version (ESV)

¹⁵ And the LORD routed Sisera and all his chariots and all his army before Barak by the edge of the sword. And Sisera got down from his chariot and fled away on foot.

In the Bible, you have Biblical prose, and Biblical poetry.

Prose: language that is not poetry: (1) writing or speech in its normal continuous form, without the rhythmic or visual line structure of poetry **(2)** ordinary style of expression: writing or speech that is ordinary or matter-of-fact, without embellishment.

Poetry: literature in verse: (1) literary works written in verse, in particular verse writing of high quality, great beauty, emotional sincerity or intensity, or profound insight **(2) beauty or grace:** something that resembles poetry in its beauty, rhythmic grace, or imaginative, elevated, or decorative style.

We have a beautiful example of both of these forms of writing-communication in chapters four and five of the book of Judges. Judges Chapter 4 is a prose account of Deborah and Barak, while Judges Chapter 5 is a poetic account. As we have learned from the above, poetry is less concerned with accuracy than evoking emotions. Poetry has a license to say things like what we find in of 5:20, which is in the poetry chapter: "from heaven the stars fought." This can be said and the reader is expected to not take the language literally. What we can surmise from it though, is that God was acting against Sisera in some way, there was divine intervention.

Procedures for Handling Bible Difficulties

1. You need to be completely convinced a reason or understanding exists.

2. You need to have total trust and conviction in the inerrancy of the Scripture as originally written down.

3. You need to study the context and framework of the verse carefully, to establish what the author meant by the words he used. In other words, find the beginning and the end of the context that your passage falls within.

4. You need to understand exegesis: find the historical setting, determine author intent, study key words, and note parallel passages. You need to slow down and carefully read the account, considering exactly what is being said

5. You need to find a reasonable harmonization of parallel passages.

6. You need to consider a variety of trusted Bible commentaries, dictionaries, lexical sources, encyclopedias, as well as books on Bible difficulties.

7. You should investigate as to whether the difficulty is a transmissional error in the original text.

8. You must always keep in mind that the historical accuracy of the biblical text is unmatched; that thousands of extant manuscripts some of which date back to the second century B.C. support the transmitted text of Scripture.

9. We must keep in mind that the Bible is a diverse book when it comes to literary styles: narrative, poetic, prophetic, and apocalyptic; also containing parables, metaphors, similes, hyperbole, and other figures of speech. Too often, these alleged errors are the result of a reader taking a figure of speech as literal, or reading a parable as though it is a narrative.

10. The Bible student needs to understand what level that the Bible intends to be exact in what is written. If Jim told a friend that 650 graduated with him from high school in 1984, it is not challenged, because it is all too clear that he is using rounded numbers and is not meaning to be precise.

Review Question

- Can the Bible be trusted? Explain.
- What are some practical principles for overcoming Bible difficulties?
- Are there contradictions in the Bible? Explain.
- Are there mistakes in the Bible? Explain.
- Are there scientific errors in the Bible? Explain.
- What are some procedures for handling Bible difficulties

CHAPTER 10 Dealing With Bible Difficulties

By R. A. Torrey

Before taking up those specific difficulties and alleged "contradictions" in the Bible, which have caused the most trouble to seekers after truth, let us first consider how difficulties should be dealt with.

Honestly

Whenever you find a difficulty in the Bible frankly, acknowledge it. Do not try to obscure it. Do not try to dodge it. Look it square in the face. Admit it frankly to whoever mentions it. If you cannot give a good, square, honest explanation, do not attempt any at all. Those, who in their zeal for the infallibility of the Bible have attempted explanations of difficulties that do not commend themselves to the honest, fair-minded man, have done untold harm. People have concluded that if these are the best explanations, then there are really no explanations at all, and the Bible instead of being helped has been injured by the unintelligent zeal of foolish friends. If you are not really convinced that the Bible is the Word of God, you can far better afford to wait for an honest solution of a difficulty than you can afford to attempt a solution that is evasive and unsatisfactory.

Humbly

Recognize the limitations of your own mind and knowledge, and do not for a moment imagine that there is no solution just because you have found none. There is, in all probability, a very simple solution, even when you can find no solution at all.

Determinedly

Make up your mind that you will find the solution if you can by any amount of study and hard thinking. The difficulties of the Bible are our heavenly Father's challenge to us to set our brains to work. Do not give up searching for a solution because you cannot find it in five minutes or ten minutes. Ponder over it and work over it for days if necessary. The work will be more beneficial than the solution does. There is a solution somewhere, and you will find it if you will only search for it long enough and hard enough.

Fearlessly

Do not be frightened when you find a difficulty, no matter how unanswerable or how insurmountable it appears at first sight. Thousands of men have encountered just such difficulties, and still the old Book has withstood the test of time, being the bestseller that will never be touch, in the untold billions of copies. The Bible that has stood eighteen centuries of rigid examination, and of incessant and awful assault, is not likely to go down before your discoveries or before the discharges of any modern critical guns. To one who is at all familiar with the history of critical attacks on the Bible, the confidence of those modern critics who think they are going to annihilate the Bible at last is simply amusing.

Patiently

Do not be discouraged because you do not solve every problem in a day. If some difficulty persistently defies your very best efforts at a solution, lay it aside for a while. Later it will likely be resolved, and you will wonder how you were ever perplexed by it.

Scripturally

If you find a difficulty in one part of the Bible, look for another scripture to throw light upon it and dissolve it. Nothing explains scripture like scripture. Repeatedly people have come to me with some difficulty in the Bible that had greatly staggered them, and asked for a solution. I have been able to give a solution by simply asking them to read some other chapter and verse, and the simple reading of that scripture has thrown such light upon the passage in question that all the mists have disappeared and the truth has shone as clear as day.

Prayerfully

It is simply wonderful how difficulties dissolve when one looks at them on his knees. Not only does God open our eyes in answer to prayer to behold wonderful things out of His law, but He also opens our eyes to look straight through a difficulty that seemed impenetrable before we prayed. One great reason why many modern Bible scholars have learned to be destructive critics is because they have forgotten how to pray.

Review Question

- What are some ways that we can deal with Bible difficulties?

CHAPTER 11 View of Bible Difficulties

By R. A. Torrey

Updated By Edward D. Andrews

Every careful student and every thoughtful reader of the Bible finds that the words of the Apostle Peter concerning the Scriptures, that there are some things in them hard to be understood is true. The apostle Peter says of Paul's letters, "as *he does* also in all his [Paul's] letters, speaking in them about these *things*, in which there are some *things* **hard to understand**, which the ignorant and unstable distort to their own destruction, as *they* also *do* the rest of the scriptures." (2 Peter 3:16, LEB) If this were true of Peter, how much more so of us 2,000 years removed, of a different language and culture? This is abundantly true for us! Who of us has not found things in the Bible that have puzzled us, yes, that in our early Christian experience have led us to question whether the Bible was, after all, the Word of God? We find some things in the Bible, which it seems impossible to reconcile with other things in the Bible. We find some things which seem incompatible with the thought that the whole Bible is of divine origin and absolutely inerrant.

It is not wise to attempt to conceal the fact that these difficulties exist. It is the part of wisdom, as well as of honesty, to frankly face them and consider them.

What shall we say concerning these difficulties that every thoughtful student will eventually encounter?

The first thing we have to say about these difficulties in the Bible is that from the very nature of the case *difficulties are to be expected.*

Some people are surprised and staggered because there are difficulties in the Bible. For my part, I would be more surprised and staggered if there were not. What is the Bible? It is a revelation of the mind and will and character and being of an infinitely great, perfectly wise and absolutely holy God. God Himself is the Author of this revelation. However, one would ask, to who specifically is the revelation made? To men, to finite beings who are imperfect in intellectual development and consequently in knowledge, and who are imperfect in character and consequently in spiritual discernment. The wisest man measured on the scale of eternity is only a babe, and the holiest man compared with God is only an infant in moral development. Therefore, there must from the very necessities of the case, be difficulties in such a revelation from such a source made to such persons. In addition, when the finite are attempting to understand the infinite, there is bound to be difficulty. When the ignorant contemplate the utterances of one perfect in knowledge, there must be many things hard to be understood, and some things, which to their immature and inaccurate minds appear absurd. When beings whose moral judgments as to the hatefulness of sin and as to the awfulness of the penalty that it demands, listen to the demands of an absolutely holy Being, they are bound to be staggered at some of His demands; and when they consider His dealings, they are bound to be staggered at some of His dealings. These dealings will appear too severe, too stern, and too harsh.

It is plain that there must be difficulties for us in such a revelation as the Bible has proved to be. If someone should hand me a book that was as simple to me as the multiplication table, and say, "This is the Word of God; in it He has revealed His whole will and wisdom," I should shake my head and say, "I cannot believe it; that is too easy to be a perfect revelation of infinite wisdom." There must be in any complete revelation of God's mind and will and character and being, things hard for the beginner to understand; and the wisest and best of us are but beginners.

The second thing to be said about these difficulties is that a difficulty in a doctrine, or a grave objection to a doctrine, does not in any way prove the doctrine to be untrue.

Many people think that it does. If they come across some difficulty in the way of believing in the divine origin and absolute inerrancy and infallibility of the Bible, they at once conclude that the doctrine is exploded. That is very illogical. They should stop a moment and think, and learn to be reasonable and fair.

There is scarcely a doctrine in science generally believed today, that has not had some great difficulty in the way of its acceptance.

When the Copernican theory (the earth revolves around the sun and not vice versa), now so universally accepted, was first proclaimed, it encountered a very grave difficulty. If this theory were true, the planet Venus should have phases as the moon has, but no phases could be discovered by the best glass then in existence. However, the positive argument for the theory was so strong that it was accepted in spite of this apparently unanswerable objection. When a more powerful glass was made, it was found that Venus had phases after all. The whole difficulty arose, as most; all of those in the Bible arise, from man's ignorance of some of the facts in the case.

The nebular hypothesis (the formation of the solar system) is commonly accepted in the scientific world today. Nevertheless, when this theory was first announced, and for a long time afterward, the movements of the planet Uranus could not be reconciled with the theory. Uranus seemed to move in just the opposite direction from that in which it was thought it ought to move in accordance with the demands of the theory. However, the positive arguments for the theory were so strong that it was accepted in spite of the inexplicable movements of Uranus.

If we apply to Bible study the commonsense logic recognized in every department of science (with the exception of Biblical criticism, if that be a science), then we must demand that if the positive proof of a theory is conclusive, it must be believed by rational men in spite of any number of difficulties in minor details. He is a shallow thinker who gives up a well-attested truth because there are some apparent facts, which he cannot reconcile with that truth. In addition, he is a very shallow Bible scholar who gives up his belief in the divine origin and inerrancy of the Bible because there are some supposed facts that he cannot reconcile with that doctrine. There are in the theological world today many shallow thinkers of that kind.

The third thing to be said about the difficulties in the Bible is: there are many more, and much greater, difficulties in the way of the doctrine that holds the Bible to be of human origin, and hence fallible, than there are in the way of the doctrine that holds the Bible to be of divine origin, and hence infallible.

Turning the Tables

Oftentimes a man will put forth some difficulty and say, "How do you explain that, if the Bible is the Word of God?" You may not be able to answer him satisfactorily. Then he thinks he has you cornered. Not at all, turn on him, and ask him, "How do you account for the fulfilled prophecies of the Bible if it is of human origin? How do you account for the marvelous unity of the Book? How do you account for its inexhaustible depth? How do you account for its unique power in lifting men up to God?" For every insignificant objection he can bring to your view of the Bible, you can bring very many more deeply significant objections to his view of the Bible. Moreover, any candid man who desires to know and obey the truth will have no difficulty in deciding between the two views.

Some time ago a young man, who was of a bright mind and unusually well read in skeptical, critical, and agnostic literature, told me he had given the matter a great deal of candid and careful thought, and as a result he could not believe the Bible was of divine origin.

I asked him, "Why not?"

He pointed to a certain teaching of the Bible that he could not and would not believe to be true.

I replied, "Suppose for a moment that I could not answer that specific difficulty; that would not prove that the Bible is not of divine origin. I can bring you many things far more difficult to account for on the hypothesis that the Bible is not of divine origin than on the hypothesis that the Bible is of divine origin. You cannot deny the fact of fulfilled prophecy. How do you account for it if the Bible is not God's Word? You cannot shut eyes to the marvelous unity of the sixty-six books of the Bible, written under such divergent circumstances and at periods of time so remote from one another. How do you account for it if God is not the real Author of the Book back of the forty or more human authors? You cannot deny that the Bible has a power, to save men from sin, to bring men peace and hope and joy, to lift men up to God, that all other books taken together do not possess. How do you account for it if the Bible is not the Word of God in a sense that no other book is the Word of God?"

The objector did not answer. The difficulties that confront one who denies that the Bible is of divine origin and authority are far more numerous and vastly more weighty than those which confront the one who believes it to be of divine origin and authority.

The fourth thing to be said about the difficulties in the Bible is: *the fact that you cannot solve a difficulty does not prove it cannot be solved, and the fact that you cannot answer an objection does not prove at all that it cannot be answered.*

It is remarkable how often we overlook this very evident fact. There are many who, who meet a difficulty in the Bible and give it a little thought and can see no possible solution, at once jump at the conclusion that a solution is impossible, and so they give up their faith in the inerrancy of the Bible and in its divine origin. Any man should have a sufficient amount of modesty, being so limited in knowledge, to say, "Though I see no possible solution to this difficulty, someone a little wiser than I might easily find one."

If we would only bear in mind that we do not know everything, and there are a great many things that we cannot solve now which we could very easily solve if we only knew a little more, it would save us from all this foolishness. We ought never to forget that there may be a very easy solution to infinite wisdom even for that which to our finite wisdom, or ignorance, appears unsolvable. What would we think of a beginner in algebra who, having tried in vain for half an hour to solve a difficult problem, declared that there was no possible solution to the problem because he could find none!

A man of unusual experience and ability one day left his work and drove a long distance to see me, as he was in great uneasiness of mind because he had discovered what he believed to be a flat contradiction in the Bible. He had lain awake all night thinking about it. It had defied all his attempts at reconciliation, but when he had fully stated the case to me, in a very few moments I showed him a very simple and satisfactory solution of the difficulty. He went away with a happy heart. Nevertheless, why had it not occurred to him at the outset that, though it appeared impossible to him to find a solution, after all, someone else might easily discover a solution? He supposed that the difficulty was an entirely new one, but it was one that had been faced and answered long before either he or I were born.

The fifth thing to be said about the difficulties in the Bible is that *the seeming defects of the Book are exceedingly insignificant when put in comparison with its many and marvelous areas of excellence.*

It certainly reveals great perversity of both mind and heart that men spend so much time focusing on and exaggerating such insignificant points, which they consider defects in the Bible, and pass absolutely unnoticed the incomparable beauties and wonders that adorn and glorify almost every page. This is even taking place in some prominent institutions of learning, where men are supposed to be taught to appreciate and understand the Bible and where they are sent to be trained to preach its truth to others. These institutions are spending much more time on minute and insignificant points that seem to point toward an entirely human origin of the Bible than is spent upon studying and understanding and admiring the unparalleled glories that make this Book stand apart from all other books in the world. What would we think of any man who in studying some great masterpiece of art concentrated his whole attention upon what looked like a flyspeck in the corner? A large proportion of the much boasted about "critical study of the Bible" is a laborious and scholarly investigation of supposed flyspecks. The man who is **not** willing to squander the major portion of his time in this intellectualized investigation of flyspecks but prefers to devote it to the study of the unrivaled beauties and majestic splendors of the Book is counted in some quarters as not being "scholarly and up to date."

The sixth thing to be said about the difficulties in the Bible is that *they have far more weight with superficial readers than with profound students.*

Take a man like Colonel Ingersoll, who was very ignorant of the real contents and meaning of the Bible, or that class of modern preachers who read the Bible for the most part for the sole purpose of finding texts to serve as pegs to hang their own ideas. To such superficial readers of the Bible these difficulties seem of immense importance, but to one who has learned to meditate upon the Word of God day and night they have scarcely any weight at all. That rare man of God, George Müller, who had carefully studied the Bible from beginning to end more than one hundred times, was not disturbed by any difficulties he encountered; but to the man who is reading it through for the first or second time there are many things that perplex and stagger.

The seventh thing to be said about the difficulties in the Bible is that *they rapidly disappear upon careful and prayerful study.*

How many things there are in the Bible that once puzzled and staggered us, but which have since been perfectly cleared up and no longer present any difficulty whatever! Every year of study finds these difficulties disappear more and more rapidly. At first they go by ones, and then by twos, and then by dozens, and then by scores. Is it not reasonable then to suppose that the difficulties that remain will all disappear upon further study?

Review Question

- How have some reacted when they discovered there are Bible difficulties?
- How should we view Bible difficulties
- How can we turn the table on Bible critics?

CHAPTER 12 Some Types of Bible Difficulties

By R. A. Torrey

Updated by Edward D. Andrews

All the difficulties found in the Bible can be included under ten general headings:

The Text from which our English Bible was Translated

No one, as far as I know, holds that the English translation of the Bible is absolutely infallible and inerrant. The doctrine held by many is that the Scriptures as originally given were absolutely infallible and inerrant, and that our English translation is a *substantially accurate* rendering of the Scriptures as originally given.

We do not possess the original manuscripts of the Bible. These original manuscripts were copied many times with great care and exactness, but naturally, some errors crept into the copies that were made. We now possess so many good copies that by comparing one with another, we can tell with great precision just what the original text was. Indeed, for all practical purposes the original text is now settled.

Update: After Torrey's death in 1928, we have made the extremely important discovery over 100 papyrus manuscripts that date before 300 C.E. Quite a few date to the second century, with one small fragment being dated to about 125 C.E. The modern textual scholar can now say with certainty that we have establish the Greek New Testament to a ninety-nine percent reflect of the originally publish book(s). Moreover, we have more than 100 English translations today, with many of them being a very good representation of the Hebrew and Greek in English: NASB, ESB, HCSB, LEB, and others. **Edward D. Andrews**

There is not one important doctrine, which hangs upon any doubtful reading of the text. However, when our Authorized Version (KJV) was published in 1611, some of the best manuscripts were not within reach of the translators, and the science of textual criticism was not so well understood as it is today, and so the translation was made from an imperfect text. Not a few of the apparent difficulties in the Bible arise from this source.

For example, we are told in John 5:4 that "an angel went down at a certain season into the pool, and troubled the water: whosoever then first after the troubling of the water stepped in was made whole of whatsoever disease he had." This statement for many reasons seems improbable and difficult to believe, but upon investigation, we find that it is all a mistake of the copyist. Some early copyist, reading John's account, added in the margin his explanation of the healing properties of this intermittent medicinal spring. A late copyist embodied this marginal note in the body of the text, and so it came to be handed down and got into the Authorized Version (KJV). Very properly, it has been omitted from the Revised Version.

Note: It is omitted from almost all of our modern-day translations as well, with the exception of the NASB and the HCSB, which retained it out of esteem to the KJV. **Edward S. Andrews**

The discrepancies in figures in different accounts of the same events as, for example, the differences in the ages of some of the kings as given in the text of Kings and Chronicles, doubtless arise from the same cause, errors of copyists. Such an error in the matter of figures would be very easy to make, as in the Hebrew; letters, and letters that appear very much alike have a very different value as figures denote numbers. For example, the first letter in the Hebrew alphabet denotes one, and with two little points above it, no larger than flyspecks, it denotes a thousand. The twenty-third or last letter of the Hebrew alphabet denotes four hundred, but the eighth letter of the Hebrew alphabet that looks very much like it and could be easily mistaken for it, denotes eight. A very slight error of the copyist would therefore make an utter change in figures. The remarkable thing when one contemplates the facts in the case is that so few errors of this kind have been made.

Inaccurate Translations

For example, in Matthew 12:40 Jonah is spoken of as being in "the whale's belly." Many a skeptic has made a mockery over the thought of a whale with the peculiar construction of its mouth and throat swallowing a man. However, if the skeptic had only taken the trouble to look the matter up, he would have found the word translated "whale" really means "sea monster" [or great fish] without any definition as to the character of the sea monster. We will take this up more in detail in considering the story of Jonah. Therefore, the whole difficulty arose from the translator's mistake and the skeptic's ignorance. Many skeptics today are so densely ignorant of matters clearly understood by many Sunday school children that they are still harping in the name of scholarship on this supposed error in the Bible.

False Interpretations of the Bible

What the Bible teaches is one thing, and what men interpret it to mean is oftentimes something widely different. Many difficulties that we have with the Bible arise not from what the Bible actually says, but from what men interpret it to mean.

A striking illustration of this is found in Genesis 1. If we were to take the interpretation put upon this chapter by many, it would indeed be difficult to reconcile it with much that modern science regards as established. However, the difficulty is not with what Genesis 1 says, but with the interpretation put upon it. There is no contradiction whatever between what is really proven by science and what is really said in Genesis 1.

Another difficulty of the same character is with Jesus' statement that He would be three days and three nights in the heart of the earth. Many interpreters would have us believe that He died Friday and rose early Sunday morning, and the time between these two is far from being three days and three nights. However, it is a matter of biblical interpretation, and the trouble is not with what the Bible actually says, but with the interpretation that men put upon the Bible. We will take this matter up at length below by Edward D. Andrews.

Matthew 12:40 How many days was Jesus in the tomb?

Some argue for three days, based on Jesus' words,

Matthew 12:40 English Standard Version (ESV)

⁴⁰ For just as Jonah was three days and three nights in the belly of the great fish, so will the Son of Man be three days and three nights in the heart of the earth.

This would seem to suggest a full 72 hours. However, we should not set aside similar expressions that may allow us to get at the intent of the words. Many times in Scripture, three days does not always mean a full 72 hours of three days. For example, look at the words of Reheboam,

1 Kings 12:5, 12 English Standard Version (ESV)

⁵ He said to them, "Go away for three days, then come again to me." So the people went away. ¹² So Jeroboam and all the people came to Rehoboam the third day, as the king said, "Come to me again the third day."

You see that the king told the people to go away for three days, and then return to him. But you als will notice that they returned on the third day, which was not a full 72 hours of three days. Now, consider what Jesus said of himself, something that Scripture repeatedly says,

Luke 24:46 English Standard Version (ESV)

⁴⁶ and said to them, "Thus it is written, that the Christ should suffer and **on the third day** rise from the dead

Now, if he had remained in the grave for a full 72 hours of three days, it mean that he would have been raised on the fourth day. Jewish days ran from sundown to sundown. Jesus died on Friday afternoon about 3:00 p.m., Nisan 14, 33 C.E.

- Jesus' death Friday Nisan 14, about 3:00 p.m. (Matt 27:31-56; Mk 15:20-41; Lu 23:26-49; Jn 19:16-30)
- Jesus was in Tomb before sundown Friday evening (Matt 27:57-61; Mk 15:42-47; Lu 23:50-56; Jn 19:31-42)
- Jesus in tomb all of Nisan 15th from sundown Friday to sundown Saturday, which began Nisan 16 (Matt 27:62-66)
- Jesus resurrected early Sunday morning of Nisan 16th (Matt 28:1; Mk 16:1; Lu 24:1; Jn 20:1)

Therefore, Jesus was dead and in the tomb for at least a period of time on Friday Nisan 14, was still in the tomb during the course of the whole day of Nisan 15, and spent the nighttime hours of Nisan 16 in the tomb.

- Now after the Sabbath, toward the dawn of the first day of the week, Mary Magdalene and the other Mary went to see the tomb. (Matt 28:1)
- When the Sabbath was past, Mary Magdalene, Mary the mother of James, and Salome bought spices, so that they might go and anoint him. (Mk 16:1)

- But on the first day of the week, at early dawn, they went to the tomb, taking the spices they had prepared. (Lu 24:1)
- Now on the first day of the week Mary Magdalene came to the tomb early, while it was still dark, and saw that the stone had been taken away from the tomb. (Jn 20:1)

Certain women came to the tomb on Sunday morning, it was still dark, he had already been resurrected. Thus, Jesus had been in the tomb for parts of three days.

A Wrong Conception of the Bible

Many think that when you say the Bible is the Word of God, of divine origin and authority, you mean that God is the speaker in every utterance it contains; but this is not at all, what is meant. Oftentimes it simply records what others say—what good men say, what bad men say, what inspired men say, what uninspired men say, what angels and demons say, and even what the devil says. The record of what they said is from God and absolutely true, but what those other persons are recorded as saying may be true or may not be true. It is true that they said it, but what they said may not be true.

For example, the devil is recorded in Genesis 3:4 as saying, "You will not surely die." It is true that the devil said it, but what the devil said is not true, but an infamous lie that shipwrecked our race. That the devil said it is God's Word, but what the devil said is not God's word but the devil's word. It is God's Word that this was the devil's word.

Very many careless readers of the Bible do not notice who is talking, God, good men, bad men, inspired men, uninspired men, angels or devil. They will tear a verse right out of its context regardless of the speaker and say, "There, God said that." However, God said nothing of the kind. God's Word says that the devil said it or a bad man said it or a good man said it or an inspired man said it, or an uninspired man said it, or an angel said it. What God says is true, namely, that the devil said it, or a bad man, or a good man, or an inspired man, or an uninspired man, or an angel. However, what they said may or may not be true.

It is very common to hear men quote what Eliphaz, Bildad or Zophar said to Job as if it were necessarily God's own words because it is recorded in the Bible, in spite of the fact that God disavowed their teaching and said to them, "you have not spoken of me what is right" (Job 42:7). It is true that these men said the thing that God records them as saying, but often they gave the truth a twist and said what is not right. A very large share of our difficulties thus arises from not noticing who is speaking. The Bible always tells us, and we should always note it. Below, under the subheadings of "the Case of Job" and "The Comforters" Andrews demonstrates how the erroneous interpretations come about.

The Case of Job

What we have covered thus far will help us understand one of the more complex books of the Bible, the book of Job.

Job was a "blameless and upright man, who fears God and turns away from evil." Job was living the happy life; he had seven sons and the daughters. He was a wealthy landowner. "He possessed 7,000 sheep, 3,000 camels, 500 yoke of oxen, and 500 female donkeys, and very many servants, so that this man was the greatest of all the people of the east." (1:3) Even so, he is not a materialistic person; he was simply following a proverb like the above, 'if you work hard, your efforts will be blessed.'

Job 1:13-19; 2:7-8 English Standard Version (ESV)

^{13}Now there was a day when his sons and daughters were eating and drinking wine in their oldest brother's house, ^{14}and there came a messenger to Job and said, "The oxen were plowing and the donkeys feeding beside them, ^{15}and the Sabeans fell upon them and took them and struck down the servants with the edge of the sword, and I alone have escaped to tell you." ^{16}While he was yet speaking, there came another and said, "The fire of God fell from heaven and burned up the sheep and the servants and consumed them, and I alone have escaped to tell you." ^{17}While he was yet speaking, there came another and said, "The Chaldeans formed three groups and made a raid on the camels and took them and struck down the servants with the edge of the sword, and I alone have escaped to tell you." ^{18}While he was yet speaking, there came another and said, "Your sons and daughters were eating and drinking wine in their oldest brother's house, ^{19}and behold, a great wind came across the wilderness and struck the four corners of the house, and it fell upon the young people, and they are dead, and I alone have escaped to tell you." $^{2:7}$So Satan went out from the presence of the LORD and struck Job with loathsome sores from the sole of his foot to the crown of his head. ^{8}And he took a piece of broken pottery with which to scrape himself while he sat in the ashes.

The Comforters

Job 4:7-8 English Standard Version (ESV)

⁷"Remember: who that was innocent ever perished? Or where were the upright cut off? ⁸As I have seen, those who plow iniquity and sow trouble reap the same.

Eliphaz in an attempt at dealing with Job's atrocities assumes Job's tragedies are a result of his own actions. Eliphaz has reasoned wrong by taking a proverb and making it an absolute. In essence, he asks Job, 'do those that are innocent die? When have those that live a righteous life been destroyed?' Eliphaz goes on by saying, 'my experience suggests that it is those who are doing wrong and entertain bad that will get back what they gave out.' In other words, Eliphaz is assuming that only the wicked reap bad times.

Job 5:15 English Standard Version (ESV)

¹⁵But he saves the needy from the sword of their mouth and from the hand of the mighty.

Eliphaz again assumes that Job is at fault. Eliphaz is assuming that it was Job's great riches, which were ill gotten, and this is why he is suffering. Is Eliphaz's statement wrong in and of itself? No, God does rescue the poor from the oppressive, by their following his counsel on the right way to live. However, this is no absolute; saying all who live by God's will and purposes will never be mistreated. Moreover, the whole idea is misplaced, in that maybe Job is the rich oppressor and this is his punishment from God.

Job 8:3-6 English Standard Version (ESV)

³Does God pervert justice? Or does the Almighty pervert the right? ⁴If your children have sinned against him, he has delivered them into the hand of their transgression.⁵If you will seek God and plead with the Almighty for mercy, ⁶if you are pure and upright, surely then he will rouse himself for you and restore your rightful habitation.

Bildad too is stating true statements, but in absolute terms that are misplaced when it comes to Job, or anyone. Certainly, God does not pervert justice. Therefore, Bildad is right on that, but his application and understanding is what is twisted, as he assumes that children died because they had sinned, and justice was being meted out to them. Again, in verse 5-6, we have a true thought, in that if one is in an impure state, and turns to God with pleadings, he will restore them. However, in verses 5-6,

Bildad is assuming that Job is unrighteous, because he sees that proverb as an absolute.

As can be seen from the above, one must be aware that proverbs are not absolutes, but are general truths. True enough, there are likely a couple of exceptions to this rule, but that would not negate this rule, and approach of correct interpretation of proverbs.

In the Psalms, we have sometimes, what God said to man and that is always true; but on the other hand, we often have what man said to God, and that may or may not be true. Sometimes, and far oftener than most of us see, it is the voice of the speaker's personal vengeance or despair. This vengeance may be and often is prophetic, but it may be the wronged man committing his cause to Him to whom vengeance belongs (Romans 12:19), and we are not obliged to defend all that he said. In the Psalms, we have even a record of what the fool said, "There is no God" (Psalm 14:1). Now it is true that the fool said it, but the fool lied when he said it. It is God's Word that the fool said it, but what God reports the fool as saying is not God's own word at all but the fool's own word.

Therefore, in studying our Bible, if God is the speaker we must believe what He says. If an inspired man is the speaker, we must believe what he says. If an uninspired man is the speaker, we must judge for ourselves, it is perhaps true, perhaps false. If it is the devil who is speaking, we do well to remember that he was a liar from the beginning; but even the devil may tell the truth sometimes.

The Language in Which the Bible was Written

The Bible is a book of all ages and for all kinds of people, and therefore it was written in the language that continues the same and is understood by all, the language of the common people and of appearances. It was not written in the terminology of science.

Thus, for example, what occurred at the Battle of Gibeon (Joshua 10:12–14) was described in the way it appeared to those who saw it, and the way in which it would be understood by those who read about it. There is no talk about the refraction of the sun's rays, and so forth, but the sun is said to have *"stood still"* (or tarried) in the midst of heaven. It is one of the perfections of the Bible that it was not written in the terminology of modern science. If it had been, it would never have been understood until the present day, and even now it would be understood only by a few. Furthermore, as science and its terminology are constantly changing, the Bible if written in the terminology of the science of today would be out of date in a few years; but being written in just the language chosen, it has proved the Book for all ages, all lands and all conditions of men.

Other difficulties from the language in which the Bible was written arise from the fact that large portions of the Bible are poetical and are written in the language of poetry, the language of feeling, passion, imagination and figure. Now if a man is hopelessly matter-of-fact, he will inevitably find difficulties with these poetical portions of the inspired Word.

For example, in Psalm 18 we have a marvelous description of a thunderstorm, but let the dull, matter-of-fact fellow get hold of that, for example, verse 8: "Smoke went up from his nostrils, and devouring fire from his mouth; glowing coals flamed forth from him," and he will be head over heels in difficulty at once. However, the trouble is not with the Bible, but with his own stupid, thickheaded plainness.

Our Defective Knowledge of the History, Geography and Usages of Bible Times

For example, in Acts 13:7 Luke speaks of "the deputy" (more accurately "the proconsul," see English Standard Version) of Cyprus. Roman provinces were of two classes, imperial and senatorial. The ruler of the imperial provinces was called a propraetor, of a senatorial province a proconsul. Up to a comparatively recent date, according to the best information we had, Cyprus was an imperial province and therefore its ruler would be a propraetor, but Luke calls him a proconsul. This certainly seemed like a clear case of error on Luke's part, and even the conservative commentators felt forced to admit that Luke was in slight error, and the destructive critics were delighted to find this "mistake." Further and more thorough investigation has brought to light the fact that just at the time of which Luke wrote the senate had made an exchange with the emperor whereby Cyprus had become a senatorial province, and therefore its ruler was a proconsul. Luke was right after all, and the literary critics were themselves in error.

Repeatedly further researches and discoveries, geographical, historical and archaeological, have vindicated the Bible and put to shame its critics. For example, the book of Daniel has naturally been one of the books that unbelievers and destructive critics have most hated. One of their strongest arguments against its authenticity and truthfulness was that such a person as Belshazzar was unknown to history, that all historians agreed that Nabonidus was the last king of Babylon, and that he was absent from the city when it was captured. Therefore, Belshazzar must be a purely mythical character, and the whole story legendary and not historical. Their argument seemed very strong. In fact, it seemed unanswerable. However, Sir H. Rawlinson discovered at Mugheir and other Chaldean sites clay cylinders on which Belshazzar (Belsaruzar) is named by Nabonidus as his eldest son. Doubtless he reigned as regent in the city during his father's absence, an indication of which we have in his proposal to make Daniel third ruler in the kingdom (Daniel 5:16). He himself being second ruler in the kingdom, Daniel would be next to him. So the Bible was vindicated again.

The critics asserted most positively that Moses could not have written the Pentateuch because writing was unknown in his day. However, recent discoveries have proved beyond a question that writing far antedates the time of Moses. So the critics have been compelled to give up their argument, though they have had the bad grace to hold on stubbornly to their conclusion.

The Ignorance of Conditions under Which Books Were Written and Commands Given

For example, to one ignorant of the conditions, God's commands to Israel as to the extermination of the Canaanites seem cruel and horrible. However, when one understands the moral condition to which these nations had sunk, the utter hopelessness of reclaiming them and the weakness of the Israelites themselves, their extermination seems to have been an act of mercy to all succeeding generations and to themselves.

The Many-Sidedness of the Bible

The broadest-minded man is one-sided, but the truth is many-sided, and the Bible is all-sided. Therefore, to our narrow thought one part of the Bible seems to contradict another.

For example, religious men as a rule are either Calvinistic or Arminian in their mental makeup. In addition, some portions of the Bible are decidedly Calvinistic and present great difficulties to the Arminian type of mind, while other portions are decidedly Arminian and present difficulties to the Calvinistic type of mind. However, both sides are true. Many men in our day are broad-minded enough to be able to grasp at the same time the Calvinistic side of the truth and the Arminian side of the truth; but some are not, so the Bible perplexes, puzzles and bewilders them. The trouble is not with the Bible, but with their own lack of capacity for comprehensive thought.

Expansion: These schools of doctrinal positions are initially established religious leaders and their followers, such as John Calvin and Jacob Arminius. There are even more, such as the Lutheran, from Martin Luther, The Wesleyan, from John Wesley, and the Mennonites, from Menno Simons, and Society of Friends (Quakers) under George Fox. Actually, I would disagree with Torrey here, I believe that he should have used his earlier point of argument, it boils down to the truth of the Bible as being absolute, but man may misinterpret that truth. Therefore, it will lay concealed until discovered. This misinterpretation does not refute the infallibility or inerrancy of Scripture. Actually, doctrine plays no part in inerrancy of Scripture. Whether one believes the earth was created in six literal 24-hour days, or six creative periods called days, has no impact on the doctrine of inerrancy. The Bible is inerrant and one of those interpretations is wrong and the other is correct. This has to do with the person interpreting the Bible, not the inerrancy of the Bible. **Edward D. Andrews**

Therefore, Paul seems to contradict James, and James seems sometimes to contradict Paul; and what Paul says in one place seems to contradict what he says in another place. However, the whole trouble is that our narrow minds cannot take in God's large truth.

The Bible has to do with the Infinite, and our Minds are Finite

It is necessarily difficult to put the facts of infinite being into the limited capacity of our finite intelligence, just as it is difficult to put the ocean into a pint cup. To this class of difficulties belong those connected with the Bible doctrines of the Trinity and of the divine-human nature of Christ. To those who forget that God is infinite, the doctrine of the Trinity seems like the mathematical monstrosity of making one equal three. However, when one bears in mind that the doctrine of the Trinity is an attempt to put into forms of finite thought the facts of infinite being, and into material forms of expression the facts of the spirit, the difficulties vanish. The simplicity of the Unitarian conception of God arises from its shallowness.

The Dullness of our Spiritual Perception

The man who is farthest advanced spiritually is still so immature that he cannot expect to see everything yet as an absolutely holy God sees it, unless he takes it upon simple faith in Him. To this class of difficulties belong those connected with the Bible doctrine of eternal punishment. It often seems to us as if this doctrine cannot be true, must not be true, but the whole difficulty arises from the fact that we are still so blind spiritually that we have no adequate conception of the awfulness of sin, and especially of the awfulness of the sin of rejecting the infinitely glorious Son of God. However, when we become so holy, so like God, that we see the enormity of sin as He sees it, we shall have no difficulty with the doctrine of eternal punishment.

Expansion: Torrey is like many other Calvinist or Lutheran minded individuals, he wishes to follow the evidence, but instead, desires to call those, who do not find this doctrine Biblical, spiritually blind. I hope that even the most conservative reader can see that as dismissive. Without arguing the evidence, I will say that once again, the truth is biblical, and we must follow it objectively, and not allow theological bias to cloud our judgment. I am recommending that you read the following articles.[131]
Edward D. Andrews

As we look back over the ten classes of difficulties, we see they all arise from our imperfection, and not from the imperfection of the Bible. The Bible is perfect, but we, being imperfect, have difficulty with it. As we grow more and more into the perfection of God, our difficulties grow ever less and less, and so we are forced to conclude that when we become as perfect as God is, we shall have no more difficulties whatever with the Bible.

Review Question

- Explain some of the different types of Bible difficulties?

---

[131] **Hellfire - Eternal Torment?**
http://www.christianpublishers.org/hellfire-eternal-torment
Hellfire - Is It Just?
http://www.christianpublishers.org/hellfire-is-it-just

Bibliography

Akin, Daniel L. *The New American Commentary: 1, 2, 3 John*. Nashville, TN: Broadman & Holman , 2001.

Aland, Kurt and Barbara. *The Text of the New Testament*. Grand Rapids: Eerdmans, 1987.

Alden, Robert L. *Job, The New American Commentary, vol. 11* . Nashville: Broadman & Holman Publishers, 2001.

Anders, Max. *Holman New Testament Commentary: vol. 8, Galatians, Ephesians, Philippians, Colossians*. Nashville, TN: Broadman & Holman Publishers, 1999.

—. *Holman Old Testament Commentary - Proverbs* . Nashville: B&H Publishing, 2005.

Anders, Max, and Doug McIntosh. *Holman Old Testament Commentary - Deuteronomy*. Nashville: B&H Publishing, 2009.

Anders, Max, and Steven Lawson. *Holman Old Testament Commentary - Psalms: 11*. Grand Rapids: B&H Publishing, 2004.

Anders, Max, and Trent Butler. *Holman Old Testament Commentary: Isaiah*. Nashville, TN: B&H Publishing, 2002.

Andrews, Edward D. *The Text of the New Testament: A Beginner's Guide to New Testament Textual Criticism*. Cambridge, OH: Bible-Translation.Net Books, 2012.

Andrews, Stephen J, and Robert D Bergen. *Holman Old Testament Commentary: 1-2 Samuel*. Nashville: Broadman & Holman, 2009.

Archibald, Hunter, H. *Interpreting the Parables. London:SCM*. Philadephia: Westminster, 1980.

Arndt, William, Frederick W. Danker, and Walter Bauer. *A Greek-English Lexicon of the New Testament and Other Early Christian Literature. 3rd ed.* . Chicago: University of Chicago Press, 2000.

Arnold, Clinton E. *Zondervan Illustrated Bible Backgrounds Commentary Volume 2: John, Acts.* . Grand Rapids, MI: Zondervan, 2002.

—. *Zondervan Illustrated Bible Backgrounds Commentary Volume 3: Romans to Philemon*. Grand Rapids: Zondervan, 2002.

—. *Zondervan Illustrated Bible Backgrounds Commentary Volume 4: Hebrews to Revelation.* Grand Rapids, MI: Zondervan, 2002.

—. *Zondervan Illustrated Bible Backgrounds Commentary: Matthew, Mark, Luke, vol. 1.* Grand Rapids, MI: Zondervan, 2002.

Baer, Daniel. *The Unquenchable Fire.* Maitland, FL: Xulon Press, 2007.

Barclay, William. *The Letter to the Hebrews (New Daily Study Bible).* Louisville, KY: Westminster John Knox Press, 2002.

Barker, Kenneth L., and Waylon Bailey. *The New American Commentary: vol. 20, Micah, Nahum, Habakkuk, Zephaniah.* Nashville, TN: Broadman & Holman Publishers, 2001.

Barnett, Paul. *The Birth of Christianity: The First Twenty Years (After Jesus, Vol. 1)* . Grand Rapids, MI: Wm. B. Eerdmans , 2005.

Benner, David G., and Peter C Hill. *Baker Encyclopedia of Psychology and Counseling (Second Edition).* Grand Rapids: Baker Books, 1985, 1999.

Bercot, David W. *A Dictionary of Early Christian Beliefs.* Peabody: Hendrickson, 1998.

Bergen, Robert D. *The New American Commentary: 1-2 Samuel.* Nashville: Broadman & Holman, 1996.

Blenkinsopp, Joseph. *Isaiah 56-66: A New Translation with Introduction and Commentary.* New York: Anchor Bible, 2003.

Blomberg, Craig. *The New American Commentary: Matthew.* Nashville, TN: Broadman & Holman Publishers, 1992.

Boa, Kenneth, and William Kruidenier. *Holman New Testament Commentary: Romans.* Nashville: Broadman & Holman, 2000.

Borchert, Gerald L. *The New American Commentary: John 1-11* . Nashville, TN: Broadman & Holman Publishers, 2001.

Borchert, Gerald L. *The New American Commentary vol. 25B, John 12–21.* Nashville: Broadman & Holman Publishers, 2002.

Brand, Chad, Charles Draper, and England Archie. *Holman Illustrated Bible Dictionary: Revised, Updated and Expanded.* Nashville, TN: Holman, 2003.

Breneman, Mervin. *The New American Commentary, vol. 10, Ezra, Nehemiah, Esther*. Nashville: Broadman & Holman Publishers, 1993.

Briley, Terry R. *The College Press NIV Commentary: Isaiah*. Joplin, MO: ollege Press Pub, 2000.

Brisco, Thomas V. *Holman Bible Atlas, Holman Reference*. Nashville, TN: Broadman & Holman Publishers, 1998.

Brooks, James A. *The New American Commentary: Mark (Volume 23)*. Nashville: Broadman & Holman Publishers, 1992.

Bruce, F. F. *The New International Commentary on the New Testament: The Epistle to the Hebrews (Revised)*. Grand Rapids, MI: William B. Eermans Publishing Company, 1990.

Butler, Trent C. *Holman New Testament Commentary: Luke*. Nashville, TN: Broadman & Holman Publishers, 2000.

Butler, Trent C. *Holman Old Testament Commentary - Hosea, Joel, Amos, Obadiah, Jonah, Micah* . Nashville: Broadman & Holman Publishers, 2005.

Caba, Tedl et al.,. *The Apologetics Study Bible: Real Questions, Straight Answers, Stronger Faith*. Nashville: Holman Bible Publishers, 2007.

Calloway, Brent A. *THE BOOK OF JAMES: CPH CHRISTIAN LIVING COMMENTARY*. Cambridge: Chriwstian Publishing House, 2015.

Carpenter, Eugene E., and Philip W Comfort. *The Holman Treasury of Key Bible Words: 200 Greek and 200 Hebrew Words Defined and Explained*. Nashville: Broadman & Holman Publishers, 2000.

Carson, D. A, and Douglas J Moo. *An Introduction to the New Testament*. Grand Rapids, MI: Zondervan, 2005.

Carson, D. A. *New Bible Commentary: 21st Century Edition*. 4th ed. Downers Grove: Inter-Varisity Press, 1994.

Cole, R. Dennis. *THE NEW AMERICAN COMMENTARY: Volume 3b Numbers*. Nashville: Broadman & Holman Publishers, 2000.

Comfort, Philip. *Encounterring the Manuscripts: An Introduction to New Testament Paleography and Textual Criticism*. Nashville: Broadman & Holman, 2005.

Comfort, Philip W. *New Testament Text and Translation Commentary.* Carol Stream: Tyndale House Publishers, 2008.

Comfort, Philip, and David Barret. *The Text of the Earliest New Testament Greek Manuscripts.* Wheaton: Tyndale House Publishers, 2001.

Cooper, Lamar Eugene. *The New American Commentary, Ezekiel, vol. 17.* Nashville, TN: Broadman & Holman Publishers, 1994.

Cooper, Rodney. *Holman New Testament Commentary: Mark.* Nashville: Broadman & Holman Publishers, 2000.

Cottrell, Peter, and Maxwell Turner. *Linguistics and Biblical Interpretation.* Downers Grove: InterVarsity Press, 1989.

Cruse, C. F. *Eusebius' Eccliatical History.* Peabody, MA: Hendrickson, 1998.

Dockery, David S, and George H. Guthrie. *The Holman Guide to Interpreting the Bible.* Nashville: Broadman & Holman Publishers, 2004.

Dockery, David S. *HOLMAN CONCISE BIBLE COMMENTARY Simple, straightforward commentary on every book of the Bible.* Nashville: Broadman & Holman, 1998.

Dockery, David S., and Trent C. Church, Christopher L. Butler. *Holman Bible Handbook* . Nashville, TN: Holman Bible Publishers, 1992.

Easley, Kendell H. *Holman New Testament Commentary, vol. 12, Revelation.* (Nashville, TN: Broadman & Holman Publishers, 1998.

Ellingworth, Paul. *The Epistle to the Hebrews: A Commentary on the Greek Text.* Grand Rapids, MI: W.B. Eerdmans, 1993.

Elwell, Walter A. *Evangelical Dictionary of Theology (Second Edition).* Grand Rapids: Baker Academic, 2001.

Ferguson, Everett. *Backgrounds of Early Christianity.* Grand Rapids, MI: Wm. B. Eerdmans, 2003.

Galli, Mark, and Ted Olsen. *131 Christians Everyone Should Know* . Nashville, TN : Broadman & Holman Publishers, 2000.

Gangel, Kenneth O. *Holman New Testament Commentary: Acts.* Nashville, TN: Broadman & Holman Publishers, 1998.

Gangel, Kenneth O. *Holman New Testament Commentary, vol. 4, John*. Nashville, TN: Broadman & Holman Publishers, 2000.

—. *Holman Old Testament Commentary: Daniel*. Nashville: Broadman & Holman Publishers, 2001.

Garrett, Duane A. *Proverbs, Ecclesiastes, Song of Songs, The New American Commentary, vol. 14*. Nashville: Broadman & Holman Publishers, 1993.

—. *The New American Commentary: Vol. 14 (Proverbs, Ecclesiastes, Song of Songs)*. Nashville: Broadman & Holman Publishers, 1993.

Geisler, Norman L, and William E Nix. *A General Introduction to the Bible*. Chicago: Moody Press, 1996.

George, Timothy. *The New American Commentary: Galatians*. Nashville, TN: Broadman & Holman Publishers, 2001.

Greenlee, J Harold. *Introduction to New Testament Textual Criticism*. Peabody: Hendrickson, 1995.

Guthrie, Donald. *Introduction to the New Testament (Revised and Expanded)*. Downers Grove, IL: InterVarsity Press, 1990.

Guthrie, George H. *The NIV Application Commentary: Hebrews*. Grand Rapids, MI: Zondervan, 1998.

Hoerth, Alfred. *Archaeology and the Old Testament*. Grand Rapids: Baker, 1998.

House, Paul R. *The New American Commentary: 2 Kings*. Nashville: Broadman & Holman Publishers, 2001.

Johnson, W. Ronald. *How Would They Hear if We Do Not Listen?* Nashville: Broadman & Holman Publishers, 1994.

Keener, Craig S. *The IVP Bible Background Commentary: New Testament*. Downer Groves, IL: InterVarsity Press, 1993.

Keil, Carl Friedrich, and Franz Delitzsch. *Commentary on the Old Testament*. Peabody, MA: Hendrickson, 2002.

Kistemaker, Simon J. *Baker New Testament Commentary: Hebrews*. Grand Rapids: Baker Books, 1984.

Kistemaker, Simon J, and Hendriksen William. *New Testament Commentary: Exposition of the Gospel According to Luke*. Grand Rapids: Baker Book House, 1953-2001.

Kistemaker, Simon J, and William Hendriksen. *New Testament Commentary: Exposition of Paul's Epistle to the Romans* . Grand Rapids, MI : Baker Book House , 1953-2001.

—. *New Testament Commentary: vol. 15, Exposition of Hebrews.* Grand Rapids: Baker Book House, 1953-2001.

—. *New Testament Commentary: vol. 19, Exposition of the Second Epistle to the Corinthians.* Grand Rapids, MI:: Baker Book House, 1953-2001.

Kistemaker, Simon J., and William Hendriksen. *Exposition of the First Epistle to the Corinthians, vol. 18, New Testament Commentary.* Grand Rapids, MI: Baker Book House, 1953–2001.

Larson, Knute. *Holman New Testament Commentary, vol. 9, I & II Thessalonians, I & II Timothy, Titus, Philemon.* Nashville, TN: Broadman & Holman Publishers, 2000.

Lea, Thomas D, and David Allen Black. *The New Testament: Its Background Message.* 2d ed. Nashville, TN: B & H Academic, 2003.

Lea, Thomas D. *Holman New Testament Commentary: Hebrews, James.* Nashville, TN: Broadman & Holman Publishers, 1999.

Lea, Thomas D., and Hayne P. Griffin. *The New American Commentary, vol. 34, 1, 2 Timothy, Titus.* Nashville: Broadman & Holman Publishers, 1992.

Lightfoot, Neil R. *How We Got the Bible.* Grand Rapids, MI: Baker Books, 1963, 1988, 2003.

Macarthur, John. *Fool's Gold: Discerning Truth in an Age of Error.* Wheaton: Crossway Books, 2005.

MacArthur, John. *Pastoral Ministry: How to Shepherd Biblically.* Nashville: Thomas Nelson, 2005.

—. *The MacArthur Bible Commentary.* Nashville: Thomas Nelson, 2005.

Martin, D Michael. *The New American Commentary 33 1, 2 Thessalonians* . Nashville, TN: Broadman & Holman, 2001, c1995 .

Martin, Glen S. *Holman Old Testament Commentary: Numbers.* Nashville: Broadman & Holman Publishers, 2002.

Mathews, K. A. *The New American Commentary vol. 1A, Genesis 1-11:26* . Nashville: Broadman & Holman Publishers, 2001.

Matthews, K. A. *The New American Commentary Vol. 1B, Genesis 11:27-50:26*. Nashville: Broadman and Holman Publishers, 2001.

McRaney, William. *The Art of Personal Evangelism*. Nashville: Broadman & Holman, 2003.

Melick, Richard R. *The New American Commentary: Philippians, Colossians, Philemon, electronic ed., Logos Library System*. Nashville: Broadman & Holman Publishers, 2001.

—. *The New American Commentary: vol. 32, Philippians, Colissians, Philemon*. Nashville, TN : Broadman & Holman Publishers, 2001.

Metzger, Bruce M. *The Text of the New Testament: Its Transmission, Corruption, and Transmission*. New York: Oxford University Press, 1964, 1968, 1992.

Metzger, Bruce M. *A Textual Commentary on the Greek New Testament*. New York: United Bible Society, 1994.

Miller, Stephen R. *The New American Commentary: Volume 18 Daniel*. Nashville: Broadman & Holman Publishers, 1994.

Mounce, Robert H. *Romans: The New American Commentary 27*. Nashville: Broadman & Holman, 2001, c1995.

Mounce, Robert H. *The New American Commentary: Vol. 27 Romans*. Nashville, TN: Broadman & Holman Publishers, 2001.

Mounce, William D. *Mounce's Complete Expository Dictionary of Old & New Testament Words*. Grand Rapids, MI: Zondervan, 2006.

Mounce, William D. *Basics of Biblical Greek Grammar*. Grand Rapids: Zonervan, 2009.

Niessen, Richard. "The virginity of the `almah in Isaiah 7:14." *Bibliotheca Sacra 137* , 1980: 133-50.

Oswalt, John N. *The NIV Application Commentary: Isaiah*. Grand Rapids, MI: Zondervan, 2003.

Outlaw, W. Stanley. *The Book of Hebrews* . Nashville, TN: Randall House, 2005.

Pink, Arthur Walkington. *An Exposition of Hebrews*. Swengel, PA: Bible Truth Depot, 1954.

Polhill, John B. *The New American Commentary 26: Acts*. Nashville: Broadman & Holman Publishers, 2001.

Pratt Jr, Richard L. *Holman New Testament Commentary: I & II Corinthians, vol. 7*. Nashville: Broadman & Holman Publishers, 2000.

Richards, E. Randolph. *Paul And First-Century Letter Writing: Secretaries, Composition and Collection*. Downers Grove: InterVarsity Press, 2004.

Richardson, Kurt. *The New American Commentary Vol. 36 James*. Nashville: Broadman & Holman Publishers, 1997.

Robertson, A. T. *An Introduction to the Textual Criticism of the New Testament*. London: Hodder & Stoughton, 1925.

Robinson, Darrell W. *Total Church Life: How to be a First Century Chrurch*. Nashville, TN: Briadman and Holman, 1997.

Rooker, Mark F. *The New American Commentary, vol. 3A, Leviticus*. Nashville: Broadman & Holman Publishers, 2000.

—. *Holman Old Testament Commentary: Ezekiel*. Nashville: Broadman & Holman Publishers, 2005.

—. *Leviticus: The New American Commentary*. Nashville: Broadman & Holman, 2001.

Schreiner, Thomas R. *The New American Commentary: 1, 2 Peter, Jude*. Nashville: Broadman & Holman, 2003.

Scott, Julius J. Jr. *Jewish Backgrounds of the New Testament*. Grand Rapids, MI: Baker Academic, 1995.

Smith, Gary. *The New American Commentary: Isaiah 1-39, Vol. 15a*. Nashville, TN: B & H Publishing Group, 2007.

—. *The New American Commentary: Isaiah 40-66, Vol. 15b*. Nashville, TN: B&H Publishing, 2009.

Souter, Alexander. *The Text and Canon of the New Testament*. New York: Charles Scribner's Sons, 1913.

Sproul, R. C. *What Is Faith?* Lake Mary: Reformation Trust, 2010.

Stein, Robert H. *A Basic Guide to Interpreting the Bible: Playing by the Rules*. Grand Rapids: Baker Books, 1994.

—. *The New American Commentary: Luke.* Nashville, TN: Broadman & Holman, 2001, c1992.

Stott, John. *The Letters of John (Tyndale New Testament Commentaries).* Downers Grove: IVP Academic, 2009.

Stuart, Douglas K. *The New American Commentary: An Exegetical Theological Exposition of Holy Scripture EXODUS.* Nashville: Broadman & Holman, 2006.

Taylor, Richard A, and Ray E Clendenen. *The New American Commentary: Haggai, Malachi, , vol. 21A .* Nashville, TN: Broadman & Holman Publishers, 2007.

Thomas, Robert L. *Revelation 1-7: An Exegetical Commentary .* Chicago, IL: Moody Publishers, 1992.

Tuck, Robert. *A Handbook of Biblical Difficulties: Or Reasonable Solutions of Perplexing Things in Sacred Scriptures (Reprint).* New York: Bible House, 2012.

Walls, David, and Max Anders. *Holman New Testament Commentary: I & II Peter, I, II & III John, Jude.* Nashville: Broadman & Holman Publishers, 1996.

Walton, John H. *Zondervan Illustrated Bible Backgrounds Commentary (Old Testament) Volume 1: Genesis, Exodus, Leviticus, Numbers, Deuteronomy.* Grand Rapids, MI: Zondervan, 2009.

Walton, John H. "Isaiah 7:14: what's in a name?" *Journal of the Evangelical Theological Society 30*, 1987: 289-306.

Weber, Stuart K. *Holman New Testament Commentary, vol. 1, Matthew.* Nashville, TN: Broadman & Holman Publishers, 2000.

Wegner, Paul D. *A Student's Guide to Textual Criticism of the Bible: Its History Methods & Results.* Downers Grove: InterVarsity Press, 2006.

Westcott, B. F., and Hort F. J. A. *The New Testament in the Original Greek, Vol. 2: Introduction, Appendix.* London: Macmillan and Co., 1882.

Wilkins, Michael, and Craig A. Evans. *The Gospels and Acts (The Holman Apologetics Commentary on the Bible).* Nashville: B & H Publishing Group, 2013.

Wolf, Herbert M. "Solution to the Immanuel Prophecy in Isaiah 7:14-8:22." *Journal of Biblical Literature 91* , 1972: 449-56.

Wood, D R W. *New Bible Dictionary (Third Edition)*. Downers Grove: InterVarsity Press, 1996.

Wright, N. T. *Hebrews for Everyone*. London: Westminster John Knox Press, 2003.

www.ingramcontent.com/pod-product-compliance
Lightning Source LLC
Chambersburg PA
CBHW022357040426
42450CB00005B/223